Necia Chronister
Domestic Disputes

Interdisciplinary German Cultural Studies

Edited by
Irene Kacandes

Volume 28

Necia Chronister
Domestic Disputes

―

Examining Discourses of Home and Property
in the Former East Germany

DE GRUYTER

ISBN 978-3-11-109012-2
e-ISBN (PDF) 978-3-11-067397-5
e-ISBN (EPUB) 978-3-11-067400-2
ISSN 1861-8030

Library of Congress Control Number: 2020947732

Bibliographic information published by the Deutsche Nationalbibliothek
The Deutsche Nationalbibliothek lists this publication in the Deutsche Nationalbibliografie; detailed bibliographic data are available on the Internet at http://dnb.dnb.de.

© 2022 Walter de Gruyter GmbH, Berlin/Boston
This volume is text- and page-identical with the hardback published in 2021.
Cover Image: *Taxi nach Rathenow*. Thomas Golze (Jörg Pose) entschuldigt sich bei Edith Strombach (Inge Meysel) für seinen ruppigen Ton, mit dem er sie vor die Türe setzte, als sie Ansprüche auf ihr altes Haus geltend machen wollte. / Thomas Golze (Jörg Pose) apologizes to Edith Strombach (Inge Meysel) for his rude tone when she tried to claim her old house and he threw her out of the house. Copyright: ZDF/Arbor TV Tutzing.
Printing and binding: CPI books GmbH, Leck

www.degruyter.com

For, and always with, Eric

Acknowledgments

For me, home and work have never been inextricable. While I refuse to live in the office, I do prefer to work at home. In the age of COVID-19, quarantines, and stay-at-home orders, writing about the concept of home while also spending an unprecedented amount of time in my own home has given me a new appreciation for the emotional, material, and psychological meanings of this unique space. It also reminds me how dangerous it is, especially now, to be without a home or to be in a home that is unsafe. Even in the best of circumstances, being at home for long stretches of time can be isolating, as many of us have experienced, and so for me, this pandemic has made it all the more urgent to acknowledge the personal and professional connections that have supported me and this work. Just as home and work overlap and mesh for me, so have the ideas, feedback, and support of so many people during this project.

First, I want to thank the people who have generously devoted time and attention to responding to chapter drafts. In particular, the insights of Melinda Cro, Eric Hoffpauir, and Sara Luly have impacted the shape to this project. I would also like to thank Irene Kacandes and the editorial team at De Gruyter for their guidance and for providing a wonderful publishing experience. Many thanks to my dear friend John Holmes for his help interpreting BADV statistics and his partner, Sven Vollrath, for helping me find direction early in my research. I also want to thank the coalition of Women in German for cultivating an atmosphere that encourages the rigorous and constructive exchange of ideas. In particular, I would like to acknowledge Hester Baer, Mareike Hermann, Jennifer Creech, and Bradley Boovy for hosting GSA seminars on feminist and queer approaches to German Studies in 2015 and 2016, which introduced me to theory that I used in this monograph. I especially want to thank Hester Baer for her unwavering support and guidance whenever I have needed it. I would also like to thank my colleagues, Kathleen Antonioli, Ljudmila Bilkić, Derek Hillard, and Sara Luly, as well as our graduate students Dylan McCullough and Heidi Summers, for helping cover my service duties in the department while I was away on sabbatical to write. To Eric Hoffpauir, my partner in life, I am grateful for the countless conversations about these novels, movies, and stories that you have not read or seen yourself, but were willing to help me think through. I also would like to thank my mom, Sharla Robbins, for so many conversations about my work on the phone on Sundays. And I would like to thank my dad, Rick Chronister, for his encouragement throughout the process.

My research on homes has required me to leave my own at times and make trips to Germany to visit archives and meet with artists. I could not have done this without the financial support of Kansas State University, who funded research for this project in the form of University Small Research Grants in 2012 and 2020 and a Faculty Enhancement Grant in 2014. I would like to thank Sonja Blattner, Knut Böser, and Harald Reichebner for taking the time to talk with me about their work during my various trips to Berlin, as well Alexandra Dexheimer and Helene Lorenz at ZDF, Christine Scherer at NDR, Julia Riedel at the Stiftung Deutsche Kinemathek, and Ramona Schröder at the Bundesanstalt für vereinigungsbedingte Sonderaufgaben for providing me with materials that are not available commercially or in library circulation. Thanks go as well to the staff at the Bundesarchiv in Berlin, the Staatsbibliothek zu Berlin, and the city archives of Leipzig and Magdeburg, who assisted me with archival research. Thanks also to Stephan Moll at ZDF for helping me secure permission to use the cover image. Many, many thanks to Eric, for taking over the duties of parenting all those times I was away for research.

Without the love, encouragement, and patience of my husband, daughter, parents, grandparents, and siblings, this book would not exist. Thank you, Nola, for your enthusiasm about your mom being an author, which made me feel like a good example and a rock star. Thanks also for making me put work down and play once in a while. Thanks above all else to Eric, for all the reasons I have mentioned already – for your intellectual exchange, emotional support, and willingness to take on more than half of the parenting duties – but also for your patience and for being a wonderful partner in life. Your sustained support over the years has made it possible for me to write this book, and I am forever grateful for that.

Finally, because I live in Northeastern Kansas and work for a state institution, I would like to acknowledge that the state of Kansas is historically home to many Native nations, including the Kaw, Osage, and Pawnee, among others. Furthermore, Kansas is the current home to four federally recognized Native nations: the Prairie Band Potawatomie, the Kickapoo Tribe of Kansas, the Iowa Tribe of Kansas and Nebraska, and Sac and Fox Nation of Missouri in Kansas and Nebraska.

Contents

Introduction
Home in the East —— 1

Chapter 1
Home in the East as a Bureaucratic Nightmare: On Property Claims, Media Representations, and the Informative Function of Television Movies —— 20
      A Deeply Flawed System —— 21
      Informative Fiction in Television: *Taxi to Rathenow* —— 38

Chapter 2
Home in the East as a Site of Competing Histories: *Our House* (Griesmayr, 1991) and *The Same Old Song* (Stöckl, 1992) —— 50
      Patrilineal *Heimat*, Patrilineal History in *Our House* —— 51
      Matrilineal *Heimat* and History in *The Same Old Song* —— 63
      Heimat as Material Engagement, Not Family History —— 70

Chapter 3
Home in the East as a Capitalist Battlefield: *The Brocken* (Glowna, 1992) and *No More Mr. Nice Guy* (Buck, 1993) —— 73
      Commodifying Community in *The Brocken* —— 75
      The Cruelty of Capitalism in *No More Mr. Nice Guy* —— 86
      Spaces of Resistance? —— 95

Chapter 4
Home in the East as an Instrument of the Patriarchy: Judith Hermann's "Summerhouse, Later" (1998) and *Where Love Begins* (2014) —— 98
      Home as an Overdetermined Place in "Summerhouse, Later" —— 101
      Deterritorialized Home as a Nightmare in *Where Love Begins* —— 111
      Is There a Reterritorialization? —— 121

Chapter 5
Home in the East as a Threat to Men's Control: Peter Schneider's *Eduard's Homecoming* (1999) and Karen Duve's *Rain* (1999) —— 123
      Property, History, and Emasculation in *Eduard's Homecoming* —— 126

Threatening Women, Threatening Landscapes in *Rain* —— 137
Gendered Anxieties, Gendered Fantasies —— 150

Chapter 6
Home in the East as a Thing of the Past: Jenny Erpenbeck's *Visitation* (2008) and Kathrin Gerlof's *Now That's a Story* (2014) —— 153
The Erratic Linearity of Time in Jenny Erpenbeck's *Visitation* —— 155
Time as Accountability in Kathrin Gerlof's *Now That's a Story* —— 167
The Threatening Inevitability of (In)justice —— 178

Chapter 7
Home in the East as Corporate Overlord: Juli Zeh's *Unterleuten* (2016) —— 181
The Alien Invasion of Capitalism, or Not Recognizing the Sociomateriality —— 185
Violent Capitalism(s) —— 190
The Fallacy of Misrecognition —— 197

Coda
Home in the East as an Ongoing Issue: Sonja Blattner's *drüben* Series and the Importance of Considering Medium —— 200

Works Cited —— 208
Primary Texts —— 208
Secondary Literature and Theoretical Works —— 209
Laws, Legal Decisions, and Treaties —— 217

Index —— 220

Introduction
Home in the East

> "I'm still here. My country's going west.
> WAR ON THE COTTAGES, THE PALACES TAKE THE REST!"
> - Volker Braun from the poem "Property"
> 10. August 1990[1]

> "The courts work slowly and are not on our side."
> - Hedwig Gottwald in Kathrin Gerlof's *Now That's a Story*[2]

On September 30, 1991, just days before the first anniversary of German unification, the television station ZDF aired a made-for-television movie titled *Our House* (*Unser Haus*, Griesmayr, 1991).[3] In this film, the fall of the Berlin Wall and German unification offer the protagonist, Kurt Wrede, a hitherto unthinkable possibility: that he might have a legal claim to his childhood home, the lakeside house his father built outside of Potsdam. For Kurt, this house represents a *Heimat* that has been restricted to him since he was thirteen years old, when his mother made the decision to flee from East Germany to West Berlin with her children. In claiming the house, however, Kurt must face the fact that another family has inhabited it for nearly four decades and also has a right to call it their home. Both families have a legal claim to the house and, perhaps more importantly for the German television audience, sentimental attachment to it. A feud soon ensues over rights to the house, creating a compelling interfamily drama that asks, at its heart, who has a right to call a place home.

Rather than celebrate the triumph of national unification as one might expect on this first anniversary, *Our House* depicts one of the prime challenges

---

[1] "Da bin ich noch: mein Land geht in den Westen. / KRIEG DEN HÜTTEN FRIEDE DEN PALÄSTEN." Volker Braun, "Das Eigentum," *Die Zeit*, Aug. 9, 1990, https://www.zeit.de/1990/33/das-eigentum. My translation adapted from those of Michael Hofmann, David Constantine, and Karen Leeder. See: Volker Braun, "Property," trans. Michael Hofmann, *Poetry* 173, no. 1 (1998): 53; Volker Braun, "Property," trans. David Constantine and Karen Leeder, *Rubble Flora: Selected Poems* (New York: Seagull Books, 2014), 46.
[2] "Die Gerichte arbeiten langsam und sind nicht auf unserer Seite." Kathrin Gerlof, *Das ist eine Geschichte* (Berlin: Aufbau Verlag, 2014), 206. All translations from the German into English are my own unless otherwise indicated.
[3] Parts of this introductory chapter, as well as chapter 2 and the coda appeared originally as Necia Chronister, "Domestic Disputes: Envisioning the Gender of Home in the Era of Re-privatization in Eastern Germany," in *Heimat Goes Mobile – Hybrid Forms of Home in Literature and Film*, ed. Gabriele Eichmanns and Yvonne Franke (Newcastle: Cambridge Scholars Publishing, 2013), 146–169. Published here with the permission of Cambridge Scholars Publishing.

that the new republic faced: determining property rights. As the two Germanys unified and the former East Germany prepared to enter the market economy, it was imperative to determine who would own what property. *Our House* depicts on a familial level both the promise and the uncertainty that many Germans faced in this unprecedented historical and political moment. Some 95% of East Germany's assets, which included housing, had been controlled by the government or cooperatives, so the privatization process of the 1990s would be sweeping.[4] This led not only to animosities between Easterners and Westerners in competition for properties, as we will soon see, but it also would force the nation to answer once again for its troubled past.

The premise of *Our House* hinges on the particular way in which homes were awarded in the new system. According to article 14 of the West German Basic Law (*Grundgesetz*), to which the "new states" from the former East were now beholden, citizens who had been expropriated, were coerced into selling their property, or fled to escape persecution by the German government at any time dating back to National Socialism were entitled to their relinquished property. While article 14 had been written into the West German Basic Law in 1949 to respond to the expropriation and political persecution of Jews and other groups under the Nazi regime, in the era of unification it extended to those who had lost property in the eastern part of Germany as well, either during the Nazi era or in the German Democratic Republic (the official name of East Germany, hereafter referred to as the GDR).

This article in the Basic Law would lead to widespread uncertainty about the just ownership of properties in the former East Germany, as there are numerous reasons why one would have lost or abandoned property in this part of Germany over the course of the twentieth century. Under National Socialism, Jewish and other persecuted people were routinely expropriated or coerced to sell homes and businesses for the purposes of "Aryanization," were removed from their property, or fled to escape. Confiscated real estate then went to those favored by the Nazi party. After World War II, the occupying Soviet forces implemented a massive land reform, confiscating millions of acres from large landholders and known Nazis and redistributing the land among the unpropertied. Much of this same land, however, would be collectivized once again and turned into industrial farmlands later in the GDR. Finally, those who left the GDR for the West over

---

[4] Peter H. Merkl, "An Impossible Dream? Privatizing Collective Property in Eastern Germany," in *German Unification: Process and Outcomes*, ed. M. Donald Hancock and Helga A. Welsh (Boulder, San Francisco, and Oxford: Westview Press), 200.

the country's forty-year existence relinquished their property, submitting it, knowingly or not at the time, for confiscation by the state.

While article 14 of the Basic Law was meant to correct an unjust history, for many residents of the former East Germany in the 1990s, it felt like another round of expropriation by the government. As we will see in chapter 1, owning a home outright did not guarantee one's entitlement to it if a claimant emerged who had been expropriated in the past. During the privatization efforts of the 1990s, most properties in the former East Germany that were not marked for business investment became available for previous owners or their heirs to claim, and consequently, many of the current residents found their sense of security to be threatened. The titles of book-length journalistic works that focused on the privatization of businesses, such as *Raid in the East* (*Raubzug Ost*, Huhn, 2009), *The German Gold Rush* (*Der deutsche Goldrausch*, Laabs, 2012), and *The Great Expropriation* (*Die große Enteignung*, Köhler, 1994) foreground such anxiety, likening the privatization of the former East Germany to other historical practices of expropriation, particularly the plunder of others' property (as in "raid") or resources (as in "gold rush").

However, these and other book-length journalistic works paint only part of the picture, profiling the *Treuhandanstalt* (*Treuhand* for short, or Trust Agency), the governmental agency that oversaw the privatization of East German commercial properties, and largely disregarding issues pertaining to residential properties.[5] To date, no book-length study profiles the housing disputes that took place in the eastern part of Germany following unification. Only shorter-form reporting in magazines, newspapers, and televised news programs cover home ownership disputes during this era. A similar incongruity exists in the academic scholarship. While a body of work in the disciplines of business, political science, history, and law review has been devoted to studying the privatization of East German business and industry, little attention has been paid to the effects of privatization efforts on houses and their inhabitants.

This monograph is the first extended study to examine the discourses that arose from the privatization of residential properties, and it does so by offering an interpretation of fictional television programming, film, prose fiction, and paintings that depict Westerners acquiring or attempting to acquire a house in the former East Germany, either by presenting a historical claim, inheriting it from a family member who lived there, or purchasing it at low market prices

---

5 The *Treuhandanstalt* quickly gained notoriety among East Germans for the perception that it placed business interests over the good of the people. Because of its particular cultural meaning and the fact that it is historically unique, I will refer to it in the German original in this monograph.

after unification. While a review of short form news reporting in chapter 1 will lend important context for the readings of fiction in this study, fictional productions are the study's focus. Made-for-television films, cinematic releases, prose fiction, and paintings are the primary cultural artifacts that we can turn to for extended and nuanced depictions of the changing property relations of the 1990s in the former East Germany and the enduring philosophical, cultural, and emotional impact of those policies into the present day.

The cultural productions examined in this monograph dramatize anxieties about social disenfranchisement in the former East, and as I will show in the following chapters, such depictions have changed over time. As one can surmise by the book titles listed above, the earliest portrayals frame the privatization of East German assets in wholly adversarial, and often colonialist, terms. (This will be true of the earliest fictional depictions as well.) On the day that German unification officially took place, October 3, 1990, the East German newspaper *Neues Deutschland* announced that "the full-scale attack on the GDR as a country, on GDR land, has begun."[6] While *Neues Deutschland*, formerly the official party newspaper of the Socialist Unity Party of the GDR, can hardly be considered a neutral source, a number of national news outlets from the West soon followed suit. For example, the news magazine *Der Spiegel* declared in 1992 that "the run on GDR land was off"[7] thereby likening the opening of the East for investment to the US-American colonialist practice of the land run.

In chapter 1, I take a closer look at these news media and the case studies they present in order to provide contextual information for the analysis of fiction and visual material in the chapters to follow. Drawing together case studies presented in law review journals and the news media, I outline the historical circumstances that resulted in the expropriation or abandonment of properties over the course of the twentieth century and explain the legal parameters under which an individual or family could lay claim to a house in the former East. In this chapter, I also take a close look at one of the first fictional productions to appear, the made-for-television film *Taxi to Rathenow* (*Taxi nach Rathenow*, Engel 1991), in order to demonstrate the informational value of made-for-television films for the national audience at that time.

The made-for television films and cinematic releases discussed in chapters 1–3 make invaluable cultural artifacts. Produced and released quickly, these films addressed the new property relations as the laws and policies were

---

[6] "Der Großangriff auf das Land DDR, auf DDR-Land hat begonnen." Quoted in "Die Lage ist trostlos," *Der Spiegel*, Oct 8, 1990 and Wolfgang Gehrmann und Nikolaus Piper, "Der Häuserkampf," *Die Zeit* (Hamburg, Germany) March 20, 1992.

[7] "Der Run auf DDR-Land brach los." "Alte Rechte neues Unrecht," *Der Spiegel*, June 26, 1992.

being written and implemented. For example, according to production notes, *Taxi to Rathenow* was shot within about a month and appeared roughly two months after shooting wrapped.[8] Because they were produced quickly, they could speak directly to the anxieties of the time. In chapter 2, I examine the made-for-television film *Our House* and the independent cinematic release *The Same Old Song* (*Das alte Lied*, Stöckl 1992), both of which depict property disputes as feuds between two families who hail from the West and the East. In these films, claimants are framed as invaders from the West who threaten Easterners' financial security, and, to cast further doubt on their justifications for claiming a house, the Western family in each of these films has a Nazi past. Nevertheless, the Westerners do have some redeeming qualities, and as allegories of the national parts, the families must find a way to settle their differences. In both films, an emerging friendship among the youth of the families represents the hope for a true unification of the two Germanys.

While the films discussed in chapter 2 depict Easterners as victims of Western neocolonial aggression, chapter 3 presents two films in which resourceful Easterners outwit Westerners and defeat them at their own game. In *The Brocken* (*Der Brocken*, Glowna 1992) and *No More Mr. Nice Guy* (*Wir können auch anders*, Buck 1993), Easterners quickly learn the rules – and tricks – of the capitalist system in order to frustrate Westerners' attempts to acquire property. While on their surface, these films offer a counter narrative to that of the neocolonial Western invasion, I argue that they actually show a different kind of Western invasion taking place, as neoliberalism, the driving force behind privatization, was already becoming entrenched as a mindset among Easterners by the early 1990s.

By the end of the decade, depictions of the new property relations began to appear in prose fiction as well, but these texts quickly departed from narratives of East versus West. Instead, the houses themselves became the adversaries to those Westerners who acquire and inhabit them. In the texts examined in chapters 4 and 5, the houses wield an eerie agency of their own, posing existential threats to their inhabitants that recall, but do not fully align with, the trope of the haunted house. In chapter 4, I examine Judith Hermann's short story "Summerhouse, Later" ("Sommerhaus, später," 1998) and interpret her novel *Where Love Begins* (*Aller Liebe Anfang*, 2014) as an extension of that previous work. In these two narratives, houses threaten to fall in on or otherwise fail to protect their female inhabitants, serving as either symbols of the patriarchy or overt

---

[8] "Taxi nach Rathenow," press material, *ZDF Presseproduktion Berlin*. "Unser Haus," press material, *ZDF Presseproduktion Berlin*. Many thanks to the Stiftung deutsche Kinemathek for access to these materials.

mechanism of male control over women. However, in Peter Schneider's *Eduard's Homecoming* (*Eduards Heimkehr*, 1999) and Karen Duve's *Rain* (*Regenroman*, 1999), examined in chapter 5, the male protagonists are no longer "kings of their castles." Instead, the houses they acquire pose existential threats to them – whether financial, social, or physical – and trigger masculinity crises. In reading chapters 4 and 5 of this monograph together, it becomes clear that the concerns of Westerners in these scenarios are strongly gendered: that women are made vulnerable by the choices the men around them make, while men are vulnerable to more abstract social forces.

In chapters 6 and 7, I examine texts with collective protagonists who must fact antagonists that are largely invisible and intangible in nature. In Jenny Erpenbeck's *Visitation* (*Heimsuchung*, 2008) and Kathrin Gerlof's *Now That's a Story* (*Das ist eine Geschichte*, 2014), discussed in chapter 6, time is the unwieldy foe of the main characters, whose personal or family histories catch up with them in the present day and force many of them, justifiably or not, out of their homes. In both novels, humans have committed grave injustices against one another – displacement, exploitation, murder – and the forward march of time guarantees that no one can safely claim a space for themselves in the present day for very long. In chapter 7, the invisible hand of capitalism poses the main threat to a small community in Juli Zeh's *Unterleuten* (2016). In this novel, a small town is driven to violence by the competition over a land contract with a clean energy firm. I demonstrate how Zeh draws on the materiality of *Heimat* to highlight the apparently immaterial nature of capitalism and to depict home ownership by Westerners in the East as a form of gentrification that soon brings with it more invisible capitalist interventions on a community.

This monograph ends with a coda rather than a conclusion since the discourses on the privatization of homes in the former East Germany are still developing and new cultural productions on this topic continue to appear. Focusing on the paintings of Berlin-based visual artist Sonja Blattner, I consider houses at the interface of materiality, emotion, interdependence with humans, and their independence from us as agentic entities. Blattner paints houses in the former East Germany that stand empty because they are up for sale. Her paintings bring out the dignity and personality of these often run-down houses, casting them as organic beings that have emerged out of their material environments. Blattner's paintings bring together many of the themes addressed in the narrative-driven productions discussed in this monograph: the materiality of house and home; our emotional connection to structures; houses as real estate; and houses marking the conjunction of a troubled national history, a present that is structured largely by the market, and an uncertain future.

In examining house and home in the news media, television, film, prose fiction, and painting, this monograph builds on the work of other scholars who have enriched our understanding of the meaning of home. For example, social scientist Shelley Mallett showcases the breadth and complexity of scholarship on the concept of home in her ambitious survey of the work done in anthropology, architecture, human geography, philosophy, psychology, and sociology. According to her survey, home is conventionally understood to be the locus of family, belonging, and stasis. It "holds symbolic power as a formative dwelling place, a place of origin and return, a place from which to embark upon a journey."[9] Home as a place from which we originate and to which we can always return is, however, a decidedly middle-class and heteronormative construct since it takes for granted financial stability, reproductive sex as a person's origin, and a supportive family structure. As such, home in this conventional form functions much better as a psychological or literary trope than a universal truth. Mallett then goes on to examine the concept of home from a variety of critical frameworks that untether it from a particular place or family structure. Home can also be "the lived experience of locality" and "a practice, the diverse way people 'do' and feel home."[10] It can be "an expression or symbol of the self," a source or expression of independence, "a place one can be oneself freely," and a site of identity.[11] Such notions liberate home from being merely and restrictively one kind of place with a set type of inhabitants, instead casting it as a dynamic experience that shapes and is shaped by the individual practicing it. The cultural productions discussed in this monograph certainly play on the tension between these two notions: home as the static place of origin and home as something practiced.

Literary studies have long conceived of home in such multidimensional ways, exploring its symbolic, psychological, and material meanings through the experiences of fictional characters. Perhaps the most important study on homes in German Studies recently is Monika Shafi's monograph *Housebound: Selfhood and Domestic Space in Contemporary German Fiction* (2012). In her introduction, Shafi writes that homes in contemporary German literature are "a prime site of identity, powerfully registering conditions of contemporary life."[12] According to Shafi, they give us a glimpse of selfhood as it is impacted upon lo-

---

9 Shelley Mallett, "Understanding Home: A Critical Review of the Literature," *The Sociological Review* 52, no. 1 (February 2004): 63. doi:10.1111/j.1467–954X.2004.00442.x
10 Shelley Mallett, "Understanding Home," 79.
11 Shelley Mallett, "Understanding Home," 82–83.
12 Monika Shafi, *Housebound: Selfhood and Domestic Space in Contemporary German Fiction* (Rochester: Camden House, 2012), 4.

cally, nationally, and transnationally in the domestic sphere through negotiations of material comfort and the utopian ideal of home as refuge.[13] In the works examined here in *Domestic Disputes*, the notion of home as the site of family and childhood memories, comfort, and refuge runs counter to the financial realities of the house as an investment, financial burden, or legal liability. The illusion of a domestic sphere that provides the conditions for conventional family dynamics or gender roles is disrupted by the upheaval of the property relations, the houses themselves often posing threats to those who inhabit or are vying for them. Some of these narratives put forth a scenario of ruined dreams by foiling a character's fantasy of inheriting or being awarded a house. In others, old claims to a house are dug up and dusted off, making the ever-presence of the Nazi past apparent.

These various and differentiated narratives that respond to the phenomenon of housing disputes in the former East Germany pose deep social, philosophical, and existential questions. To what extent is home tied to our ability to inhabit a space in this world? Who is allowed to inhabit what space when? Who has a right to home and *Heimat*? Why is our property central to our identities, or perhaps: what is the nature of the relationship between self, space, and stuff? Who and what are the real threats to our security: the individuals we compete with, the economic structures within which we live, or other, more abstract forces like time and history? The cultural productions discussed in this monograph – from those made-for-television movies produced quickly as the phenomenon of housing disputes unfolded in the early 1990s to the novels and paintings that have appeared well into the twenty-first century – express deeply held fears about the fragility of a social order that regulates our position in the material world through home ownership or the rightful occupation of a house.

While the chapters of this monograph bring together texts based on similarities in their narratives, particularly how their narratives expose certain anxieties about home in the former East Germany, a number of themes reappear across chapters. The most prevalent is the presentation of home as *Heimat*. This German concept has no direct translation into English, but refers to a rather pastoral notion of home in which there exists an organic harmony between one's house, the local community, the landscape, and folk tradition. In its conventional definition, *Heimat* is rural, innocent and timeless, anti-modern, and impervious to national politics and economic influence. It is typically the place of one's childhood, the place where one feels an unequivocal belonging to house, landscape, and community. *Heimat* is a powerful concept in the German culture,

---

13 Monika Shafi, *Housebound*, 4–6.

and several of the narratives discussed in this monograph invoke it to suggest that a particular character has a greater claim to a house than another character, to emphasize a character's sense of attachment to home, or to express a character's need for belonging within that space.

In his ambitious study that attempts a comprehensive theory of *Heimat*, Peter Blickle describes how central *Heimat* is to the German imaginary:

> *Heimat* is a crucial aspect in German self-perceptions; it represents the fusional anti-Enlightenment thinking in German Romanticism; it is the idealization of the pre-modern within the modern; it unites geographic and imaginary conceptions of space; it is a provincializing, but disalienating, part of German bourgeois culture; it reflects modern German culture's spatialized interiority; it combines territorial claims with a fundamental ethical reassurance of innocence; and, to achieve this combination, it uses a patriarchal, gendered way of seeing the world.[14]

As Blickle points out, *Heimat* is a multifaceted concept that only feigns simplicity. It is rooted in a bourgeois fantasy that imagines simple, working-class life to be wholesome, comfortable, and leisurely. This fantasy serves a psychological purpose, as *Heimat* promises to be where the alienated modern individual can be healed by gaining an almost pre-linguistic, polymorphous sense of belonging to community and landscape.[15] Finally, and most importantly for the topic of property disputes, *Heimat* imagines territorialism to be innocent; it supposes an eternal and ahistorical occupation of a place by a certain group of people, thereby endeavoring to strip the implications of history from the particularities of place.

Of course, *Heimat* only feigns to be apolitical and ahistorical, having always harbored a (usually exclusive, but sometimes inclusive) notion of who belongs where when. In its most notorious implementation, *Heimat* served the genocidal blood-and-soil spatial politics of National Socialism. As Celia Applegate and Johannes von Moltke have demonstrated, National Socialism capitalized on the rhetoric of *Heimat* popularized during the Weimar Republic, which offered a pastoral escape from the hustle and bustle of modern life, particularly in Berlin. The Nazis, however, altered the *Heimat* ideal from a place of "escape" to one of "return," thereby employing a nativist rhetoric that supported their vision of a deep-

---

14 Peter Blickle, *Heimat: A Critical Theory of the German Idea of Homeland* (Rochester: Camden House, 2002), 1–2.
15 Peter Blickle, *Heimat*, 12.

ly rooted "Aryan" pastoral Germany.[16] The Nazis simultaneously employed what von Moltke calls a "militant pastoralism," shifting the purview of *Heimat* from the local particular to the national.[17] Thus *Heimat* was utilized for national political purposes, such that "*Heimatschutz*" (protection of the homeland) connected a focus on protecting nature and landscape with an expanionist war and the programmatic expulsion and murder of millions of Jewish people and others who did not fit the Nazi ideal citizenry. To date, the concept of *Heimat* is fraught with racial overtones. A recent collection of essays by immigrants and Germans with immigrant heritage, *Eure Heimat ist unser Albtraum* (*Your Heimat is Our Nightmare*, 2019) illustrates just how closely tied the notion of *Heimat* remains to whiteness in Germany, as people of color are continually othered, marginalized, and unprotected.[18]

Heimat remains a prominent concept in German society, and some important recent scholarship has worked to rehabilitate it, showing how it has, in some eras, been employed to help Germans face change and fluctuations in social demographics. Johannes von Moltke has shown how the *Heimat* films of the 1950s functioned to reconcile the regionalism and traditions of *Heimat* with rapid modernization and the influx of outsiders into the German post-war nation, including expellees from the Eastern provinces, refugees from Eastern Europe, and soldiers returning late from the war. *Heimat* films also often feature a character who introduces new technologies and consumer products into the *Heimat* community, thereby integrating modernizing aspects of the nation into the values and traditions of the local *Heimat*.[19] Other scholars debate whether *Heimat* can exist in urban, suburban, or even cosmopolitan settings, and *Heimat* as something one can adopt has become a useful way of thinking about the status of minority populations in Germany. Heike Henderson and Friederike Eigler, for example, discuss the extent to which Turkish-German authors have broadened the concept of *Heimat* by framing their own narratives of migration within this register.[20]

---

[16] Johannes von Moltke, *No Place Like Home: Locations of Heimat in German Cinema* (Berkeley: University of California Press, 2005), 53–55. Celia Applegate, *A Nation of Provincials: The German Idea of Heimat* (Berkeley: University of California Press, 1990), 205.

[17] Johannes von Moltke, *No Place Like Home*, 53.

[18] Fatma Aydemir and Hengameh Yaghoobifahah, eds., *Eure Heimat ist unser Albtraum* (Berlin: Ullstein fünf, 2019).

[19] For an overview of the *Heimat* film genre, see Johannes von Moltke, *No Place Like Home*, 21–35.

[20] See Heike Henderson, "Re-Thinking and Re-Writing Heimat: Turkish Women Writers in Germany," *Women in German Yearbook* 13 (1997): 226. Friederike Eigler, "Critical Approaches to Heimat and the 'Spatial Turn,'" *New German Critique* 38, no. 1 (2012): 39.

It is perhaps not surprising that *Heimat* has gained new attention in both popular productions and scholarly works in the post-unification era. Applegate, Blickle, Elizabeth Boa, and Rachel Palfreyman, among others, agree that *Heimat* has proven to be most popular in times of nation building or when the nation is in flux. Blickle situates *Heimat* as an

> antinational construct that historically has always served to support a broad and not clearly defined nationalism. [...] Whenever deep shifts in the self-definition of Germany as a nation took place, *Heimat* was there to counterbalance (in the case of loss of territory and its accompanying phantom pains) and to help integrate (in the case of expansions).[21]

Applegate's explanation of the term's history reinforces this point. *Heimat* has etymological roots dating back to the Medieval period, but was "rescued from the archaic German" in the literature of late eighteenth century amidst widespread legal reforms in the German-speaking world. The concept gained strength among intellectuals during the Romantic era, when the German language became central to the project of developing a *Kulturnation*. Eventually, *Heimat* was popularized in the late nineteenth century as a means of celebrating diverse regional cultures under the umbrella of the nation.[22] To that point, Boa and Palfreyman consider *Heimat* to be a foil to modernity, serving as a reply to the swift changes the late nineteenth century brought: "Heimat literature was one aspect of a great variety of activities and institutions – in part reactionary, in part practically reformist, in part idealistically utopian [...] which can be seen as responses to Germany's rapid modernization."[23] This combination of being reactionary, reformist, and utopian makes *Heimat* particularly powerful in times of social upheaval. Eigler even argues that the anti-modernity inherent in *Heimat* can be seen as productive today in light of the spatial turn in cultural geography and literary studies, in which space as a dimension becomes the privileged object of inquiry over time. *Heimat* then warrants re-examination as a possible countercurrent to modernity's increasing time-space compression in the age of advanced globalization.[24]

The 1990s saw a number of dramatic shifts: the re-configuration of the German nation, pervasive social changes and a geographical restructuring in Europe, the privatization of post-Communist states (including East Germany), the

---

21 Peter Blickle, *Heimat*, 47.
22 Celia Applegate, *A Nation of Provincials*, 4–7.
23 Elizabeth Boa and Rachel Palfreyman, *Heimat – A German Dream: Regional Loyalties and National Identity in German Culture 1890–1990* (Oxford: Oxford University Press, 2000), 2.
24 Friederike Eigler, "Critical Approaches to Heimat and the 'Spatial Turn,'" 30.

official formation of the European Union with largely unrestricted travel across its internal borders, the advancement of globalization, and the increase in digital spaces. Accordingly, *Heimat* has come under increased scrutiny in response to concerns about Germany's place in global politics. An article titled "Basic Need: What is Heimat?" in the popular magazine *Stern online* from 2004 considers what *Heimat* means in this era: "What is Heimat? Is it a place? A feeling? In the age of globalization, economic crisis, and changing values, many Germans are discovering how important it is to feel at home somewhere."[25] The definitions that the article proposes do not differ substantially from the ones just discussed. *Heimat* is a place (of one's origin or of one's choosing) in which one feels a sense of belonging. It is a place connected with memories and one's language, and it can serve as an escape from the cold politics and economy of the outside world. The article also points out the impossibility of *Heimat*: "Heimat demands stasis that does not exist. Life demands change. For that reason, any Heimat achieved is almost already a lost Heimat."[26] Indeed, whether concerned with the nation or with social change, theorists of *Heimat* seem to agree on a few basic principles: *Heimat* is a utopian space, a mythologized version of home that relies on a nostalgic sense of loss and a need for belonging.

While theorists like Blickle conceive of *Heimat* primarily in emotional and psychological terms, the television, films, and prose fiction discussed in this monograph throw into sharp relief just how intensely the materiality of home was felt by those who stood to lose theirs. This brings us to the second major theme to reappear across chapters: the materiality of home. In all of the texts and films discussed in this monograph, houses are not merely the containers of human activity, and home is not an a priori condition of human life. Instead, home is an entanglement of house (the physical structure), its inhabitants, the spaces it delineates, the emotions we attach to it, the relationships it harbors, and the social meaning it holds. As such, home as a concept is a rich site for investigating the complex emotional, political, financial, and existential implications of privatization on a personal and familial level. While house, home, and *Heimat* are terms that often cannot be fully unentangled, I try in this mono-

---

[25] "Grundbedürfnis: Was ist Heimat?" *Stern Online*, Dec 15, 2004, https://www.stern.de/politik/deutschland/grundbeduerfnis-was-ist-heimat–3554102.html. Originally: "Grundbedürfnis: Was ist Heimat?" / "Was ist Heimat? Ist es ein Ort? Ein Gefühl? Im Zeitalter von Globalisierung, Wirtschaftskrise und Wertewandel entdecken viele Deutsche, wie wichtig es ist, sich irgendwo zu Hause zu fühlen."
[26] "Grundbedürfnis: Was ist Heimat?" Originally: "Heimat will Stillstand, den es nicht gibt. Das Leben will den Wechsel. Deswegen ist jede Heimat, kaum dass sie errungen wurde, immer auch schon verlorene Heimat."

graph to keep a distinction between them when possible for the sake of clarity. I refer to houses when it is important to foreground the physical structure, home when the emotional stakes are more important, and *Heimat* when that particular cultural concept is employed in the primary text. There are moments, however, when the three overlap so completely that a disentanglement is impossible.

To explore the notion of home as a material practice and entanglement, I turn to Karen Barad's concept of intra-activity. In her monograph *Meeting the Universe Halfway*, Karen Barad draws on the theories of quantum physicist Niels Bohr to shift our understanding of materiality from an atomistic view to a performative and relational one. For Barad, materiality does not exist as an a priori condition. Rather, the basic building block of reality is what she calls the "intra-action," the entangled way in which entities materialize through relationships. In Barad's view, materiality is how we perceive the universe having gone through "agential cuts," a process by which substance differentiates itself from other substance, excluding it, and thus making itself known. Materiality is "the universe making itself intelligible to another part in its ongoing differentiating intelligibility and materialization."[27]

For Barad, nothing exists before the "agential cut" out of which matter emerges. Her neologism "intra-action" emphasizes this relationality of all matter, as opposed to the term "interaction," which would suppose individual, independent entities that pre-exist their relationships.[28] The agential cut is an articulation of boundaries, an iterative relationship, and the way in which materiality practices agency. Barad maintains that everything emerges through agential cuts, even humans, and so in chapter 2, I consider *Heimat* in this paradigm as a "particular material (re)configuring" out of which the human subject "phenomenon" arises and changes throughout their life.[29] A reading of *Heimat* in such a way suggests that subjectivity itself is material and *Heimat* is not static, but rather a "phenomenon" of the world in its endless "becoming."[30] This means that *Heimat*, and those who interact with it – and intra-act from within it – are not ahistorical, but materially and historically situated, active, and culpable.

In chapter 5, I build on Barad's philosophy by pairing it with Stacy Alaimo's concept of the "trans-corporal space," which further theorizes the enmeshment of the human within its material environment. According to Alaimo, the natural world and the human one are mutually constitutive of one another and are both

---

27 Karen Barad, *Meeting the Universe Halfway: Quantum Physics and the Entanglement of Matter and Meaning* (Durham: Duke University Press, 2007), 176.
28 Karen Barad, *Meeting the Universe Halfway*, 33.
29 See Karen Barad, *Meeting the Universe Halfway*, 136.
30 Karen Barad, *Meeting the Universe Halfway*, 139.

shaped by the same forces. She writes that the "'body' and 'nature' are comprised of the same material, which has been constituted, simultaneously, by the forces of evolution, natural and human history, political inequities, cultural contestations, biological and chemical processes, and other factors too numerous to list."[31] For Alaimo, as for Barad, the material world does not exist as the a priori condition for human activity, but is also iterative, belonging to the world of discourse. She calls for an understanding of materiality in which "nonhuman nature or the human body can 'talk back,' resist, or otherwise affect its cultural construction."[32]

Indeed, in the narratives discussed in this monograph, houses in particular do talk back and resist. Dilapidation, decay, crumbling, and warping are ways in which materials assert their own agency against the structure that humans try to impose on them. The constant negotiation between dilapidating materials and humans who repair them form a particular intra-action of humans, environment, and technology. According to Alaimo, by recognizing that we are not materially distinct entities from our physical environment or one another, we can be freed from the "delusions of grandeur that place us far above a base nature."[33] Concomitantly, this understanding allows us to conceive of other agencies and organizing principles active in nature that are separate from, but on par with, human subjectivity.

While the privatization of the former East Germany makes the materiality of house, home, and *Heimat* all the more evident in these texts and visual productions, its driving force, the spread of neoliberalism in the East, is continually represented as abstract and non-material. Privatization appears to be happening from faraway, the result of decisions made by faceless bureaucrats and lawyers in the West, and thus not arising from the material systems in which the characters operate and over which they have control. In order to discuss the reach of neoliberalism in these texts, I turn to work by David Harvey, Wendy Brown, and Raewyn Connell. In his monograph, *A Brief History of Neoliberalism*, Harvey describes the mechanism driving the spread of neoliberalism across Europe and the United States as "the construction of consent." The neoliberal revolution of Margaret Thatcher and Ronald Reagan instrumentalized a rhetoric of individual freedom to garner popular support to deregulate industries and markets, bust unions, withdraw federal funding from numerous social institutions, and priva-

---

31 Stacy Alaimo, "Trans-Corporal Feminisms and the Ethical Space of Nature," in *Material Feminisms*, ed. Stacy Alaimo and Susan Hekman (Bloomington and Indianapolis: Indianapolis University Press), 257.
32 Stacy Alaimo, "Trans-Corporal Feminisms," 242.
33 Stacy Alaimo, "Trans-Corporal Feminisms," 258.

tize where possible.³⁴ This construction of consent plays out on an individual level in the films and texts discussed in this monograph, as many of the characters are incentivized to comply with the system in order to optimize their personal freedom within it. Others who do not consent are compelled to flee, seeking a space as yet untouched by the market.

Of course, economic forces alone do not detemine the material circumstances that the characters face. In several of these narratives, the Nazi and Communist pasts play a significant role in who is awarded a house. The premises of these films and texts hinge on the unique intersection of economics, politics, and history in the former East Germany of the 1990s. While the films from the early 1990s, particularly *Our House* and *The Same Old Song*, address the Nazi past directly, it takes on a more complicated role in the prose fiction of the 2000s. To discuss the presentation of historical responsibility in Jenny Erpenbeck's *Visitation* and Kathrin Gerlof's *Now That's a Story*, I turn to Aleida Assmann's list of strategies for denying historical responsibility for National Socialism and the Holocaust that she identifies operating in German culture today. These strategies include offsetting (that is, relativizing suffering), externalizing (pointing blame at others), erasure, remaining silent, and falsification.³⁵ While these terms describe the tactics the characters in *Now That's a Story* employ to defend their rights to their homes, Assmann's taxonomy does not account for the full commercialization of the past that we see in *Visitation*. In Erpenbeck's novel, Germans are no longer ashamed of the Nazi past by the turn of the millennium. Rather, the fact that the house at the center of the novel was built by an architect who worked on Albert Speer's Germania project becomes a selling point for real estate agents.

A final theme to appear across chapters in this monograph is the way in which the privatization of houses in some ways disrupted, and in some ways reified, conventional gender norms. In most of the narratives discussed in this monograph, the conventional gender order is only ever destabilized temporarily, although two exceptions stand out. Ula Stöckl's film *The Same Old Song* portrays a matrilineal inheritance structure and Karen Duve's novel *Rain* imagines a largely female East German society. While the other texts and films in question do not portray gender roles in a very progressive or experimental manner, there are moments in which they cast a critical eye on conventional gender dynamics. Particularly the stories of Judith Hermann depict the ways in which

---

34 See David Harvey, *A Brief History of Neoliberalism* (Oxford and New York: Oxford University Press, 2005), 39–63.
35 Aleida Assmann, *Shadows of Trauma: Memory and the Politics of Postwar Identity*, trans. Sarah Clift (New York: Fordham University Press, 2016), 141–153.

men's decisions about property can be detrimental to women. To discuss the female characters kept in relative captivity in Hermann's works, I draw on Sigrid Weigel's broad study of femininity in modern European philosophy and literature. Surveying the depiction of women at home in European cultural productions from the eighteenth through the twentieth century, Weigel concludes that the socialization of girls to become wives constitutes a colonization of women, and houses serve as a key tool of the patriarchy.[36]

At the same time, two other novels that appeared at the turn of the millennium depict newly acquired homes as the main threat to their owners' masculinity. In Peter Schneider's *Eduard's Homecoming* and Karen Duve's *Rain*, the male protagonists are overwhelmed by the financial and material demands of owning a home in the East, which triggers their masculinity crises. Indeed, Claudia Breger and other scholars in German Studies have identified a widespread preoccupation with the fragility of masculinity in Germany at the turn of the millennium. To contextualize this dynamic in these two novels, I turn to work by Klaus-Michael Bogdal and Wolfgang Schmale, two scholars working at the intersections of German Studies and Masculinity Studies. Both scholars highlight the role that property ownership has played in the dominant masculinity construct in Europe since the eighteenth century. Not only has the (male) ownership of property been the driving force behind the delineation of public and private spaces in modern society, and thereby reified male and female gender roles; property ownership has often been requisite for the full participation in political life.[37] Moreover, the hegemonic masculinity construct typically requires men to occupy the provider and protector role within the family and thus has often been available only to men with the means to own property.[38] Both Bogdal and Schmale argue that German society expanded its view of acceptable masculinities in the second half of the twentieth century, a change that accelerated at the turn of the millennium. This challenge to the hegemonic masculinity construct perhaps explains the widespread concern about conventional masculinity in the popular media and fiction around the year 2000.

In chapter 5, I turn to another scholar who takes a long view on gender in the European imaginary to examine the masculinity crises at play in *Eduard's Home-*

---

[36] Sigrid Weigel, *Topographien der Geschlechter* (Reinbek bei Hamburg: Rowohlt Taschenbuch Verlag, 1990), 128–131.
[37] Wolfgang Schmale, *Geschichte der Männlichkeit in Europa (1450–2000)* (Vienna, Cologne, and Weimar: Böhlau Verlag, 2003), 194.
[38] Klaus-Michael Bogdal, "Hard-Cold-Fast: Imagining Masculinity in the German Academy, Literature, and the Media," in *Conceptions of Postwar German Masculinity*, ed. Roy Jerome (Albany: State University of New York Press, 2001) 29.

coming and *Rain*. In his foundational work, *Male Fantasies*, Klaus Theweleit famously traces German literary and artistic depictions of water as a trope of men's anxiety about the threat of women's "uncontainability."³⁹ In this tradition, women appear as dangerous and seductive water nymphs, naiads, nixies, and mermaids, associated with flooding and the watery earth.⁴⁰ By contrast, men have historically depicted themselves as "steeled up" to protect against the "flowing" and "soft" femininity of mothers, lovers, and war enemies (who are often feminized in war propaganda).⁴¹ The "steeled up" male body represents the opposite of the abject feminine in the German imaginary, according to Theweleit. This suggests another possible dimension in a monograph about houses. Often seen as a "second skin," houses variably succeed or fail at "steeling up" to protect their male inhabitants from the threats of the outside world.

As this monograph demonstrates, the destabilization of property relations in the former East Germany triggered a wave of cultural productions that address anxieties about home by employing themes of *Heimat*, the materiality of houses, neoliberalism, the Nazi past, and the construction of gender. Home has perhaps always been a site where issues of material and emotional security intersect, where belonging should secure one's role within the family and in society, and where one might shut out, if only temporarily, society's demands. The restructured property relations in the former East, which left so many people vulnerable, makes the fragility of home evident. An emotional tie to *Heimat* no longer guarantees one's belonging there. The Nazi past cannot be escaped or obscured in the domestic realm when it might be the cause of one's loss of home. The financial and material demands of home can no longer allow men and women to occupy conventional gender roles as though they were natural, nor can they allow dreams of inheritance to continue to promise wealth and security. Home and *Heimat* are no romantic or sentimental ideals in these scenarios, but rather, are continued social and material intra-actions.

This book has a relatively narrow focus, examining cultural productions in which Westerners enter the East in order to acquire a residential property, either during or following the era of privatization. In Chapter 7, I address the privatization of a business as part of a discussion about Westerners purchasing homes and settling in the former East. Otherwise, the privatization of non-residential properties is outside the purview of this monograph. Fictional narratives that depict the privatization of commercial properties and the work of the *Treuhand*,

---

39 Klaus Theweleit, *Male Fantasies*, trans. Stephen Conway, Erica Carter, and Chris Turner (Minneapolis: University of Minnesota Press, 1987), 236–310.
40 Klaus Theweleit, *Male Fantasies*, 274.
41 Klaus Theweleit, *Male Fantasies*, 229–310.

such as Günther Grass's novel *A Broad Field* (*Ein weites Feld*, 1995), Stefan Heym's volume of stories and essays *Filz: Thoughts on the Newest Germany* (*Filz: Gedanken über das neuste Deutschland*, 1992), Rolf Hochhuth's play *Westerners in Weimar: Scenes from an Occupied Land* (*Wessis in Weimar: Szenen aus einem besetzten Land*, 1993), and Ingo Schulze's *Simply Storys* (1999) could be rich source material for further research. I also do not examine cultural productions in which the acquisition of residential property in the East by a Westerner is treated only peripherally, as in Yadé Kara's novel *Selam Berlin* (2003), or where homes in the East play other roles, as in Thomas Arslan's film *Vacation* (*Ferien*, 2007) or Christian Petzold's film *Jerichow* (2008).

Homelessness is not a central topic of this study, but it does arise in some limited instances, overtly when I examine Detlev Buck's film *No More Mr. Nice Guy*, but more often as an implicit threat to those who stand to lose their homes, such as in *Our House* and *The Same Old Song*. Similarly, while squatting and other non-conventional living arrangements are an important part of the residential landscape of the former East Germany, squatters play a role only in my treatment of Peter Schneider's novel *Eduard's Homecoming*. Finally, while this book does address the destabilization of gender roles, their reinforcement, the varying dangers posed to women and men at home, and the inability of houses to protect them, certain issues pertaining to home, gender, sexuality, and protection are largely missing from the corpus of primary texts. Domestic violence, for instance, is not a central focus of my work, although it does come up in my discussion of Judith Hermann's *Where Love Begins*. Issues of LGBTQ+ belonging, dangers at home, homelessness, and chosen family barely appear in these works, and issues of race even less. Rather, the corpus of primary texts examined here, determined for its presentation of the changing property relations that followed unification, depict characters and families that are largely white and heteronormative.

I kept the parameters of this study narrow in order to highlight the issue of changing property relations resulting from German unification and the privatization of the former East Germany. These narratives are limited as general social and historical analyses; however, I submit that they present the challenges of home in powerfully emotional, personal, and nuanced ways. In examining these homes and the characters who vie for them, we see how the history of expropriation and displacement in this part of Germany in the twentieth century reverberates into the present, creating emotional, financial, and familial instabilities. Moreover, the disputes over these homes mark a unique moment in the discursive history of homes as property, happening before the sub-prime mortgage crisis of the late-2000s that would come to associate home ownership explicitly with speculation, predatory lending, and finance capitalism. The homes under discussion in *Domestic Disputes* thus show the interface of the personal, the material, and discourse at a crucial point in the development of neoliberalism. We see that when home, as the cornerstone of social intelligibility and financial stability, is threatened, so is one's position in society. These narratives reveal the fragility of home as *Heimat* and refuge that so many Germans have counted upon until now.

Chapter 1
Home in the East as a Bureaucratic Nightmare: On Property Claims, Media Representations, and the Informative Function of Television Movies

In 1992, the weekly newspaper *Die Zeit* published an article titled "Der Häuserkampf" ("Urban Warfare"), a report on the widespread mistrust Easterners felt toward Westerners in the era of property disputes. One of the most poignant images in this article is a warning sign spotted on a front lawn in Zeesen, near Berlin, which read: "For people hostile to this property (Westerners), entering is strictly prohibited. Enter at your own risk."[1] By 1992, many Easterners feared that Westerners would take their property, and the article quotes a number of locals who anticipated previous owners – or new speculators – coming for their homes. "If one comes in here, I'll go at him with a pitchfork" says one woman.[2] Another man states that he would rather burn his house down than relinquish it to a Westerner since he would face homelessness if forced out: "If it's decided that I have to evacuate this house, I'll torch it. In jail I'll at least be warm and won't have to sleep under a bridge."[3] Such statements attest to the desperation many felt as they awaited expropriation.

People who stood to lose their homes in the era of unification faced a complex, and largely opaque, bureaucratic system governing the ways in which properties were awarded. Although property rights were to be determined principally on the historical ownership of a home, there are more than a few discrepancies among the law review journals and news reports of the time about how that principal would be carried out. The lack of agreement among legal experts resulted not only in variations in the implementation of the law, but also in more general public confusion. In this chapter, I bring together the pertinent laws, as interpreted in law review journal articles and news reports, to provide an overview of the bureaucratic hurdles that both Easterners and Westerners faced when making or disputing property claims. I will also outline the historical cir-

---

[1] "Für grundstücksfeindliche Personen (Wessis) ist das Betreten dieses Grundstücks strengstens untersagt. Betreten nur auf eigene Gefahr." Wolfgang Gehrmann und Nikolaus Piper, "Der Häuserkampf." *Die Zeit* (Hamburg, Germany) March 20, 1992.
[2] "Wenn hier einer reinkommt, gehe ich mit der Mistforke auf ihn los." Wolfgang Gehrmann und Nikolaus Piper, "Der Häuserkampf."
[3] "Wenn entschieden wird, daß ich das Haus räumen muß, fackele ich die Hütte ab. Im Knast habe ich es wenigstens warm, muß nicht unter der Brücke schlafen." Ibid.

cumstances that led Westerners into the East to claim property. Case studies from the news media will further enrich the discussion, as they convey the sense of insecurity that many Easterners felt in the face of complex bureaucratic procedures. Finally, an examination of one of the first fictional narratives to address housing disputes, the made-for-television movie *Taxi to Rathenow* (*Taxi nach Rathenow*, Engel 1991), demonstrates the essential role that fictional television productions played in informing a larger public about property policy in the privatizing East.

A Deeply Flawed System

In order to understand the anxiety, vulnerability, and mistrust that many Easterners felt about the changing property relations, one must realize just how completely the processes of German unification had put Easterners at a disadvantage to their Western counterparts. Instead of merging the two states to create a new Germany, as many had hoped, unification was achieved through the dissolution of the German Democratic Republic (GDR) and the absorption of its territory, people, assets, and debts into the Federal Republic of Germany (FRG). The *Treaty of 31 August 1990 between the Federal Republic of Germany and the German Democratic Republic on the Establishment of German Unity* (hereafter Unification Treaty)[4] provided for German unification according to the terms outlined in the preamble and article 23 of the *Grundgesetz*, or Basic Law, of West Germany.[5] The West German government had always considered unification an inevitability, and the preamble of the Basic Law, ratified in May 1949, went so far as to call it a duty of the German people: "The entire German people is called upon to accomplish, by free self-determination, the unity and freedom of Germany."[6] By placing this statement in the preamble of its own constitution, the FRG embedded the concept of a provisional GDR into its very framework. Furthermore, article 23 provided the means for this unification:

---

4 *Vertrag zwischen der Bundesrepublik Deutschland und der Deutschen Demokratischen Republik über die Herstellung der Einheit Deutschlands*
5 The Unification Treaty also determined the reorganization of the GDR's administrative districts into five federal states and addressed the major legal and financial issues pertaining to unification.
6 "Das gesamte Deutsche Volk bleibt aufgefordert, in freier Selbstbestimmung die Einheit und Freiheit Deutschlands zu vollenden." Source of translation: "The Basic Law of the FRG (23 May 1949)." CVCE, University of Luxembourg, https://www.cvce.eu/content/publication/1999/1/1/7fa618bb-604e-4980-b667-76bf0cd0dd9b/publishable_en.pdf.

> For the time being, this Basic Law shall apply in the territory of the Laender [sic] Baden, Bavaria, Bremen, Greater Berlin, Hamburg, Hesse, Lower Saxony, North Rhine-Westphalia, Rhineland-Palatinate, Schleswig Holstein, Wuerttemberg-Baden and Wuerttemberg-Hohenzollern. It shall be put into force for other parts of Germany on their accession.[7]

The administrative districts of the GDR would join the FRG upon agreeing to adhere to the West German Basic Law. Upon unification, the West German Basic Law and the civil rights it guarantees would apply to the territories of the GDR, replacing East German law.

To expedite unification, the East German government voted to dissolve itself and take the path outlined by the FRG rather than negotiate a wholly new constitution with West Germany, which would have been cumbersome and legally unprecedented. While the government opted for this path to unification because it was most expeditious, many Easterners felt betrayed by that decision, seeing unification taking place on Westerners' terms. At the same time, many Westerners were also dissatisfied with this decision since it required the West to assume the debts and toxic assets of the former East Germany. Many Westerners felt financially burdened by special taxes designed to cover the bureaucratic and legal costs of unification, infrastructure updates, and environmental clean-up in the East.

This absorption into a foreign system was evident in almost all aspects of everyday life in East Germany. In preparation for entering the market economy, the East German government passed the *Law for the Sale of People's Structures* in March 1990, seven months before unitification officially took place. This law made the GDR's commercial property available to local, Western, and foreign investors for purchase, which soon resulted in the widespread closure of East German enterprises and, subsequently, high unemployment rates.[8] Workers in many sectors, especially professionals in education, academia, the government, and journalism, lost not only their jobs, but also their professional credentials. Some were required to go through retraining to keep their positions, whereas oth-

---

7 "Dieses Grundgesetz gilt zunächst im Gebiete der Länder Baden, Bayern, Bremen, Groß-Berlin, Hamburg, Hessen, Niedersachsen, Nordrhein-Westfalen, Rheinland-Pfalz, Schleswig-Holstein, Württemberg-Baden und Württemberg-Hohenzollern. In anderen Teilen Deutschlands ist es nach deren Beitritt in Kraft zu setzen." Translation source ibid.

8 *Gesetz über den Verkauf volkseigener Gebäude.* This law allowed private parties to purchase state-owned structures in East Germany for business purposes and provided an exception to article 20 of the GDR's civil code, which prohibited the private acquisition of people's property if it was to be used for business. See Michael J. Thomerson, "German Reunification: The Privatization of Socialist Property on East Germany's Path to Democracy," *Georgia Journal of International and Comparative Law* 21, no. 1 (1991): 128.

ers were fired and replaced by professionals from West Germany. While that law from March 1990 opened up East German assets for investment and purchase from the outside, the *Treaty Establishing a Monetary, Economic and Social Union*, signed on May 18, 1990, is widely considered to have been the first concrete step in the actual unification process.[9] In addition to making the Deutsche Mark the official currency of both lands and rendering the Ostmark obsolete as of July 1990, it established the legal basis for East Germany's transition from a planned socialist economy to a market economy.

A fundamental question in transitioning to the Western economic system was how the ownership of property would be determined. After World War II, West Germany had adopted a social market economy that allowed for individual or joint ownership of private property and operated on a system of full, transferable ownership.[10] Under the East German constitution, by contrast, property was largely considered means of production and was owned collectively as the people's property. This meant that all commercial property would eventually be organized into *volkseigene Betriebe* (VEBs, enterprises owned by the East German people) or grouped into larger *Kombinate* (combines). Eventually, all land and most homes would also belong to the state. For all practical purposes, however, state ownership of property was in title only, as the properties' residents, or those who operated businesses or farms on them, held the responsibility of maintenance.[11] In instances in which ownership was possible, the state served as a kind of holding corporation so that ownership by any private individual was in practice a form of trusteeship. The owner could acquire various rights, including possession and use, but the free transfer of properties between private individuals was prohibited. The state also reserved the right of first purchase on any property for sale, as well as the right to review all property transactions

---

9 *Vertrag über die Schaffung einer Währungs-, Wirtschafts- und Sozialunion zwischen der Deutschen Demokratischen Republik und der Bundesrepublik Deutschland.* Translation source: "Treaty Establishing a Monetary, Economic and Social Union (Bonn, 18 May 1990)," CVCE, University of Luxembourg, https://www.cvce.eu/en/obj/treaty_establishing_a_monetary_economic_and_social_union_bonn_18_may_1990-en-9847e49d-43c7-4c0e-b625-ff732673a06e.html

10 Rainer Frank, "Privatization in East Germany: A Comprehensive Study," *Vanderbilt Journal of Transnational Law* 27 (1994): 827; Michael J. Thomerson, "German Reunification, 124."

11 Dorothy Ames Jeffress, "Resolving Rival Claims on East German Property upon German Unification," *The Yale Law Journal* 101, no. 2 (1991): 531; Rainer Frank "Privatization in East Germany: A Comprehensive Study," 829; and Peter H. Merkl, "An Impossible Dream? Privatizing Collective Property in Eastern Germany," in *German Unification: Process and Outcomes*, ed. M. Donald Hancock and Helga A. Welsch (Boulder: Westview Press, 1994), 200.

for approval. Typically, transfer was only allowable if it preserved the property's assigned function under the planned economy.[12]

Article 14 of the West German Basic Law guarantees the right of citizens to own private property. Thus, domestic, commercial, and other assets owned by the East German state were to be privatized in order for the East German administrative districts to enter the FRG as states (*Länder*). Article 14 also guarantees citizens the right to compensation for unjust expropriation, which complicated the way in which property rights would be determined. Given the many waves of expropriation that had taken place over the course of the twentieth century within what constituted the current boundaries of the GDR, historical concerns had to be taken into consideration when determining private ownership of formerly state-held properties. During the Nazi era, Jews and other victims of the regime had lost real estate and moveable property because they had been dispossessed through confiscation, coerced into selling property during efforts to "Aryanize" businesses, compelled to flee, expelled from their communities, and/or robbed upon arrival at ghettos and camps. During the period of Soviet occupation following the World War II, the Soviet Military Administration in Germany (SMAD) seized nearly one third of the occupied territory, confiscating all real estate over 100 hectares (approximately 250 acres) in order to punish former affiliates of the Nazi party, claim war reparations for the Soviet Union, and restructure the land to serve the transition to Communism.[13] Many of the large land holdings previously owned by the nobility were divided into small plots and distributed to landless workers and German refugees from further East. Later, in a campaign that was officially launched at the Second Party Congress of the SED in July 1952 and lasted into the 1960s, the GDR restructured properties again in order to collectivize farmlands and create large-scale industry. While citizens were not formally required to relinquish their property in these collectivization efforts as they had been under Soviet occupation, the government practiced coercive measures, applying economic pressure to force private businesses into bankruptcy, strong-arming private landowners who owed money to the gov-

---

12 Rainer Frank, "Privatization in East Germany: A Comprehensive Study," 829.
13 Under *Befehl Nr. 124 der sowjetischen Militäradministration für Deutschland* (Order No. 124 of the Soviet Military Administration in Germany) of October 30, 1945, the Soviets dismantled 3843 firms by 1948. Of these, 676 were sent to the Soviet Union. See Arnd Bauerkämper, "Collectivization and Memory: Views of the Past and the Transformation of Rural Society in the GDR from 1952 to the Early 1960s," *German Studies Review* 25, no. 3 (May 2002): 216; Jonathan Doyle "A Bitter Inheritance: East German Real Property and the Supreme Constitutional Court's 'Land Reform' decision of April 23, 1991," *Michigan Journal of International Law* 13, no. 4. (1992): 844; Peter H. Merkl, "An Impossible Dream?" 201.

ernment, and confiscating property through criminal sentencing. Many poorer citizens who were unable to consolidate the small plots they had been appointed under SMAD were among the first to hand over their properties voluntarily.[14]

Emigration also played a role in the state's consolidation efforts. Early on, when citizens fled the GDR without official permits, the government placed their property under the control of a curator; later, the state simply confiscated such properties. Landowners who emigrated legally were often required to sell their property far below market value to someone deemed acceptable by Communist party functionaries. However, just as with cases of illegal emigration, this system eventually gave way to simple confiscation by the state. In 1972, a final comprehensive round of expropriations took place, the government confiscating almost all remaining small and mid-sized private businesses and turning them into VEBs. By 1990, over 95% of all property in the GDR was owned either by the government or communally, with private property constituting about 4.7%.[15]

As part of the negotiations of the Unification Treaty in 1990, representatives from both the GDR and FRG agreed on a means of compensating citizens and non-citizens for lands expropriated as far back as the Nazi period. West Germany had been issuing restitution and compensation to Jews persecuted during the Nazi era and their heirs since 1953 under the *Luxemburger Abkommen* (Luxembourg Agreement). This agreement, which was signed in September 1952 and took effect in March 1953, stipulated that West Germany would compensate Jews persecuted during the Nazi era via the Conference on Jewish Material Claims against Germany (JCC) for loss of livelihood, health, liberty, economic standing, or property. As part of the Unification Treaty, Germany was obligated to negotiate with the JCC on restitution claims that had not already been addressed or had been addressed insufficiently, including those in the former East Germany.[16]

For cases of expropriation that took place after the Nazi era, two forms of reparation were under consideration: financial compensation and restitution-in-kind. Given that property lines had been restructured extensively since 1945 and that the restoration of properties to their former owners would result in a

---

[14] For more on land collectivization, see Arnd Bauerkämper, "Collectivization and Memory."
[15] Peter H. Merkl, "An Impossible Dream?" 200.
[16] Karen Heilig, "From the Luxembourg Agreement to Today: Representing a People," *Berkeley Journal of International Law* 20 (2002): 183–190. The JCC was often declared the official heir of Jews who had lost property in the former East during the Nazi era. Once awarded to the JCC, the properties were typically sold and the proceeds distributed among benefactors of the organization.

large-scale dislocation of current residents, officials from the GDR pushed for financial compensation over restitution. The FRG, on the other hand, feared the financial cost of compensation and favored restitution-in-kind. Initial estimates of compensation approximated eight billion Deutsche Mark (approximately six billion USD), a sum that was unfeasible for Germany's struggling economy.[17] The *Joint Declaration of the Governments of the Federal Republic of Germany and the German Democratic Republic on the Settlement of Open Property Questions* of June 15, 1990 (hereafter "Joint Declaration") announced the compromise. Restitution-in-kind would be the preferred method of reparation, but financial (or other) compensation would be available in certain cases.[18] Whenever possible, the physical property would be restored to the previous owner, but compensation would be awarded out of a central fund in cases in which the return of property would cause a social hardship, for example when the property in question served as a housing project; where the purpose of the land had changed in nature, such as residential areas that had been converted to industrial or business areas; for property that housed a commercial enterprise that provided jobs; and, in theory if not always in practice, when the current owner had acquired the property through a good faith purchase. In those instances when property could not be restored to a previous owner, compensation could take place in the form of money, land of comparable value, or shares in company stock. Any previous owner with a valid claim on a property also had the option of receiving financial compensation instead of restitution of the physical property. Claims were considered invalid if the property had been acquired through dishonest means, such as the abuse of power, corruption, coercion, or fraud.[19] The principle of "restitution before compensation" ("Rückgabe vor Entschädigung") was later formalized in the *Law on the Regulation of Open Property Questions*

---

17 This estimate would eventually seem modest in comparison to the actual overall cost of unification. In 1994, Merkl cited current estimates at about one hundred billion Deutsche Mark in compensation claims alone, and in 1997 Stack estimated nine hundred billion DM (six hundred billion USD) in overall costs connected with unification. Peter H. Merkl, "An Impossible Dream?" 203; Heather M. Stack, "The 'Colonization' of East Germany?: A Comparative Analysis of German Privatization," *Duke Law Journal* 46, no. 5 (March 1997): 1222.
18 *Gemeinsame Erklärung der Regierungen der Bundesrepublik Deutschland und der Deutschen Demokratischen Republik zur Regelung offener Vermögensfragen*
19 For explanations of the Joint Declaration, see Dorothy Ames Jeffress, "Resolving Rival Claims" 536–537; Michael J. Thomerson, "German Reunification," 128–130; and Heath M. Stack, "The 'Colonization' of East Germany?" 1222–224.

(hereafter "Property Law") of September 23, 1990 and finally, in the Unification Treaty itself.[20]

The Joint Declaration addressed property that either was confiscated by the state or went into trusteeship administration when a citizen fled from the GDR. Its most controversial provision was that properties expropriated under Soviet occupation, May 8, 1945 to October 6, 1949, were not to be considered subject to restoration or compensation. Because the GDR did not officially exist at the time of the Soviet expropriations, and because the expropriations took place under a foreign power, the unified German government had no jurisdiction to reverse them.[21] Moreover, this stipulation had been a condition on which the Soviets had agreed to German unification during the Two-Plus-Four Treaty negotiations, and thus a judicial reversal of the policy would constitute an intervention in international affairs. Aside from this legal quagmire, more practical considerations came into play. The Soviet land reforms in Germany had been so vast – a total area of about eight million acres or nearly one third of all property in the former East Germany – that it was not feasible to restore properties as they had stood in 1945. Moreover, many of the records from the SMAD occupation had been destroyed. The lack of available and reliable records would have made restitution of those properties nearly impossible and slowed the entire process of restitution in the former East Germany considerably.

The provision was controversial, and in the ensuing years, plaintiffs representing over 10,000 instances of SMAD expropriations took their cases before the *Bundesverfassungsgericht* (Federal Constitutional Court).[22] The most common argument that claimants presented for restitution of properties confiscated under SMAD was grounded in article 3(1) of the Basic Law, "All persons shall be equal before the law."[23] These claimants argued that restoring properties during one era of expropriations and disregarding another era constituted discrimination, violating the guaranteed right that all persons be treated equally. The decision

---

20 *Gesetz zur Regelung offener Vermögensfragen*. See also Jessica Heslop and Joel Roberto, "Property Rights in the Unified Germany: A Constitutional, Comparative, and International Legal Analysis," *Boston University International Law Journal* 11 (1993): 257; Joseph Zeller and Tatiana Wait, "Safeguarding Propert Claims in the Former GDR," *International Financial Law Review* 11, no. 3 (Mar 1992).
21 Jonathan J. Doyle, "A Bitter Inheritance: East German Real Property and the Supreme Constitutional Court's 'Land Reform' decision of April 23, 1991," 853–855; Rainer Frank, "Privatization in Eastern Germany," 823; Dorothy Ames Jeffress, "Resolving Rival Claims" 530–543; Peter H. Merkl, "An Impossible Dream?" 201.
22 Peter H. Merkl, "An Impossible Dream?" 201.
23 "Alle Menschen sind vor dem Gesetz gleich." Translation source: *Basic Law of the Federal Republic of Germany*, Deutscher Bundestag, https://www.btg-bestellservice.de/pdf/80201000.pdf

not to restore properties confiscated by the SMAD intensified many Easterners' feelings of being disregarded in the new system where decisions were being made from Western viewpoints.

The Federal Constitutional Court ruled that the unification agreement with the Soviet Union must take priority over German constitutional principles.[24] Instead of considering the SMAD expropriations equivalent to those that took place later in the GDR, they should be treated like wartime losses, similar to property ceded to Poland and the Soviet Union.[25] In 1994, however, the *Law for Public Compensatory Payment for Expropriations Based on the Law or Sovereignty of Occupation, which Cannot Be Made Reversible* was passed, which amended this decision and guaranteed the right of those who had lost economic assets during the SMAD expropriations to partial financial compensation. It also upheld the principle that land could not be returned.[26] Plaintiffs nevertheless continued to push for restitution of properties, and as late as 2004, such challenges were taken before the Federal Constitutional Court and struck down.[27]

The scale of the restitution and compensation cases filed between 1990 and 1996 was monumental, totaling over 1.2 million claims on nearly 2.5 million properties.[28] *Der Spiegel* reported in 1992 that in Rostock more than 10,000 restitution cases were pending, in Leipzig 48,000, and in East Berlin 110,000.[29] Some of the most desired properties lie just outside Berlin. In Zepernick, located within an hour's commute from Berlin, claims by Westerners and foreigners were pending on more than half the houses.[30] In Kleinmachnow, in similar proximity to Berlin, eight out of ten houses had claims pending.[31] Many of these claims

---

[24] Decision of April 23, 1991, "Entscheidung des Bundesverfassungsgerichts BVerfGE, 1BvR 1170/90, 1174/90, 1175/90 (FRG)."
[25] Peter H. Merkl, "An Impossible Dream?" 201; Rainer Frank, "Privatization in Eastern Germany: A Comprehensive Study," 823–824.
[26] *Gesetz über staatliche Ausgleichsleistungen für Enteignungen auf besatzungsrechtlicher oder besatzungshoheitlicher Grundlage, die nicht mehr rückgängig gemacht werden können* (Ausgleichsleistungsgesetz – AusglLeistG).
[27] Decision of 26 October 2004, "Entscheidung des Bundesverfassungsgerichts BVerfG, 2 BvR 1038/01 – paras. (1–159)."
[28] Mark Blacksell, et al., "Settlement of Property Claims in Former East Germany," *Geographical Review*. 86, no. 2 (Apr. 1996): 198. This difference in numbers reflects the fact that a single claim filed could pertain to multiple properties.
[29] "Alte Rechte neues Unrecht," *Der Spiegel*, June 26, 1992. n. pag.
[30] Stephen Kinzer, "Anguish of East Germans Grows with Property Claims by Former Owners," *The New York Times*, June 5, 1992. n. pag.
[31] "Alte Rechte neues Unrecht," n. pag.

came from large landholding families that had been dispossessed during the Nazi or SMAD eras. *Die Welt* reported in 2003 on a case in which 600 plots in Teltow-Seehof were under consideration to be returned to the heirs of the Saberskys, a Jewish family of industrialists who had been coerced to sell to Nazi functionaries.[32] The million square meters of land in question in Kleinmachnow had similarly belonged to the family of an influential Jewish building developer, Adolf Sommerfeld, who had fled to Palestine after being shot and injured by SA men and whose business was then seized and "Aryanized." After unification, the rightful ownership of much of the family's former property was now in question, leaving the current residents of Kleinmachnow fearful of being displaced.[33] There was also the singular instance of the SMAD having expropriated an entire village. According to *Der Spiegel*, the bulk of the assets of Spechthausen, a town in Brandenburg, including a school, a church, and a former paper factory, had once belonged to the Hankwitz family but was seized under SMAD orders when the family fled to the West. In 1992, the heirs of the Hankwitz family, now located in Bavaria, attempted to claim the family's former property. Their claim was denied on the basis that Article 143 amended the Basic Law to exempt SMAD expropriations from restitution laws after unification, much to the relief of the current residents.[34]

To manage the overwhelming volume of restitution cases, the government created the *Amt zur Regelung offener Vermögensfragen* (Office for the Regulation of Open Property Questions).[35] Located regionally, these offices handled claims on non-commercial property and worked in conjunction with the *Treuhand* (Trust Agency), which dealt with the privatization of commercial properties. Citizens could file claims on non-commercial properties with local governmental agencies in the area where the claimant (or, in the cases of heirs, the deceased) had lived in the GDR, and in order to minimize confusion, the Federal Justice of Ministry in Bonn processed claims pertaining to victims of Nazi persecution and any claims from abroad.[36] Local tribunals would assess property value and rule on the bulk of disputes between conflicting claimants.[37]

---

[32] Lothar Rölleke, "Rückgabe vor Entschädigung: Im größten Restitutionsprozess geht es um 1400 Grundstücke in Teltow und Kleinmachnow," *Die Welt* 94, April 23 2003. n. pag.
[33] Ibid.
[34] "Alte Rechte neues Unrecht," n. pag.
[35] The Office for the Regulation of Open Property Questions was established by the Law for the Privatization and Reorganization of People's Property of July 1, 1990.
[36] Nicholas Hancock and Hans-Dieter Schulz-Gebeltzig, "Recovering Expropriated Property in Eastern Germany," *New Law Journal*. 1 March 1991. n. pag.
[37] Dorothy Ames Jeffress, "Resolving Rival Claims," 528.

While it was advantageous for local governments to decide on property claims – that is, it gave local authorities a voice in determining how properties in their communities would be awarded – such a decentralized system made the process of privatization difficult to coordinate.[38] The Property Law was amended a number of times to attract investors, and as noted above, even the Basic Law underwent an amendment in order to protect the stipulation in the Joint Declaration that exempted SMAD expropriations from restitution. Such modifications led to widespread confusion over the laws and shifting deadlines for those wishing to file claims. For example, one of the first filing deadlines – for individuals or organizations wishing to claim property lost during expropriations after 1972 – was moved up from January 31, 1991 to October 13, 1990. This shortened deadline caught claimants off guard, and lawyers encouraged their clients to file their claims even if they had not filed by October since it was uncertain whether that deadline was absolute.[39] Another deadline that pertained to claims made from abroad, particularly those regarding expropriations during the Nazi era and those who had abandoned property within the former GDR, was set for March 31, 1991, but, as an article in the *New Law Journal* from earlier in that month makes clear, lawyers were uncertain about the firmness of that deadline as well.[40]

In addition to the complications that resulted from the ever-shifting bureaucracy, many problems arose due to the tumultuous history of the area over the course of the twentieth century. It was feasible that a property could have been confiscated or abandoned during the Nazi era, again during the Soviet occupation, and once or more in the GDR. Even heirs within the same family were sometimes in competition for the same property. In fact, *Der Spiegel* reported on an extreme case in which a house on the island Rügen had twelve different claims pending.[41] Political regime changes over the course of the twentieth century had also resulted in cities and streets being renamed, which further complicated the processing of property claims. One would have been hard pressed in 1992, for example, to find a surviving Adolph-Hitler-Straße or Stalinallee, as had existed in previous decades. Local government officials often had to engage in investigative work to figure out the location of a claim. As one official reported to *Der Spiegel* "It can happen that a postcard comes from an Australian village with the message, 'My grandmother owned a beautiful corner house on Adolf-

---

[38] Dorothy Ames Jeffress, "Resolving Rival Claims," 544.
[39] Nicholas Hancock and Hans-Dieter Schulz-Gebeltzig, "Recovering Expropriated Property in Eastern Germany," n. pag.
[40] Ibid.
[41] "Alte Rechte, neues Unrecht," n. pag.

Hitler-Street.' And the consultants in the office for the management of pending property issues have to search like detectives in the property registries or the city archives."⁴²

Legal analysts Nicholas Hancock and Hans-Dieter Schulz-Gebeltzig of *New Law Journal* warned their readership – presumably property rights lawyers in the United State – of such difficulties: "Claimants often have only the haziest information about property in eastern Germany. It is imperative to act quickly in such cases. Land registers in the ex-GDR – where they exist at all – are generally in a sorry state and so claims must be particularized precisely when they are lodged. Street names are often of little assistance in identifying a property because they may have been changed several times since 1933 as a result of political developments. Thus, in many cases there is no alternative to on-the-spot research."⁴³

Aside from the renamed streets, Hancock and Schulz-Gebeltzig point out another complicating factor in determining the private ownership of properties: the GDR had kept notoriously poor records.⁴⁴ While East German law, similar to that of West Germany, required the transfer of ownership to be recorded in the *Grundbuch* (property register), the system broke down in East Germany in the 1970s.⁴⁵ *Der Spiegel* profiled a case in 1990, in which Claus Nuscheler, a plumber originally from Brandenburg who had fled to the West in 1977 and settled in Hessen, attempted to claim his former home after unification. Upon returning to the home, he found that the house and land now belonged to Robert Rosenthal, previously an officer of the East German National People's Army who had had close ties to the SED (East German Socialist Unity Party) and was now a banker. Since the property register was missing, Nuscheler had little recourse with the Office for

---

42 Ibid. "Da kann es geschehen, daß aus einem australischen Dorf eine Postkarte kommt, auf der es heißt: 'Meine Großmutter besaß ein wunderschönes Eckhaus an der Adolf-Hitler-Straße.' Und schon müssen die Referenten im Amt zur Regelung offener Vermögensfragen wie Detektive in Grundbüchern oder im Stadtarchiv recherchieren."
43 Nicholas Hancock and Hans-Dieter Schulz-Gebeltzig, "Recovering Expropriated Property in Eastern Germany," n. pag.
44 See also Peter H. Merkl, "An Impossible Dream?" 203.
45 Dorothy Ames Jeffress, "Resolving Rival Claims," 531. According to the German Land Register Act, which dates back to 1897, any change in the rights to a property must be recorded in the land register in order to be valid (with few exceptions). The land register lists current and previous owners of a property, any third parties who might have rights to it, and a description of its characteristics. There is no national land registry; the land registry falls under the jurisdiction of local courts. See "Grundbuchordnung," *Gesetze im Internet*, Bundesministerium der Justiz und für Verbraucherschutz, https://www.gesetze-im-internet.de/gbvfg/GBV.pdf

the Regulation of Open Property Questions.[46] The property registers in many areas were missing, and in those that did exist, pages were often torn from them or entries falsified, leaving the records less than trustworthy.[47]

Furthermore, the way in which the East German government had administered land caused difficulties in the era of privatization. Although GDR citizens were legally entitled to own a house, a provision in the Civil Code permitted the separate ownership of a structure and the land on which it stood.[48] The government retained ownership of the land, leaving homeowners to apply only for a *Nutzungsurkunde* (certificate of right of use).[49] This policy left many people who owned their house, but not the plot of land on which it stood, vulnerable to restitution claims on the plot.[50] It was not until March 1990, when the GDR was privatizing, that citizens could purchase land, and even those who did purchase the land on which their homes stood faced uncertainty. *Die Zeit* reported in March 1992 on Hans and Helga Kadenbach, who bought their home in 1981 after renting it for twenty years. It had become people's property after the heir of the previous owner relinquished it as a financial burden, and so the Kadenbachs bought it from the *Kommunale Wohnungsverwaltung* (Communal Housing Administration). They also received their certificate of right to use the land later that year, and, in five years, paid off the house. When land became available to purchase in 1990, they bought the plot on which it stood. However, in 1991, when they applied for a loan to update the heating in their house, they were denied on the grounds that its ownership was unclear. A restitution claim had been filed on the house from someone in Munich. The Kadenbachs installed the heating system anyway, paying out of pocket because of the necessity of the update. However, at the time of the report, they were waiting to learn whether they would be able to keep the house.[51] The article goes on to profile two other cases in which occupants of a house had made substantial updates to the prop-

---

[46] "Die Lage ist trostlos," *Der Spiegel*, Oct 8, 1990. n. pag. This story was profiled again in 1992 in "Alte Rechte neues Unrecht," n. pag.

[47] Dorothy Ames Jeffress, "Resolving Rival Claims," 543; Peter H. Merkl, "An Impossible Dream?" 204.

[48] GDR Civil Code, Paragraph 295 (2).

[49] In the mid-1970s, home ownership in the GDR was at nearly 40% of the population. By 1990, it had sunk to about 25%. See Peter H. Merkl, "An Impossible Dream?" 204; Sebastian Kohl, *Homeownership, Renting and Society: Historical and Comparative Perspectives, Homeownership, Renting and Society: Historical and Comparative Perspectives* (London and New York: Routledge), 7.

[50] Rainer Frank, "Privatization in Eastern Germany: A Comprehensive Study," 829–830.

[51] "Der Häuserkampf," n. pag.

erties they were inhabiting – either owned or were renting – and were now faced with the possibility of eviction.

Such cases make clear that, aside from the threat of displacement, Easterners often faced unforeseen complications when previous owners filed a claim on property. For example, with unclear assets, one could not expect to qualify for a bank loan.[52] Nor could one sell a property with a restitution claim on it until an official decision had been rendered.[53] This could take years and be costly for the party seeking to sell their property. *Der Spiegel* outlined a case in which Max Reinhard Neumann from Hessen inherited an empty, run-down hotel near the main train station in Leipzig. It had been confiscated in 1974 and placed under state administration. After unification, he fought for two years to regain the hotel, taking the bureaucratic steps to secure his legal claim, including having it listed in the property register with the help of a lawyer. However, when he initiated the sale of his hotel – he had identified an investor who wished to buy the property and begin renovations immediately – he was informed of another claimant to the property. Months later he was finally able to identify the competing heir to the property: his own name, Max Reinhard Neumann, was listed as the other party in the claim files. Overly complex bureaucracy – or perhaps, as he suspected, old animosities from previous SED functionaries still operating in the local government – had delayed his claim and his ability to sell.[54]

As the case of Neumann illustrates, not only did the prohibition on selling property with a pending restitution case cause problems for many, it hampered badly needed investment in the former East. Investors were often wary of initiating the purchase of property, even properties that did not have restitution claims currently on them, out of fear that a restitution case could arise.[55] This apprehension festered despite the fact that an advantage for commercial investors was written into the laws. The *Law on Special Investments in the German Democratic Republic* of August 31, 1990 provided an exception to the Property Law by empowering current owners or administers of real estate to sell or lease a property with a pending restitution claim if the property was needed to create or ensure employment, correct a shortage in housing, or develop infrastructure.[56] The law appeared as article 41 of the Unification Treaty. After unification, an additional

---

52 "Alte Rechte neues Unrecht," n. pag.
53 Heather M. Stack, "The 'Colonization' of East Germany?" 1224.
54 "Alte Rechte neues Unrecht," n. pag.
55 Heather M. Stack, "The 'Colonization' of East Germany?" 1224.
56 *Gesetz über besondere Investitionen in der Deutschen Demokratischen Republik*, Paragraph 1 and 1(2). See also Heather M. Stack, "The 'Colonization' of East Germany?" 1218–1219 and Michael J. Thomerson, "German Reunification," 131.

law was implemented to encourage investors, the *Law to Remove Impediments to Privatization of Enterprises and for the Promotion of Investments*[57] of March 28, 1991. This law allowed the *Treuhand* and other governmental agencies to sell properties encumbered by a restitution claim as long as the sale was made for the purposes of promoting investment.[58] Such provisions were controversial because they were seen as creating loopholes for potential profiteers to purchase and sell properties under the pretense of creating jobs or promoting investment, regardless of real intent.[59]

Such provisions in the law added to Easterners' feelings of vulnerability since they often resulted in decisions that favored Western and foreign investors over locals. The *Treuhand*'s main responsibility was to privatize East German commercial assets as quickly as possible according to the *Privatization and Reorganization of Publicly Owned Assets Act* of July 1, 1990 (hereafter "Trust Law").[60] In order to do so, it provided credits to the investors and existing enterprises assessed to be most likely to survive and provide jobs in the market economy. Enterprises considered to have a lesser chance of surviving on the free market were to be liquidated or declared bankrupt.[61] Because foreign and West German investors often had more access to capital, the *Treuhand* generally favored them over East Germans.[62] As legal analyst Heather M. Stack wrote in 1997,

> Although neutral on its face, in application the Trust Law favored foreign and West German investors over East Germans. […] Often, in fact, even when East Germans did possess the capital necessary to invest, more 'capable' foreign investors were favored. East German needs were thus subordinated in both the Trust Law's operation and effect.[63]

---

57 *Gesetz zur Beseitigung von Hemmnissen bei der Privatisierung von Unternehmen und zur Förderung von Investitionen*
58 Jessica Heslop and Joel Roberto, "Property Rights in the Unified Germany: A Constitutional, Comparative, and International Legal Analysis"; Heather M. Stack, "The 'Colonization' of East Germany?" 1225.
59 Dorothy Ames Jeffress, "Resolving Rival Claims," 538.
60 *Gesetz zur Privatisierung und Reorganisation des volkseigenen Vermögens*. On July 1, 1990, all socialist enterprises in East Germany were transferred to the ownership of the *Treuhand* and became companies under German corporate law. The *Treuhand* owned all shares of these companies and was responsible for assessing their viability for the free market, preparing viable businesses to sell to private interests, and shutting down those deemed unviable. See Heather M. Stack, "The 'Colonization' of East Germany?" 1218–1219 and Michael J. Thomerson, "German Reunification," 130–131.
61 Michael J. Thomerson, "German Reunification," 140 and Heather M. Stack, "The 'Colonization' of East Germany?" 1219.
62 Heather M. Stack, "The 'Colonization' of East Germany?" 1218–1219.
63 Heather M. Stack, "The 'Colonization' of East Germany?" 1221–1222.

Due to the perception that East Germans were less able to manage investments, they were left with very little ownership in their own country.[64]

What further compounded East Germans' sense of vulnerability – in addition to the Unification Treaty's policy of restitution over compensation and the *Treuhand*'s preference for foreign and West German investors over East Germans – was the lack of proper legal representation available to them. Lawyers and judges had been rare in East Germany in comparison to the West because there had been no judiciary independent from the state. In the first year of unification, there were fewer than 700 lawyers in the former GDR serving a population of about 18 million. In comparison, more than 60,000 lawyers were practicing in the West, serving a population of about 62 million.[65] Very few of the existing East German lawyers were trained as assessors or in land registry, and many were prohibited from practicing or were undergoing re-training because of ties to the former Communist regime. East Germans thus faced an unprecedented legal situation for which there was little access to representation, especially outside larger cities. West German lawyers flocked to the former East Germany, but even so, demand was impossible to meet. Moreover, they had little expertise in East German property law, which had been based on the concept of people's property, and thus were not fully competent in serving East German citizens' needs. While many West German lawyers left soon after arriving in the East, those who stayed were often met with mistrust. With capital flowing from West Germany and abroad, many Easterners feared that lawyers and judges could be bought off to make decisions in favor of foreign investors. Even when it came to paying standard legal fees, East Germans were at a disadvantage, as they were typically less able to afford costs incurred by the slow-moving bureaucracy and the legal strategies Westerners could employ to draw cases out. Many were forced to forfeit their cases out of financial strain.[66]

Without proper legal guidance, and with a shortage of qualified personnel, those with the authority to make decisions regarding property claims were slow to come to resolutions. An estimate from 1992, two years into the process of awarding properties, predicted three decades or more of paperwork, and in

---

64 Heather M. Stack, "The 'Colonization' of East Germany?" 1236–1237.
65 Mark Blacksell et al., "Search for a Unified Justice," *Geographical Magazine* 67, no. 2 (Feb 1995): 30; Peter H. Merkl, "An Impossible Dream?" 203.
66 See "Alte Rechte neues Unrecht," n. pag.; Mark Blacksell et al., "Search for a Unified Justice," 31; Dorothy Ames Jeffress, "Resolving Rival Claims," 532; Peter H. Merkl, "An Impossible Dream?" 203.

one area in Saxony, eighty-two years.[67] Indeed, to date, the restitution of noncommercial properties is ongoing. On December 31, 1994, the *Treuhand* officially closed, having sold some 6500 companies to private investors, reprivatized 1600, sold 300 to local communities, and shut down about 3700.[68] However, a State Office for the Regulation of Open Property Questions continues to exist in each federal state formerly in East Germany to process claims on residential properties, as does the Federal Office for Central Services and Unresolved Property Issues (BADV), which has taken over the duties of the former Federal Agency for the Settlement of Open Property Questions.[69] By 2015, when the BADV published the last available statistics, these local and national offices had processed over 2.3 million restitution claims plus a quarter of a million financial compensation cases pertaining to property lost during the Soviet occupation. Just over two thousand restitution cases were still pending as of 2015, as were nearly another quarter of a million financial compensation claims.[70]

While lawyers and local officials worked to interpret the new laws, their bureaucratic implications, and the shifting deadlines they created, those individuals wishing to claim property or defend against potential claims sought information in a number of ways. The German Ministry of Spatial Order, Construction, and Urban Planning published a guide in 1993 for potential buyers, especially of apartments, titled *The Privatization of Homes in the New States: Information for Prospective Buyers and Renters*.[71] Other advice books, such Rowohlt's *Unresolved Property Questions, a Guidebook: The Fight for Houses, Vacation Homes and Land Plots, on the Changing Legal Status in the New States*, were published soon after in multiple editions. These guidebooks provided comprehensive information following changes in the laws, but could do so only slowly.[72] News media were much more nimble, if also more piecemeal, in their presentation of new information to a broad German populace. In addition to the national newspapers and magazines that engaged in investigative reporting (such as *Das Handels-*

---

[67] "Alte Rechte neues Unrecht," n. pag., see also Dorothy Ames Jeffress, "Resolving Rival Claims," 532; Mark Blacksell et al., "Search for a Unified Justice," 30.
[68] Heather M. Stack, "The 'Colonization' of East Germany?" 1227.
[69] These offices are the *Landesamt zur Regelung offener Vermögensfragen*, the *Bundesamt zur Regelung offener Vermögensfragen*, and the *Bundesamt für zentrale Dienste und offene Vermögensfragen*, respectively.
[70] file:///C:/Users/nchroni/Downloads/akt_Statistik.pdf
[71] Bundesministerium für Raumordnung, Bauwesen und Städtebau, *Wohnungsprivatisierung in den neuen Bundesländern. Informationen für Kaufinteressenten und Mieter*.
[72] Dirk Brouër, et al. *Offene Vermögensfragen, ein Ratgeber: der Streit um Häuser, Datschen und Grundstücke, zur veränderten Rechtslage in den neuen Ländern* (Reinbek bei Hamburg: Rowohlt, 1995).

blatt, Der Spiegel, Die Welt, and *Die Zeit,* cited above), headlines in regional newspapers like the *Leipziger Volkszeitung* foregrounded Easterners' sense of vulnerability: "The Dispossessed Want an Avalanche of Progress," and "Dispossessed Want to Sue."[73] National and regional radio and television broadcasts were often more neutral in tone. Televised news features like ZDF's *Heute* segment "Federal Assembly: Priority for Investments in Construction / Deadlines for Previous Owners" (July 10, 1992), ORB's *Brandenburg Aktuell* segment "Land Politics in Brandenburg" (Feb 11, 1993), ARD's *Tagesschau* segment "Compensation Law Passed" (May 20, 1994), and countless others, kept viewers abreast of new developments in the politics of property reform.[74]

The processes of privatization and restitution have been complicated and delicate, requiring the German authorities to balance the nation's obligation to former owners who had been unfairly dispossessed with the needs of current residents and owners, the public interest, and the necessity of investment in the area.[75] However, the way in which privatization and restitution took place exacerbated the sense of disenfranchisement among East Germans and increased the animosities that existed between Easterners and Westerners. These animosities find themselves expressed in the news media of the time, as we have seen, but all too often in oversimplified form. As messy and complicated as the bureaucratic system was, real relationships between Eastern and Western individuals, families, and communities were at least as complicated. Among the multitudes of headlines and news segments, a handful of fictional made-for-television movies appeared that depict property disputes in a more personal and complex manner, foregrounding the personal struggles of family and family history, psychological and emotional ties to home, and economic dependence upon place, among other factors, as they center on East-West politics. Remarkably, these fictional television productions also had an informative function, imparted key policy information to a broad viewing audience as the bureaucratic processes were unfolding.

---

73 "Zwangsenteignete wollen Progresslawine," *Leipziger Volkszeitung* (Leipzig, Germany), August 4–5, 1990 and "Heim ins Eigene? Enteignete wollen einklagen," *Leipziger Volkszeitung* (Leipzig, Germany). August 30, 1990.
74 "Bundesrat: Vorrang von Investitionen im Bau/Fristen für Alteigentümer," "Bodenpolitik Brandenburg," and "Entschädigungsgesetz verabschiedet," respectively.
75 See Dorothy Ames Jeffress, "Resolving Rival Claims," 528.

Informative Fiction in Television: *Taxi to Rathenow*

As I noted in the introduction to this monograph, ZDF premiered the first television movie on the topic of property disputes just a few days before the first anniversary of German unification, an East-West allegorical drama titled *Our House* (*Unser Haus*, Griesmayr 1991). I will treat this film in more detail in chapter 2, but I mention it here because in both the priorities established for the television film's production and its narrative content, *Our House* illustrates just how consciously television executives employed films to serve the goals of national unification. *Our House* was one of six films contracted by ZDF to affiliates of DEFA (*Deutsche Film Aktiengesellschaft*, the state-owned East German film company) in order to help the East German film industry make the transition to the competitive capitalist market. In this interfamilial drama, West German actors were cast to play the Western family and East German actors played the Eastern family. The stated goals of this casting decision were to introduce the audiences from East and West to actors from the other side and to give East German actors work in the industry.[76] Among the seven public television channels broadcast nationally in 1991, ZDF held the highest audience share.[77] Its programming reached more people than any other public German television station and gave its actors considerable exposure. For this broad viewing audience, there was a clear pedagogical mission as well. As ZDF's press statement puts it, "The film should give all Germans the possibility to identify with both sides, as humans, without clichés, conceived of rather as a small bridge than a deepening of the rift."[78]

ZDF's second film of the six DEFA-contracted projects, *Taxi to Rathenow*, premiered on October 3, 1991, the first anniversary of German unification. Rather than framing the housing dispute at the center of the story solely in dramatic terms, this film also pokes fun at the bureaucratic complications of unification and lampoons Westerners' perceived superiority to Easterners. According to ZDF's original press material, it was billed as a "television comedy with mass appeal,"[79] but in fact, the film balances comedy with dramatic tension and heart-

---

[76] Dagmar Schwalm, "Unser Haus," BWZ (no date), 27. Stiftung deutsche Kinemathek.
[77] "Jährliche Zuschaueranteile seit 1990" (PDF) *Kommission zur Ermittlung der Konzentration im Medienbereich*. kek-online.de
[78] "Unser Haus," press material, *ZDF Presseproduktion Berlin*, Stiftung deutsche Kinemathek. Originally: "Der Film soll allen Deutschen die Möglichkeit geben, sich in beide Seiten einzufühlen, menschlich, ohne Klischees, eher als schmale Brücke, denn als Vertiefung der Kluft gedacht."
[79] "Taxi nach Rathenow," *ZDF Presseproduktion Berlin*, Stiftung deutsche Kinemathek. Originally: "publikumsattraktive Fernsehkomödie"

rending moments that invite viewers to identify with a number of characters' attachment to the house in question. Despite a running time of only 59 minutes, *Taxi to Rathenow* is exemplary of the films of its kind. It depicts the threat Easterners faced when Westerners wished to claim property, while at the same time representing the motivations of Westerners in a complicated but ultimately sympathetic manner. As an artifact it is equally compelling. It not only imparted key policy information to the German viewing audience at the time, but also exhibits a range of narrative topoi for framing property disputes in fiction that are recognizable in the films that I will discuss in chapters 2 and 3.

Taxi to Rathenow takes place over the course of a day, as the taxi driver Georg drives the elderly Edith Strombach from Berlin to her childhood home in Rathenow in the former East Germany. There, she plans to confront the current residents, the Golze family, about claiming the house. The film opens on a rather unremarkable scene, a high angle shot of a taxi stand. Indeed, on such a normal day, Georg cannot possibly anticipate the unusual excursion he is about to embark on. The sun is shining, and the weather is almost deceptively cheerful. In the series of medium shots that follow (the film makes use of a rather conventional cinematic scheme), we watch as a brand new Mercedes taxi enters at the back of the line. Our protagonist, Georg, emerges from it and is greeted cheerfully by the other taxi drivers. He has apparently been out of commission for some time. While the other drivers inspect his new taxi and remark on its top-of-the-line features, which include electric windows and a car phone, Georg proudly proclaims that no one will smoke in it. This is a particularly proud day for Georg, and to honor it, the other drivers allow him to skip to the front of the taxi line and take the next fare. As fate would have it, Georg answers the call to the film's other protagonist, Edith, who will lead him on a misadventure into the former East, where he will ultimately be punished for his sense of superiority as a Westerner.

For the first third of the film, the comedy centers on Edith and Georg bickering as they make their way to Rathenow, and in this way, the film introduces both characters' claims to class- and gender-based privilege. When Edith emerges from her apartment building in a well-to-do part of Charlottenburg in the former West Berlin, her habitus puts her privilege and wealth on display. She is well dressed and well accessorized, donning a broach on her blazer, pearl earrings, a hat perched neatly atop coifed hair, and a small handbag. Her style contrasts with that of Georg, who wears his shirt sleeves rolled up to nearly his elbows, a decidedly working class look. Edith proves to be a difficult customer, dictating the fare she will pay, the route Georg will take to Rathenow, and the driving speed, all the while attempting to eat and smoke in the new taxi against Georg's desperate attempts at interdiction. When Georg tries to draw on his privilege as a man in order to lay down the law with Edith, her casual disregard of Georg's authority renders it laughable. While this extended sequence plays to comical effect, it also, and more importantly, showcases the personality traits that will make Edith a tough adversary for the Golze family: her keen business instincts, tenacity, and a sense of entitlement. At the same time, Georg displays the personality trait that will lead him into trouble later in the film, his rather unfounded claim to authority.

Parallel to the comical scenes that depict Edith and Georg coming from Berlin, the Golze family is introduced in a more somber fashion as they nervously anticipate Edith's arrival. According to the letter they received from Edith's lawyers, not only does she plan to claim the home she abandoned as a young adult, but she is also petitioning for back rent for the past thirty-five years. Edith's success in this endeavor would be a devastating financial burden for the family, whose only real asset and source of stability is the house. Their income depends entirely on Thomas Golze's tractor repair shop, which is failing in the new economy. If the Golzes were to lose their house, then Thomas, his mother, his wife Kerstin, and their two children may face homelessness.

When Edith arrives at the property, the economic disparity between the two parties could not be clearer. Recognizing Edith as the claimant from the West by the Mercedes taxi in which she arrives, Kerstin slips out the back door to fetch Thomas from work, leaving her mother-in-law, the elderly Frau Golze, to greet the visitor. This first face-to-face encounter between these two women of the same generation further emphasizes their difference in class and experience. Frau Golze's modest dress and hair fixed into a bun contrast with the more sophisticated look that Edith can afford (see figs. 1.1 and 1.2). In this scene, Frau Golze's initial mistrust for Edith is emphasized visually by her unwillingness to step outside the door, as well as her depth within the frame. She is also in a superior moral position to Edith. We view Frau Golze from a slightly low angle, as though to valorize her, whereas we are put in a position of looking down on Edith, quite literally, who stands humbly within the frame in a high angle shot. At the same time, Edith is framed more closely than Frau Golze is during this initial exchange, which makes her seem more approachable than the distant Frau Golze. Soon enough, Frau Golze's good nature overcomes her intial mistrust and she invites Edith inside.

Fig. 1.1: Frau Golze upon first encounter with Edith Strombach

Fig. 1.2: Edith Strombach upon first encounter with Frau Golze

Taxi to Rathenow not only foregrounds economic disparity in the era of privatization, but it also exhibits a number of topoi that would become typical for depicting property disputes. For example, these films often feature a family of three generations living together. In *Taxi to Rathenow*, Thomas and his wife Kerstin live with their children and his mother, Frau Golze, in the house in dispute. As we will see in chapter 2, the middle generation in these films, typically a husband and wife, is responsible for the financial stability of the family and thus engages in confrontation with the threatening entity from the West (as Thomas does in *Taxi to Rathenow*). Members of the older generation are more capable of communicating with their counterpart on the other side and thereby broker peace, while the youngest generation represents the future of the *Heimat*.

Edith straddles two of these roles, as both the threat from the West and a member of the older generation that is capable of reconciliation. Through this dual role that Edith plays, both sparring with Thomas and connecting emotionally with his mother, Frau Golze, over the course of the film, the television audience gains a great deal of information about the perspectives of both Easterners and Westerners. In the scenes in which the two women converse over tea in the comfortably furnished interior of the house and, later, over cherry cake in the garden, they share memories and family stories connected with the property. In the first of these conversations, Edith (and thus the West German viewing audience) learns about the difficult circumstances under which an East German family might have come to possess a house that had been abandoned:

Mrs. Golze: We bought the house in 1959 from the KWV

Edith: KWV? I don't know what that is.

> Mrs. Golze: Communal Housing Administration. On the condition that we were to do the necessary repairs to it. My husband was a carpenter, otherwise we wouldn't have gotten it at all. It was falling apart. It stood empty for five years, after all.
>
> [...]
>
> Mrs. Golze: And when we finalized the purchase contract, we still had to pay the mortgage on the property.
>
> Edith: Mortgage? What mortgage? We owned the house free and clear.
>
> Mrs. Golze: There were five years of unpaid property taxes with compound interest.
>
> Edith: I can't believe it![80]

The exchange offers the audience useful information. Not only does Frau Golze explain how housing was administered in the GDR, the stipulations under which one might acquire a house, and the financial burdens associated with owning one; an East German audience learns through Edith's reactions that Westerners had only a partial understanding of the difficulties that owning a home in the East had entailed.

Edith also reveals her motivations for abandoning the property: "We would have gladly stayed, but after the seventeenth of June you could see where this was all headed."[81] Edith felt compelled to leave after the workers' strike in 1953, when it became clear that the GDR was willing to use military force to control its citizens. According to the Property Law, those who were compelled to flee from the GDR were now entitled to the property they had relinquished if it had gone into trustee adminstration from the state. Edith is in that very position. She further defends her right to her property by pointing out that the Golze family does not have the required entry in the property register (*Grundbuch*):

> Edith: But the house is still my property just as before. I mean, you don't have an entry in the property register.

---

80 Frau Golze: Wir haben das Haus 1959 von der KWV gekauft. / Edith: KWV? Kenne ich nicht. / Frau Golze: Kommunale Wohnungsverwaltung. Mit der Auflage die notwendigen Reparaturen vorzunehmen. Mein Mann war Tischler, sonst hätten wir es gar nicht gekriegt. Es war ja völlig runtergekommen. Stand ja über fünf Jahre leer. / [...] / Frau Golze: Und als wir den Kaufvertrag abgeschlossen haben, mussten wir auch noch die Hypothek löschen, die das Grundstück belastete. / Edith: Hypothek? Was denn für eine Hypothek? Unser Haus war immer schuldenfrei. / Frau Golze: Das waren fünf Jahre nicht bezahlte Grundsteuern mit Zins und Zinseszinsen. / Edith: Also das gibt's doch gar nicht!

81 "Wir wären gerne geblieben, aber nach dem 17. Juni hat man doch gesehen wohin der Hase läuft."

> Mrs. Golze: When we bought it, we were told that it belonged to the city. We were deceived. And we are just now learning about the missing entry in the property register.[82]

In this exchange, one sees just how vulnerable East German homeowners were after unification due to poor record keeping and the lack of transparency in the GDR. The Golze family had been unaware that the city had acquired the house through abandonment. While they had purchased the property in good faith, they knew nothing of the missing entry in the property register.

Scenes in which Kerstin and Thomas try to defend their claim to the house also provide the viewing audience with practical information. For example, in a meeting with their lawyer, Kerstin and Thomas try to understand their rights:

> Kerstin: We still have the transfer agreement. It says that we can use that property as our own.
>
> Thomas: Right! After all, we pay taxes and not a lease. That is the clearest proof that we're the owners.
>
> Lawyer: That is correct, but Westerners don't care about that. They invoke the property rights anchored in the Basic Law. We can't do anything at all right now. In terms of the law, we are in a vacuum.[83]

This scene illustrates the confusion that the incompatibility of East and West German property laws caused after unification. The transfer agreement alone is not sufficient to secure the Golze family's possession of the property because it does not align with the way in which West Germany had established possession. Thus, the Golzes' property may not be protected under the Unification Treaty. The lawyer's analogy of the new legal system to a vacuum indicates his own lack of clarity on the laws. He can provide only feeble reassurance to Thomas by pointing out that the bureaucratic wheels are moving slowly due to the overwhelming number of claims. At least this buys them time to build a legal argu-

---

[82] Edith: Naja, aber das Haus ist ja nach wie vor noch mein Eigentum. Ich meine, Sie haben keine Grundbucheintragung. / Frau Golze: Als wir es gekauft haben, hieß es, es gehört der Stadt. Man hat uns betrogen. Und das mit den Eintragungen haben wir auch erst jetzt erfahren.
[83] Kerstin: Wir haben noch einen Überlassungsvertrag. Der besagt, dass wir das Grundstück wie unser Eigentum nutzen können. / Thomas: Eben! Schließlich zahlen wir doch auch Steuern und keine Pacht. Das ist doch der klarste Beweis, dass wir Besitzer sind. / Anwalt: Das ist schon richtig, aber die im Westen kümmern das nicht. Die berufen sich auf das im Grundgesetz verankerte Eigentumsrecht. Wir können im Augenblick gar nichts machen. Momentan befinden wir uns, was die Rechtslage betrifft, in einem luftleeren Raum.

ment. Cinematically, the lawyer's point is illustrated by the long line of people sitting outside his office.

A further complication that the film highlights is the issue of renamed streets, and it does so in both dramatic and comical fashion. In an early scene, Thomas refuses to accept that the pending claim pertains to their property since the letter that initiated contact between Edith and the Golzes does not bear their actual home address: "Well, it's not even addressed to us. It says Tse-Tung Street! [...] You didn't need to accept that at all. [...] You should have sent it right back. Addressee unknown!"[84] Thomas fears that by opening the letter and discovering the contents of it, the family has tacitly acknowledged the claim. Frau Golze clarifies, certainly as much for the audience's benefit as for Thomas's, that their street, currently the Johannes R. Becher Street, was once named the Tse-Tung Street.[85] While this clarification of the street name contributes to the Golze family's worries, a parallel moment plays comically between Edith and Georg. Upon entering Rathenow, Edith is unsure of the way to her former house, and Georg asks a local taxi driver where to find the address. Upon hearing that the Tse-Tung Street does not exist, Georg relishes the opportunity to question Edith's sanity. Edith insists that her faculties of memory are intact and triumphantly attains the information they need from another taxi driver.

While the film provides the viewing audience with practical information about property decisions in the unified Germany, its goal is a larger moral pedagogy. Indeed, *Taxi to Rathenow* is exemplary for its evocation of *Heimat* to interrogate the extent to which sentimentality and personal memory should be considered legitimate anchors to a property claim. Edith is cast as a sympathetic character in large part because her motivations are not financial (although it is clear that she stands to gain financially from the claim). Rather, she wishes to bequeath it to her adopted daughter and regain access to her *Heimat* one more time as an elderly woman. It turns out, however, that Edith's return to the home and community of her youth does not actually constitute a return to her *Heimat* and results instead in a psychological tug-of-war. As Edith interacts with the Golze family, visits her old house, and strolls down the streets of Rathe-

---

84 "Na, der ist doch gar nicht an uns. Da steht Zedongstraße drauf! [...] Den hättest du überhaupt nicht anzunehmen brauchen. [...] Den hättest du gleich so wieder zurückschicken sollen, Empfänger unbekannt!"

85 The change in street names reflects the complicated political history of the GDR. A street named after Mao Tse-Tung in the early years of East Germany would have been changed after the political fallout between the Soviet Union and China in the late 1950s and early 1960s. Johannes R. Becher, a Communist since the Weimar Republic and author of the lyrics to the GDR's anthem, would become a more politically acceptable namesake for a street.

now, she is overwhelmed by her memories. At times she feels disoriented, unable to recognize her hometown: "But back then it all looked different. It was all destroyed."[86] At others, her general sense of dislocation is punctured by powerful moments of recognition as memories flood back. For example, when Edith arrives at the house of her youth, we see an idyllic scene: a wide shot of a small two-story house with a tree-shaded lawn and a white picket fence. Edith gazes at it and is instantly transported back in time through a memory – colored in sepia for the viewing audience – of her mother sending her off to school through the front gate. A horse-drawn carriage passes by as the young Edith skips off to school (see fig. 1.3). As if to emphasize the change in times since she was a child there, a Trabi passing by awakens Edith back into the present (see fig. 1.4).

Fig. 1.3: Edith's memory of home with horse and carriage (originally in sepia)

Fig. 1.4: Edith's childhood home in the present day with a Trabi (originally in color)

Memory and *Heimat* develop as entwined themes in the film, culminating in the final confrontation between Thomas and Edith. As Edith and Frau Golze sit in the garden, eating cherry cake and watching the children play, Kerstin and Thomas return from their visit to the lawyer. Tensions soon escalate as Thomas and Edith speak of their emotional ties to the home:

> Thomas: [...] this is our home and it's going to remain that way. I grew up here. My father planted the hedges. I kissed my wife for the first time under the cherry tree. Can you imagine that we might be attached to that and not let ourselves be chased out?
>
> Edith: Of course I can imagine that. Very well actually. It's the same for me. I also grew up here and the cherry tree that you kissed your wife under, I planted it, here [*waving her fingers*] with my hands. Do you think it was easy for me to move away? It was a difficult de-

---

86 "Aber damals sah das doch alles anders aus. Es war doch alles zerstört."

cision back then to give everything up. Do you really think that I don't have a right to come back here?

Thomas: It is not your Heimat anymore, not after forty years.

Edith: My dear young man, Heimat is not a question of the calendar. As long as I'm around – yeah, I know I'm an old woman – but as long as I live, I have a claim to my house and will fight for it. You can depend on that. You don't need to throw me out again. I'll go on my own.[87]

Both have invested a great deal into the house financially, emotionally, and physically. Thomas's father planted the hedges; Edith planted the cherry tree under which Thomas kissed Kerstin for the first time. Their labor and the labor of their parents have shaped the very materiality and emotionality of the place.[88]

This scene is the emotional climax of the film, but what *Taxi to Rathenow* does so brilliantly is balance such dramatic scenes with moments of socially critical comedy. While Edith is confronting the Golze family and engaging in a discussion of *Heimat*, belonging, and possession, a secondary storyline pokes fun at Georg for his unfounded sense of superiority as a Westerner. When Georg gets into trouble with the local police, the expected East-West power dynamic is reversed, and thus *Taxi to Rathenow* introduces another trope that will appear in other films of its kind. In this storyline, similar to the premises of *The Brocken* (*Der Brocken*, Glowna 1992) and *No More Mr. Nice Guy!* (*Wir können auch anders*, Buck 1993), discussed in chapter 3, Easterners are no hapless victims of Westerners' social and financial advantage. Rather, Easterners manipulate Westerners' sense of superiority to outsmart them, playing the new system in their own favor.

Georg articulates his sense of superiority over Easterners in a conversation with Edith over lunch at a lakeside restaurant. Giving Edith a knowing look,

---

87 Thomas: [...] das ist unser Zuhause und das bleibt es auch. Ich bin hier aufgewachsen. Mein Vater hat die Hecke gesetzt. Unter dem Kirchbaum habe ich zum ersten Mal meine Frau geküsst. Können Sie sich nicht vorstellen, dass man an sowas hängt und sich nicht irgendwie vertreiben lässt? / Edith: Doch. Das kann ich mir vorstellen. Sehr gut sogar. Mir geht es nämlich nicht anders. Auch ich bin hier aufgewachsen und der Kirchbaum, unter dem Sie sich geküsst haben, den habe ich gepflanzt, hier [*waving her fingers*] mit meinen Händen. Meinen Sie, es ist mir leicht gefallen, hier wegzugehen? War eine schwere Entscheidung damals, alles aufzugeben. Finden Sie wirklich, ich habe kein Recht, hierher zurück zu kommen? / Thomas: Das ist doch nicht mehr Ihre Heimat, nicht nach 40 Jahren. / Edith: Mein lieber junger Mann, Heimat ist keine Frage des Kalenders. Solange ich da bin – ja, ich weiß, ich bin eine alte Frau – aber so lange ich lebe, habe ich Anspruch auf mein Haus und ich werde darum kämpfen. Verlassen Sie sich darauf. Sie brauchen mich nicht noch einmal rauszuwerfen. Ich gehe schon von selber.
88 Such issues of materiality and invested labor, as they pertain to *Heimat*, will be investigated in further detail in chapters 2 and 5.

he complains about Easterners' laziness, their demands for handouts after unification, and the attendant costs to Westerners.

> Georg: I have driven taxis day and night for thirty years to earn what I have. But they want everything given to them. And who pays for it? We do, with our taxes. We've financed everything. Hundreds of billions, you know, and no end in sight.
>
> Edith: Such a unification has its price.
>
> Georg: Sure! But it's been borne on our backs. They don't even know what work is here. The first thing they did was strike for more pay [...]
>
> [...]
>
> Georg: What has really changed? The wall is gone, but in reality, it's still there. If you ask me, sometimes I think it would have been better to leave everything the way it was.
>
> Edith: Don't say such dumb things! The people here haven't had it easy at all in the last forty years. We need to give them time to adapt to our tempo.[89]

In this scene, Georg serves as a mouthpiece to express a broad dissatisfaction among Westerners at the time about having to finance the legal and bureaucratic costs of unification. Edith, in this sequence, puts such opinions in check.

As fate would have it, Georg is punished for his arrogance. He discovers upon leaving the restaurant that his hubcaps have been stolen – perhaps someone overheard his disparaging remarks? – and goes to the police to file a report. While at the police station, he insults the officers first for not having prevented the crime and then again for their skepticism about recovering the stolen hubcaps. As Georg grows ever more exasperated and insults the police officers for their passivity, one officer loses his patience. Asserting a rather passive-aggressive authority, he suggests that Georg must be intoxicated, detains him, and requires him to take a breathalizer test. He then uses Georg's propensity to underestimate Easterners against him: "You know, Mr. Nagel, we Easterners aren't

---

89 Georg: Ich bin dreißig Jahre lang Tag und Nacht Taxi gefahren um mir das zu verdienen, was ich habe. Aber die wollen doch alles geschenkt eben. Und wer bezahlt das? Wir, na von unseren Steuern. Wir haben alles finanziert. Hunderte von Milliarden, nicht, und kein Ende abzusehen. / Edith: So eine Wiedervereinigung kostet eben ihren Preis. / Georg: Sicher! Aber auf unserem Rücken wird das ausgetragen. Sie wissen doch hier ja nicht mal was Arbeit ist. Das Erste, was sie gemacht haben, waren Streiks für mehr Lohn [...] / [...] / Georg: Was hat sich denn verändert? Die Mauer ist zwar weg, aber in Wirklichkeit ist sie doch noch da. Also wenn Sie mich fragen, manchmal meine ich, es wäre besser jewesen, mit allet so jeblieben, wie es war. / Edith: Nun reden Sie nicht so dummes Zeug! Die Leute hier haben es wirklich nicht einfach gehabt in den letzten vierzig Jahren. Wir müssen denen schon Zeit lassen, sich an unser Tempo zu gewöhnen.

really familiar with the new devices from the West. Please have a seat. I'll call a doctor."[90] By feigning incompetence, the police officer draws out Georg's detainment and punishes him for his prejudices.[91]

Taxi to Rathenow depicts East-West dynamics in alternately comical and serious scenes that serve its larger moral pedagogy. It is clear that, given the financial disparities between Edith and the Golze family, the Golze family has far more to lose than Edith has to gain in the struggle over the house. However, the film resists villainizing Edith, fostering viewers' identification with both the Golze family as underdogs and Edith as someone who has a sentimental attachment to her childhood home. An already likeable character by the end of the film, Edith emerges as a hero when she finally refutes the notion that access to one's *Heimat* is a valid reason for claiming property. In the final scene of the film, Edith sits at the steering wheel of the taxi since the police have suspended Georg's license. Edith has been, figuratively, in the driver's seat the entire day. Now she is actually driving the taxi, having demonstrated that she is more in touch with working class sensibilities than she seemed to be initially. As the two drive back to Berlin, Edith tells Georg that she may drop her case. He protests: "But that's your *Heimat!*"[92] and she replies with a scoff, "*Heimat*, after forty years! It was different in my memory."[93] Edith's last words constitute the film's takeaway messages: that the *Heimat* ideal does not hold up well over time and is not enough to make a claim that would displace others.

Taxi to Rathenow provides an excellent example of how fiction draws a more complicated, personal, and emotional picture of competing parties' needs and motivations than many of the news media reports of the time did. In their aggregate, the news media and law review articles cited and consulted to write this chapter provide an overview of the historical circumstances and bureaucratic challenges German citizens faced within the new property relations. However, many of these news sources presented information to a German audience in a sensationalized, overly simplified, and adversarial manner. It is once we turn

---

90 "Ach, wissen Sie Herr Nagel, wir aus dem Osten sind mit den neuen Geräten aus dem Westen noch nicht so vertraut. Nehmen Sie bitte Platz. Ich rufe einen Arzt an."
91 In this sequence, the mise-en-scène plays comically, as the police officers express their inability to help Georg while a poster hangs on the wall behind them that lists ways in which citizens can protect themselves from car theft. Another poster hanging conspicuously on the wall in this scene plays more soberly. The wanted poster for members of the Red Army Faction (RAF) would have reminded viewers at that time that Detlev Rohwedder, manager of the *Treuhand*, had been murdered in his home by a suspected RAF sniper six months prior. The poster thus adds a serious dimension to this otherwise comical scene about East-West power dynamics.
92 "Das ist doch Ihre Heimat!"
93 "Heimat, nach vierzig Jahren! Die hatte ich anders in Erinnerung."

to fictional productions – television, literature, and film – that the representations of this socio-political phenomenon gain nuance and a human face.

As we will see in the chapters that follow, such cultural productions depart quickly from the lines of "us" and "them" that conventional wisdom draws and instead bring to the fore messy and contradictory human narratives. These narratives offer us multiple points of view, addressing intersecting issues of gender, class, family dynamic, region, landscape, health, and age. They delve into the intense emotional, psychological, and material need for stability that is human; the existential threat posed when one faces displacement from one's home; and the very gendered and class driven means by which the process of home privatization took place. What is obviously missing from these cultural productions and other media representations, however, is a discussion of how race and othering likely informed how policy was shaped and implemented. Our view of the changing property relations thus cannot be comprehensive, as the primary texts and media reports leave out certain marginalized voices. Acknowledging this important omission in the primary texts, we can nevertheless gain a more in-depth sense of the complex and precarious situation that many Eastern and Western Germans found themselves in when facing a property disputes than non-fictional reports have provided.

Chapter 2
Home in the East as a Site of Competing Histories: *Our House* (Griesmayr, 1991) and *The Same Old Song* (Stöckl, 1992)

As I illustrated in chapter 1, the government's decision to implement a policy of "restitution before compensation" to comply with article 14 of the Basic Law caused a myriad of problems. The system established to determine property rights was ill equipped to handle the unforeseen volume of claims by those who had been dispossessed in the eastern part of Germany over the course of the twentieth century. While the news media covered the breadth of the problem, there seems to have been a hesitancy to address its deep historical roots. News reports skirted the topic of the Nazi past except in a few cases in which claims from Jewish heirs from abroad affected a community. When it came to cases concerning non-Jewish Germans, the news media tended to frame property disputes as a contemporary problem, foregrounding the social and economic effects of policy that privileged Westerners over Easterners and drawing on the more recent past to highlight complications arising from GDR policy. Neither the news media nor *Taxi to Rathenow*, the made-for-television movie discussed in chapter 1, addresses the fact that property disputes often uncovered, and forced people to face, shameful family histories from the period of National Socialism. The two films I treat in this chapter, *Our House* (*Unser Haus*, Griesmayr 1991) and *The Same Old Song* (*Das alte Lied*, Stöckl 1992) depart from their contemporaries in this respect. They frame the question of *Heimat* not only in socio-economic terms, but also historically, as families with conflicting histories face off.

In the made-for-television movie *Our House*, the West Berliner Kurt Wrede wishes to claim the house in Potsdam that his father built before World War II, move his family there, and enjoy the *Heimat* of his childhood. However, upon arriving at the property, he learns that another family, the Gleiniches, has inhabited the house for nearly four decades and owned it for the past twelve years. Each family is certain, at least initially, that they have the legally valid claim to the house, whether based on the Wrede family's entry in the property register or the Gleinich family's possession of a deed. More importantly, each family has sentimental attachment to it. The families thus appear to be at both a legal and an emotional stalemate. However, it soon comes to light that both Kurt Wrede's and Jochen Gleinich's fathers may have engaged in nefarious actions during the Nazi and Communist eras that could jeopardize each party's claim in the courts.

Within a year, a second film appeared in cinemas that addresses these same issues but from a somewhat different angle. While *Our House* frames property disputes and German national history in terms of a patriarchal lineage and draws on a rather conventional understanding of *Heimat*, the independent film *The Same Old Song* by feminist director Ula Stöckl thematizes matrilineal inheritance, women's memory, and women's participation in Germany's problematic history. In *The Same Old Song*, the protagonist, an elderly woman named Katharina, returns to her native Dresden shortly after German unification to reconnect with the places and people of her youth. Her brother Rudolf, son Karl, and granddaughter Sophie accompany her on this trip, and the family will spend the first Christmas after unification with Katharina's former lover, the widower Alf, and his family. Katharina dreams of building the life she had always imagined but never achieved in Dresden by reuniting with Alf and merging her family with his. Part and parcel of this dream is to reclaim the house she formerly owned. However, as Katharina proceeds with her plan and confronts the family who lives there, her family (and the audience) learns that she harbors dark secrets from the Nazi era.

Both *Our House* and *The Same Old Song* frame the issue of housing disputes in terms of East(ern family) versus West(ern family), drawing lines of "us" versus "them" similar to the media reports of the time. However, neither film leaves these lines of difference intact, as history is unearthed, intervenes on, and entangles with the present. What steadies the protagonists' claims in both of these films is their emotional connection to the property as their *Heimat*. Just as in *Taxi to Rathenow*, however, the desire for *Heimat* may be compelling, but is by no means a guarantee for a successful property claim. Both *Our House* and *The Same Old Song* demonstrate that German unification was not a historical caesura that allowed citizens to leave the twentieth century behind them and focus solely on the social and legal circumstances of the present. Nor do these films allow their protagonists to disavow the political events of the twentieth century to reconstruct their *Heimat* ideal in the places of their childhood. Rather, these films show how national and family history complicate issues of space, desire, and legal rights.

Patrilineal *Heimat*, Patrilineal History in *Our House*

Although the word *Heimat* is uttered only once in *Our House* – approximately fifteen minutes before its conclusion – the film intentionally evokes associations with *Heimat* as established in the literary and visual traditions. Kurt Wrede's childhood home lies on a lake in the Brandenburg countryside, and the local landscape figures prominently in both the visual aesthetics and plot of the film. In the tradition of the *Heimat* film, lingering shots enhance the majesty of the lake and countryside, lending the viewer a sense of harmony existing between the community and the landscape (see fig. 2.1). Interior shots emphasize the *Gemütlichkeit* (inviting comfort) of home, and the hospitality and traditions of the local community, important features of the *Heimat* genre, are further presented in scenes that take place in the restaurant *Haus am See*, where locals gather for a beer and visitors can sample regional fare with a view over the lake (see fig. 2.2).

Fig. 2.1: Kurt's childhood home

Fig. 2.2: The Wrede family eating at the *Haus am See*

In addition to drawing on the visual characteristics of the *Heimat* film, *Our House* follows certain conventions of *Heimat* film narratives. In fact, the film combines two competing *Heimat* storylines in its treatment of Kurt. On the one hand, the narrative draws on the "prodigal son" topos, which recalls Edgar Reitz's genre-defining made-for-television miniseries, *Heimat* (1984), in which a member of the local community has left for big city life and now returns to seek his place in the *Heimat*, the place where he once belonged. At the same time, *Our House* is also about a harmonious community that is being threatened by an outside force – a narrative more typical of *Heimat* films of the 1950s and 60s.[1] The conflict between these two narratives, Kurt as returning son of the *Hei-*

---

[1] Johannes on Moltke has demonstrated that in the *Heimat* films of the 1950s, the "intruder" could be war returnees, expellees from the East, or even modernity itself, as the new technologies and commodities of the rapidly modernizing Germany entered the *Heimat*. *Heimat* films thus often feature a character, typically a woman, who can reconcile the values and traditions

mat and Kurt as colonizing intruder from the West, is at the crux of the film's tension. Similar to *Taxi to Rathenow*, this film asks whether Kurt has a right to his childhood home simply because it is his *Heimat* or whether he, as a Westerner, threatens the harmony and balance of the *Heimat* community with his money and class status. Kurt's uncertain position underscores the difficult ethical considerations of claiming property in the early 1990s and challenges the concept that one always has a justified claim to one's *Heimat*.

In *Our House*, *Heimat* is cast as property, and ownership of it is male – through either Kurt's line of inheritance or Jochen Gleinich's claim to the house by law. In the opening sequence of the film, when Kurt visits his childhood home for the first time since unification, he brings his son (not his wife) along, and the young Thomas surveys the property as his own. Indeed, this patriarchal and patrilineal arrangement aligns with the conventional structure of *Heimat* as Elisabeth Bütfering describes it:

> Heimat, the "beautiful estate," reveals itself to be a category of the patriarchal not least in its conceptual history. Home and yard, inherited by the son from his father, the linkage of land ownership, right of residence, right to vote, and so forth, all factor women in as part of the male estate and precludes her as an individual in her own right.[2]

Our House connects the issues of home ownership, patrilineal inheritance, and *Heimat* that Bütfering and others have outlined: that men own the *Heimat* insofar as they inherit family homes and trades, and women, by contrast, belong to and maintain the *Heimat* that men inherit. Kurt, and later Thomas, may own the house and *Heimat*, while Edith, Kurt's wife, remains a bystander in this arrangement.

---

of the *Heimat* with rapidly changing aspects of the nation. See Johannes von Moltke, *No Place Like Home* (Berkeley: University of California Press, 2005), 21–35, 114–134.

2 "Heimat, der 'schöne Besitz', offenbart sich als Kategorie des Patriarchalen nicht zuletzt in der Begriffsgeschichte. Haus und Hof, vom Vater auf Sohn vererbt, die Koppelung von Grundeigentum, Aufenthaltsrecht, Wahlrecht und so weiter, all das bezieht Frauen ein als Teil des männlichen Besitztums und schließt sie aus als Individuen aus eigenem Recht." Elisabeth Bütfering, "Frauenheimat Männerwelt. Die Heimatlosigkeit ist weiblich," in: *Heimat: Analysen, Themen, Perspektiven*, ed. Will Cremer and Ansgar Klein (Bielefeld: Westfalen-Verlag, 1990), 417. See also Rachel Palfreyman, "Reflections of the 'Heimat' Genre: Intertextual Reference in Reitz's Heimat," *German Life and Letters* 50, no. 4 (1997): 531, and Peter Blickle, *Heimat: A Critical Theory of the German Idea of Homeland* (Rochester: Camden House, 2002), 101. The "beautiful estate" is quoted from Reinhard P. Gruber, "Heimat ist, wo das Herz weh tut. 35 Fragmente eines konkreten Beitrags zu einer antiutopischen Heimatentheorie," in: *Die Ohnmacht der Gefühle. Heimat zwischen Wunsch und Wirklichkeit*, ed. Jochen Kelter (Weingarten: Drumlin, 1986), 179.

Not only property rights, but German history itself, is framed in patrilineal fashion in this film, as Kurt Wrede and Jochen Gleinich's respective claim relies on the question of whose father's crimes in the past were worse. In a showdown between Kurt and Jochen approximately two-thirds of the way through the film, both attempt to discredit the other's claim on historical bases.

> Kurt: Mr. Gleinich, we haven't yet talked about the most important thing: how you got your house.
>
> Jochen: We've already spoken too much. I don't want to anymore.
>
> Kurt: Your father was a party member. He served this unjust regime and was rewarded for it with our house.
>
> Jochen: You don't know what you're talking about.
>
> Kurt: Oh yes, I do know. My father was detained after the war by people who had a say here and your father belonged to those people.
>
> [...]
>
> Jochen: My father survived the war in a penal company that the Nazis had put him in. Your father was also a Nazi. Otherwise he wouldn't have been detained.[3]

Kurt defends his claim by suggesting that Jochen's father, a former Communist party functionary, acquired the house as a reward for having aided in the detainment of individuals and removal from their homes some decades earlier under SMAD occupation. This information is significant, because according to the Property Law, a claim could be rendered invalid if the property had been acquired through the misuse of power or unfair practices, in this case party favoritism.[4] (As discussed in chapter 1, many of these films have an informative function. A number of scenes are designed to educate the audience about the legal parameters and expected timelines of property decisions.) When Kurt accuses the Gleinich family of having acquired the home in this manner, Jochen responds by revealing that Kurt's father must have been removed from the house because

---

3 Kurt: Herr Gleinich, wir haben noch nicht über das Wichtigste gesprochen: wie Sie zu Ihrem Haus gekommen sind. / Jochen: Wir haben schon zu viel gesprochen. Ich habe keine Lust mehr / Kurt: Ihr Vater war Genosse. Und er hat diesem Unrechtsregime gedient und er ist dafür belohnt worden mit unserem Haus. / Jochen: Sie wissen nicht, wovon Sie reden. / Kurt: Doch doch, das weiß ich. Mein Vater ist nach dem Krieg abgeholt worden, von Leuten, die hier das Sagen hatten und zu diesen Leuten gehörte Ihr Vater. / [...] / Jochen: Mein Vater hat den Krieg in einer Strafkompanie überlebt, in die ihn die Nazis gesteckt hatten. Ihr Vater war ja wohl auch ein Nazi. Sonst wäre er nicht geholt worden.

4 See chapter 1 for more information about the Property Law.

of Nazi activity. The audience already knows that Kurt's father was arrested soon after the war and most likely died in prison.

Our House eventually takes the side of the Gleiniches, but it does not allow its viewers to come to easy conclusions about just property rights for either of these families. We learn that Kurt's father had not been a "convinced" Nazi, but had done what he felt was necessary in order to survive in those years. Kurt also points out that he, his mother, and his sister had been innocent, regardless of what his father had done. Kurt faced discrimination in school under the Communist regime because of his father's previous affiliation, which motivated his mother to abandon the *Heimat* and flee with her children to West Germany. While Kurt wishes to inherit the property his father cultivated, he also attempts to distance himself from his father's involvement with National Socialism. At the same time, we learn that while Herr Gleinich was devoted to Communism, he was not personally involved in the removal of people from their homes. Both Kurt and Jochen's claims to the house are potentially compromised by their fathers' respective complicity with the German regimes of the twentieth century; at the same time, neither father is cast as a criminal himself.

The film links property rights in the present with guilt in the past, such that the particularities of place are determined by their situation within the temporality of history. This connection between physical place and history is embedded in the very materiality of the house. In an early scene, we watch as Jochen negotiates with repairmen whom he has hired to fix a leak in the roof. Later, when we view Kurt's photographs of the damaged home from the immediate postwar period, we learn that the house's roof had been hit by a grenade toward the end of the war. The leaky roof is a recurring material problem resulting from that initial damage and, metaphorically, serves as a reminder that the history of National Socialism continues to assert its influence into the present day.

While the legal case will likely hinge on Kurt and Jochen's respective fathers' ties to a problematic German history, the men's wives, children, and parents give a more differentiated view of ownership of the house, its history, and perhaps even its future. Jochen's wife, Karla, resembles the women of *Heimat* narratives to the extent that she supports Jochen's fight for the home in the interest of their daughter Verena. She departs from the *Heimat* convention, however, in that she does not maintain the *Heimat* for the sake of men. Rather, she is concerned with her own daughter and, as the coach of the local girls' rowing team, the girls of the community.

Kurt's wife Edith, on the other hand, has no emotional investment in the house or *Heimat*. She enjoys her society in Berlin and does not wish to uproot her son, who has school and friends in the city. Moreover, she would prefer to avoid the hostility the family faces as affluent Westerners when visiting the lakeside community. For Edith, the house does not represent *Heimat*, but instead presents an opportunity to purchase and sell real estate for profit. Although she is, to some extent, an opportunist, she also represents a voice of reason in the film. When Kurt insists that he must inhabit his childhood home, she replies, "It's a different world now. You know, I wonder how you would want to live out there, where you are doing well and around you nobody, really nobody, can get on their feet. How do you picture that?"[5] Indeed, Edith points out the emotional conflict in which Kurt has placed himself. He no longer belongs in the *Heimat* community and could not be happy living in a place where he will be the object of animosity. Returning to the *Heimat* would mean inserting a class disparity into an area that is already economically depressed. Moreover, by pointing out that Kurt is fixated on a time and place that no longer exist, Edith refuses to participate in the role allotted to women in many *Heimat* narratives: to help integrate (male) outsiders into the community.[6]

While Edith voices the film's position regarding the property claims of Westerners – that they had best leave it alone – information divulged by the two families' elders, Frau Wrede and Herr Gleinich, further diminishes the Wrede family's claim to the house. We learn from the elder Frau Wrede that the family's roots in the area are not as deep as Kurt would like to imagine. She and Kurt's father moved from the city to build the house in 1938 because they liked to swim and hike at the lakeside. According to her, they built the house there on a whim, and she indicates no previous attachment to the place. The Wrede family has only inhabited the area for one generation before the Gleinich family moved in. In fact, of all the characters in the film, Frau Wrede is the most at peace with the changing property relations. When Kurt brings her to the old neighborhood, she inquires after the family that had previously lived next door and helped her and the children escape. A different family name is now listed on the mailbox. "Oh well," she replies, "sooner or later unfamiliar names will

---

[5] "Jetzt ist eine andere Welt. Weißt du, ich frage mich bloß wie du da draußen leben wolltest, wo es dir gut geht und ringsherum niemand, aber auch wirklich niemand, auf die Beine kommt. Wie stellst du dir das vor?"

[6] According to Heide Fehrenbach, women in 1950s *Heimat* films such as *Grün ist die Heide* (Deppe 1951) and *Schwarzwaldmädel* (Deppe 1950) often serve as "midwives to the future [and] promise a fresh start" to rehabilitate men after Nazism and integrate them into the local community. Heide Fehrenbach, *Cinema in Democratizing Germany* (Chapel Hill and London: University of North Carolina Press, 1995), 159. While Kurt himself is not a Nazi, he is the character most closely associated with the legacy of Nazism, as his father was a member of the party. Here, Edith refuses to help Kurt shed the liability of that history, as well as that of having fled to the West so that he can become a more suitable community member. For a discussion of women in *Heimat* films, see Heide Fehrenbach, *Cinema in Democratizing Germany*, 158–163.

be on all of them."[7] It is senseless to expect a place not to change, as both human life and the material conditions of home are transitory in nature.

The elderly Herr Gleinich, on the other hand, expresses a deep emotional attachment to the house. In a meeting between Frau Wrede and Herr Gleinich – as mentioned in chapter 1, the elderly generation often brokers peace in these films – Herr Gleinich describes the conditions under which he and his family had lived before moving into it. In the early years of the GDR, they lived in cramped barracks, and the Wrede family's former house was appointed to his family once it stood empty. His daughter was born in their home and his wife died there. In this meeting, approximately fifteen minutes before the end of the film, we hear the word *Heimat* uttered for the first and only time and, most significantly, in association with the Gleinich family. Frau Wrede acknowledges the rival family's claim to the house, based on the principle of *Heimat* as a place of family history and sentimental attachment: "So then it was also *Heimat* for you."[8] Uttered toward the end of the film, the elder Frau Wrede's statement is to be understood as the final word, validating the Gleinich family's claim to the home.

The film makes no clear determination about which family has a more valid legal claim, based on the historical circumstances of expropriation and appointment of properties. It also cannot make a clear case based solely on emotional and sentimental attachment. If one were to conceive of *Heimat* strictly as the place of one's childhood innocence, an aspect that many discussions of *Heimat* rely on, then it is not Kurt and Jochen, but rather, Kurt and Verena, Jochen's daughter, who should be parallel characters with a similar right to the house and landscape. When Kurt shows Thomas around the property for the first time, he points out the tree he liked to climb as a child to peer out over the lake; when he enters the house, he notes that the furniture once belonged to his grandparents. The material circumstances of his childhood remain in many ways the same as when he lived in the house. But these are also the material circumstances of Verena's childhood now. When Kurt appears at the house during Verena's thirteenth birthday party, she becomes nervous about the prospect of being forced out of her home, but her grandfather reassures her that she is part of the *Heimat*, "You belong here. No one can take that from you."[9] She belongs to the place of her childhood and therefore has an existential claim to it. Does Kurt not as well?

---

7 "Na ja," she replies, "früher oder später sind überall fremde Namen daran."
8 "Dann war es also auch Heimat für Sie."
9 "Du gehörst doch hierher. Das darf dir keiner nehmen."

Yet the film does not actually make a case for the Gleinich family by placing Verena at the center of the narrative. Rather, the central conflict revolves around Kurt and Jochen, two men of the same generation with different attachments to the land based on the age in which they inhabit(ed) it. What tips the balance in favor of the Gleinich family is their material engagement with the landscape. The film makes the case that Jochen's labor connects him just as strongly to the place as does Kurt's sentimentality. We learn during an argument between Kurt and Jochen that Jochen was brought to this area as a child at the end of the war; his childhood *Heimat* now lies in Poland and is inaccessible. Since moving into this house, he and his family have built a dock from the property onto the lake, transformed the lawn around the house from a grass field to a nicely manicured garden, and maintained the house to guard it against dilapidation. They continue to manage the roof that leaks due to damage from the war. The film suggests that the upkeep of a property might outweigh sentimental childhood attachment to *Heimat* when considering who should own a property. Material engagement with the land connects one to it as powerfully as memory does.

One of the most challenging questions for theorists of *Heimat* to answer is why this particular concept of home so powerfully connects the emotional and the social to the material. At its center, *Heimat* imagines home as a place in which an organic harmony exists among the individual, the home, the local community, and the landscape. In their respective works, Peter Blickle and Rachel Palfreyman have suggested that *Heimat* is emotionally powerful because it is a trope of loss, deriving from the psychological separation from the mother, whereby *Heimat* is associated with childhood and the womb.[10] While this interpretation is compelling, it reads *Heimat* in solely symbolic terms and disregards its material charge. This reading also fails to acknowledge the possibility of making a place of one's adulthood a *Heimat*. As the narratives discussed in this monograph demonstrate, *Heimat* extends beyond the psycho-melodrama of the family and conceives of the subject instead as belonging to the *Heimat*'s very materiality. This connection of individual to the materiality of house and landscape is deeply embedded in the German cultural understanding of home, as indicated in the fictional and non-fictional accounts of property claims discussed in the previous chapter and this one. Thus a more materially-focused investigation of *Heimat* is warranted to understand why fictional narratives and news media de-

---

10 See Blickle, *Heimat: A Critical Theory of the German Idea of Homeland*, 45, 47, and 68, and Rachel Palfreyman, "Reflections of the 'Heimat' Genre: Intertextual Reference in Reitz's *Heimat*," 530–531.

picting property disputes invoke individuals' invested labor to garner audience's sympathy for one party over another.

What is perhaps most compelling about *Heimat* is that it entangles the emotional, the social, and the material, not just within the interior of the home, but also within a particular community and landscape. *Heimat*, with its focus on traditional practices and ways of inhabiting the land, is performative in nature, requiring particular discursive practices for its maintenance as a physical space. Seen this way, the *Heimat* cannot be understood as a given material circumstance, the backdrop of one's childhood. Nor can it be understood in purely symbolic terms. Rather, *Heimat* is intensely relational, performative, and material. The work of Karen Barad supports such an interpretation of *Heimat*.

In her monograph, *Meeting the Universe Halfway*, Barad conceives of all materiality as performative and relational rather than existing in an atomistic or a priori way. For Barad, the basic building block of reality is not the atom or particle, but rather, the "intra-action," the entangled way in which entities materialize through relationships. In essence, Barad postulates that everything in the universe is made of the same abstract "stuff." During what Barad calls the "agential cut," substance differentiates itself from other substance, excluding it, and thus makes itself known as matter. Nothing material exists before the agential cut, and to express this idea, she utilizes the term "intra-action" rather than "interaction":

> The neologism "intra-action" *signifies the mutual constitution of entangled agencies.* That is, in contrast to the usual "interaction" which assumes that there are separate individual agencies that precede their interaction, the notion of intra-action recognizes that distinct agencies do not precede, but rather emerge through, their intra-action. It is important to note that the 'distinct' agencies are only distinct in a relational, not absolute, sense, that is, *agencies are only distinct in relation to their mutual entanglement; they don't exist as individual elements.*[11]

Whereas the term "interaction" supposes individual, independent entities that pre-exist their relationship to one another, "intra-action" proposes that entities emerge only through the formation of a relationship. The agential cut is an act of articulating boundaries so that two or more entities become intelligible. It is an iterative relationship formation and the way in which materiality practices agency. As an interative act, the agential cut is thus a material practice that belongs to the realm of discourse. Materiality as we understand it emerges from dis-

---

[11] Karen Barad, *Meeting the Universe Halfway: Quantum Physics and the Entanglement of Matter and Meaning* (Durham: Duke University Press, 2007), 33.

course and discourse takes shape in the performative practices of materiality. They are not collapsible into one, but rather, are mutually constitutive of one another.

According to Barad, everything is both material and discursive, emerging through agential cuts – even humans. She maintains:

> "humans" refers to phenomena, not independent entities with inherent properties but rather beings in their differential becoming, particular material (re)configurings of the world with shifting boundaries and properties that stabilize and destabilize along with specific material changes in what it means to be human.[12]

Perhaps, then, *Heimat* can be understood as a "particular material (re)configuring" out of which the human subject "phenomenon" arises and changes throughout its life. As a child, one "belongs" to the *Heimat* because one has emerged from the very material-discursive configuration of the landscape and community. Yet, at the same time, the *Heimat* is also the site of one's individuation, one's differentiation from the surrounding material-discursive world. It is the site of the "agential cuts" that make up the physical and emotional self, the exclusionary act of distinguishing oneself from the material configuration from which one has emerged. One is thus connected to the area because one is composed of the same matter; one is differentiated from it because one has carved out the self in an articulation of boundaries. *Heimat* is important not only because we feel our sameness – a deeply rooted connection with the landscape, the people, and the language because we are made of the same materiality – but also because it is crucial to our individuation. It is the first place we feel strange, the first place we see ourselves as distinct from what surrounds us, both of which set us up to venture into the world and continue our process of becoming. A reading of *Heimat* in such a way suggests that subjectivity itself is material. Materiality and discourse, subjectivity and material environment, are mutually constitutive, never wholly distinct and separate entities.

One of the most appealing aspects of *Heimat* (for many) is that it is imagined to be innocent and timeless, even anti-modern, and impervious to national politics and economic influence. As such, it is a notion that imagines home to be apolitical and innocent in the face of troubling national and international politics. However, read in Barad's terms, the *Heimat*, as a material-discursive configuration cannot be static, but is a performed phenomenon that belongs to the world in its "endless becoming."[13] This means that *Heimat* and those who

---

12 Karen Barad, *Meeting the Universe Halfway*, 136.
13 Karen Barad, *Meeting the Universe Halfway*, 139.

intra-act with and within it are not ahistorical, but historically situated, active, and culpable. For example, *Heimat* is a concept of home that has long practiced a discursive assertion of boundaries, if not strictly physical ones, to enact exclusionary social policies. For this reason, the Nazi regime made extensive use of the term *Heimat* to enact racist citizenship policies and justify genocide.[14] In his classic essay, "Wieviel Heimat braucht der Mensch?" ("How much Heimat Does a Person Need?") Jean Améry asserts that one of the greatest crimes of the Nazi regime against German and Austrian Jews was that it robbed them of their *Heimat*. He argues that German Jews not only lost their sense of security and home, but that by being driven into exile, into camps, and to death, they were also robbed of their language, their dress, and their customs, all of which are important parts of *Heimat*. As noted in the discussion of *Heimat* in the introduction to this monograph, people with a racist and narrow view on who should inhabit Germany continue to invoke *Heimat* in an exclusionary manner.

However, *Heimat* reconsidered as a performed, relational, and discursive space, part of the world in its "endless becoming," can serve a notion of home that overcomes exclusionary boundaries. Heike Henderson and Friederike Eigler, for example, have discussed the extent to which Turkish-German authors have broadened the concept of *Heimat*. Heike Henderson points out that Turkish women writers often characterize *Heimat* as a form of containment rather than cast it in a nostalgic light.[15] Taking a different perspective, Friederike Eigler argues that Turkish-German writers such as Emine Sevgi Özdamar and Feridun Zaimoğlu have broadened the scope of *Heimat* by divorcing it from a particular place and making it compatible with mobility and hybridity.[16] *Heimat* is thus a space that can be opened to, and redefined by, those who are not born in a particular place, but who make it their own through intra-activity.

If Kurt and Verena both have a claim to the house because it is the site of their individuation, their agential cuts that differentiate them from the material condition out of which they each emerged, then Jochen also has a claim to it due to the intra-actions on the property that have made him a part of this *Heimat*.

---

14 Jean Améry, "Wieviel Heimat braucht der Mensch?" in *Werke*, ed. Irene Heidelberger-Leonard (Stuttgart: Klett-Cotta, 2002). See also Friederike Eigler, "Critical Approaches to Heimat and the 'Spatial Turn'," *New German Critique* 39, no. 1 (2012): 41.
15 Heike Henderson, "Re-Thinking and Re-Writing *Heimat:* Turkish Women Writers in Germany," *Women in German Yearbook* 13 (1997): 226.
16 Friederike Eigler, "Critical Approaches to Heimat and the 'Spatial Turn'," 39. See also Elizabeth Boa and Rachel Palfreyman, *Heimat: A German Dream: Regional Loyalties and National Identity in German Culture 1890–1990* (Oxford: Oxford University Press), 207–209.

Jochen's interactions with the material configurations of the house and property have given way to new intra-actions in which both he and the *Heimat* are reconfigured. This same reasoning explains why Kurt no longer belongs there. If people are not self-contained entities per Barad, but rather open-ended phenomena, then it follows that as Kurt's material circumstances have changed, so has he. The *Heimat* might have been the material condition out of which his subjectivity emerged; it might have been the site of his first agential cuts, his individuation. But the ongoing changes in material configurations in Kurt's life have led to new intra-actions so that Kurt is now a different person than before. As his material circumstances have changed, so has his worldview, his subjectivity. He is no longer fully part of the *Heimat*.

While the *Heimat* ideal in its conventional form may represent a place where an escape from history is possible, *Our House* presents *Heimat* as the material place in which one is forced to face one's family history and reconsider one's claims to innocence in the present day. The film suggests that perhaps no one has an unproblematic claim to *Heimat* based on the patrilineal inheritance of property and history. Of course, this message borders dangerously on historical relativism: as the older generation puts the past to rest, the younger generation of adults argues over whose past is worse and concludes that neither family is really all that guilty. The film seems to suggest instead that the *Heimat* belongs to those who have made it theirs, those whose intra-actions in the landscape and resulting material reconfigurations have made them a part of it, even if the courts might not ultimately decide in this way. The film thus also argues that no one has a lasting claim to the *Heimat*, due to the material reconfigurations of every life. Yet, the film does end on an optimistic (if also heteronormative) note in the spirit of the *Heimat* film. Although the narrative ends long before the courts have made a decision about the house, the blossoming friendship between the young Thomas Wrede and Verena Gleinich suggests the possibility of a potential marriage in the future that would place the house in the possession of both families.

As demonstrated in the introduction and chapter 1, popular discourses of the time often cast the scenario of Westerners claiming lands in the East in colonialist terms. Like *Taxi to Rathenow*, *Our House* employs the *Heimat* trope in order to mitigate that type of narrative. The introduction of *Heimat* in *Our House* encourages the national television audience – from both Eastern and Western Germany – to identify with both Kurt and Jochen and thereby consider both sides of property disputes. There are no straightforward villains or heroes in the film, even if the Wrede family is wealthier and their lasting presence in the community would come at a price for the Gleinich family. By emphasizing that Kurt's interest in the house is not financial, but rather, sentimental, the film casts him as a sympathetic figure.

Our House resembles the *Heimat* films of previous decades, not only in its visual iconography and some adherence to narrative conventions, but also in its straightforward approach to addressing the nation of viewers. The message of the film seems to be: "Westerners, stay away!" voiced most directly by Edith Wrede. The film communicates to Westerners that the *Heimat* in the East will not be what they remember or imagine, that they will only destroy its security by pursuing property claims there, and that they no longer belong to that *Heimat* as they once did, given the ongoing reconfigurations of all people, materials, and circumstances.

Matrilineal *Heimat* and History in *The Same Old Song*

Ula Stöckl's 1992 film *The Same Old Song* shares the premise and many of the main themes of *Our House:* a return to the *Heimat* followed by a property dispute, family inheritance as a structuring theme, differing perspectives on *Heimat* offered across generations, and a discourse on the effects of German history on property rights in the post-unification era. However, as a feminist production, *The Same Old Song* treats these themes in a fundamentally different manner, casting both the privileges of property inheritance and the problems of German history in terms of a matriarchal lineage. Moreover, the film situates the phenomenon of property disputes among an array of issues arising in the era of unification, including the widespread job losses in the East that resulted from the restructured education and medical systems. While the protagonist, Katharina's, property dispute is one of the most poignant moments in the film and a critical element in the exposition of her character, it represents only one problem among many in unifying Germany.

The Same Old Song is no *Heimat* film, nor is it a derivation of the genre. However, it establishes *Heimat* as an important theme through its camerawork and dialog in the opening sequence. The film opens as Katharina and her family arrive in Dresden by boat on the Elbe, and viewers share their first glimpses of the city and surrounding landscape in long panning shots framing the riverbank and trees. We see snow on the ground and flocks of birds emerging along the river. (Shots of nature within the city, especially animals on the Elbe, will repeat throughout the film.) Eventually, buildings begin to appear, locating the *Heimat* in a city, and finally the iconic buildings of Dresden come into focus. The elderly Katharina appears blissful and dreamy in this opening sequence as she gazes out over the cityscape of Dresden.

As the film establishes Dresden through visual cues of the city and its surrounding landscape, the soundtrack undercuts the beauty and comfort of Katharina's romantic urban *Heimat*. The national anthem begins to play, and a woman in voiceover sings a slow and eerie version of the tabooed first stanza, which served as the official national anthem during the Nazi era. The local and the national are layered, lending us the sense that Katharina's *Heimat* is haunted by its place in the national history. Additionally, the anthem played in this context serves as a commentary on unification politics, as the third stanza of "The Song of Germany" ("Das Deutschlandlied") became the official anthem of West Germany in 1952 and continued to be the German national anthem during and following the process of unification. By alluding to the layered history of the anthem (that "same old song" referenced in the film's title), the opening sequence intimates that the politics of the Nazi era have a lingering effect in the present and that West Germany has exercised its hegemonic power in its unification with East Germany. The fact that the anthem is sung by a woman hints at a female perspective on this continuous history.

This discord between the *Heimat* ideal and the material, political realities of Dresden in 1990 are apparent not only in the juxtaposition of image and extradiegetic sound, but also in the montage of dialog that opens the film. Katharina's first utterance, "I feel like a bride, like coming home," spoken as she takes her first glimpses of Dresden since she was a young woman, reveals that a return to Dresden holds the promise of achieving an ideal of domesticity in which romantic love, marriage, and home are one and the same.[17] However, this hope, which stems from Katharina's romanticized memories of home during her adult years in Hamburg, contrasts with the sobering conversation of two East German men on the same boat, who are discussing the political and material difficulties they recognize in the new system. The men's criticisms of democracy (in which, they claim, the same parties always win) and capitalism (under which people are displaced from their homes) interrupt shots of Katharina smiling dreamily. German unification offers Katharina new hope for realizing happiness, while at the same time posing hardships for others.

Unlike *Our House*, *The Same Old Song* presents *Heimat* as a construction of desire rather than a realizable material circumstance. Katharina's brother Rudolf voices this view of *Heimat* when he questions Katharina's dream of reconciling with Alf and starting a life with him in Dresden: "Home in the past, how is that supposed to work, Kathi?"[18] Katharina answers that all of Dresden is waiting for them, confident that she is returning to the Dresden of her youth. Indeed, her nostalgia is problematic, particularly because she longs to rediscover the sense

---

17 "Mir ist so bräutlich zu Mut, wie heimkommen."
18 "Heim in die Vergangenheit, wie soll das gehen, Kathi?"

of home and belonging she felt in the period of National Socialism. Not to mention that a return to the places and spaces she once knew will prove impossible, because the events of the twentieth century have rendered many parts of a city like Dresden unrecognizable.

The material reconfigurations of the city are evident in some of the most powerful images of the film. By foregrounding the rubble that brings the past into the present, the film presents Dresden not as the static *Heimat* that Katharina hopes to return to. Rather, many sequences show the city in a state of transformation. In the sequence following Katharina's arrival in Dresden, the camera rests on three images of ruins on a hillside. The first, of a brick wall with a round window, nestled among trees and overgrown weeds (see fig. 2.3), conjures associations with Caspar David Friedrich's famous painting, *Abbey in the Oakwood* (see fig. 2.4). The wall's dilapidation is haunting. What history does it conjure? Why does it continue to stand if we have no purpose for it any longer? Wild, overgrown grass entwines itself with the human-made structure, emphasizing its forgottenness and the agency of nature in this eerily configured landscape.

Fig. 2.3: Ruins in Dresden

Fig. 2.4: *Abbey in the Oakwood*, Caspar David Friedrich (1809–1810)

The camera then rests on a second image, a low angle shot of rubble with what appears to be an angel emerging from it (see fig. 2.5). This *Posaunenengel* (trumpet angel) statue adorns the top of the nearby Lipsiusbau, an eighteenth-century building that has housed the Dresden Art Institute continuously since its construction. While the Lipsiusbau was damaged during the fire bombings of Dresden, this part of the building, and the angel perched atop, remained intact. The angel can thus be understood as a monument to the persistence of art and culture in the face of war's destruction, and indeed, the production of art will be an important theme in this film. Finally, the third still image in the sequence shows the standing ruins of a circular structure, an exterior corner of the Lipsiusbau (see fig. 2.6). Here we meet the photographer Johanna, Alf's granddaughter, who sits atop more rubble. If the image of the *Posaunenengel* rising above the ruins represents the triumph of art over destruction, then Johanna's perch atop the rubble suggests a parallel. She is following in that tradition, making art at a time when her own society as an East German is being dismantled.

Fig. 2.5: Ruins with *Posaunenengel*   **Fig. 2.6:** Johanna atop the rubble

In a parallel sequence, Sophie, Katharina's granddaughter, is also introduced as an artist who focuses on the material transformation of the city. Strolling through the iconic city center, Sophie is making a video recording of the construction underway on Dresden's classical buildings that were damaged or destroyed in bombings during World War II. The narrator introduces her as hailing from Cologne, thereby foregrounding her position as a Westerner. Whereas Johanna shows a preference for rubble, that which has been destabilized, Sophie films construction projects, that which is being re-established. Johanna and Sophie represent two views on, and engagements with, the ongoing material configurations of history.

As the film progresses, it critiques the idea that *Heimat* can have a singular material manifestation, suggesting instead that such a static notion of a place can only exist as a construction of one's desires. For Katharina, the imagined *Heimat* compensates for and, she hopes, might even correct unrequited love. We soon learn that Alf is similarly yearning for a past that can no longer be. He was never in love with Katharina, as she imagines, but rather with the beautiful Ilse, who was denounced to the Nazi regime for her political convictions, detained, and never seen again. For Alf, lost love is manifested not as a longing for *Heimat*, but rather, in visual representations of Ilse. He stores film negatives of her and spends his evenings gazing longingly at a painting for which Ilse presumably modeled. Both Katharina and Alf yearn for a return to the past, and reality provides a less desirable existence than the one they imagine for themselves. The bombings of Dresden and the loss of Ilse have contributed to a radically material, discursive, and emotional reconfiguration that makes the *Heimat* irretrievable.

Katharina's inability to realize – and indeed, lack of just entitlement to – the life she imagines for herself is brought to a critical point in the film when she attempts to claim the house she had purchased in Dresden when she was a young adult. This moment is preceded by a discussion of Dresden's past, and thus the film contextualizes Katharina's property claim within a larger narrative of German history. As Katharina, Rudolf, and Sophie stroll along the Elbe, Rudolf recalls the horrific fire bombings of Dresden and guesses at the number of corpses that must lie at the bottom of the river. Rudolf's gruesome account provides voiceover commentary for the camerawork that mimics Katharina's distracted gaze, framing images of the idyllic snow-covered landscape. Rather than responding to Rudolf, Katharina focuses on the beauty of Dresden now. She is unwilling to acknowledge the lingering presence of the past or to integrate that history into her sense of *Heimat*. However, when Katharina stops suddenly on a street corner along the Elbe, interrupting the conversation to proudly proclaim, "That is my house, your inheritance, Sophie,"[19] a dispute ensues, revealing that Katharina's past indeed has repercussions for her in the present.

This scene is what brings *The Same Old Song* into conversation with *Our House*, and three points emerge that warrant a comparison of property disputes in the two films. First, two women, rather than two men, stand at the center of the property dispute in *The Same Old Song*. Despite Rudolf's objections as the family approaches the house, Katharina addresses the woman working in its front yard, Frau Schiller, and announces herself as the owner: "That is actually my house. I would like to look around a bit."[20] Frau Schiller's indignant response plays sarcastically on the apparent class difference: "Oh, your house? And naturally you would like to have it back? [...] The madam has returned. How can I serve you, madam?"[21] Frau Schiller's retort reflects the contemporary perception among Easterners that Westerners believe themselves to be superior. Moreover, it indicates that the Schillers are aware that Westerners have been coming to the East to claim property. The name Schiller is also significant here. By giving this East German family a name connected with the very foundations of modern German culture, not to mention the former East German city of Weimar, Stöckl underlines the point that East Germans are just as entitled to property in the

---

19 "Das ist mein Haus, dein Erbe, Sophie."
20 "Das ist nämlich mein Haus. Ich möchte mich ein bisschen umgucken."
21 "Ach, Ihr Haus? Und natürlich möchten Sie es wieder haben? [...] Die gnädige Frau ist zurückgekehrt. Womit kann ich denn dienen, gnädige Frau?"

newly unified Germany as West Germans are. However, by having a woman speak for the Schiller family, Stöckl undermines the patriarchal authority attached to the name. Frau Schiller defends her property; Herr Schiller can only lend her reinforcement.

The second difference between the two films lies the way in which they address the Nazi past. Through Rudolf's attempt to placate the Schillers and persuade Katharina to leave them alone, the audience learns condemning information about Katharina. She profited from the removal of Jews from the area, buying the house at what Rudolf calls a *Schandpreis* (disgraceful price) when a Jewish family was forced to leave. When he confronts her with the actual circumstance of her purchase, "This house and this garden here have not rightfully belonged to you for one moment of your life," she replies coldly "Of course it belongs to me. I paid for it."[22] Katharina thereby reveals that she has no emotional claim to the house, but rather, a financial one. It is the one material object she can claim in order to construct the *Heimat* she wishes for in the present. By reminding Katharina that she purchased the house by exploiting the desperation of persecuted Jews, Rudolf has made sure that it cannot serve as part of an untarnished *Heimat* ideal for her.

A third significant difference is that Katharina introduces the house as "my house, your inheritance Sophie," thereby establishing matrilineal inheritance of both property and history. By depicting the property dispute in terms of matrilineal inheritance and women's problematic participation in history, the film presents a multifaceted revision to the conventions of *Heimat*, in which women support men's ownership of the land. Instead, the film frames the property dispute as a confrontation between women and a matter of matrilineal inheritance, thereby foregrounding women's active participation in both the past and the present. Even when Katharina is in the wrong, and Rudolf attempts to stop her from approaching Frau Schiller, Sophie insists on supporting her grandmother's agency. The film thus avoids any idealistic or utopian rendering of a world run by women. Ultimately, *The Same Old Song* condemns the concept of property inheritance altogether as a form of institutional injustice. As soon as the theme of inheritance is established ("your inheritance, Sophie"), it is promptly rendered illegitimate. Confiscation and cheap resale were the circumstances of Katharina's purchase of the house, and homelessness for the Schillers (as Herr Schiller indicates) would be the result if the courts were to decide in Katharina's favor.

---

22 "Dieses Haus und dieser Garten hier haben dir noch keinen Augenblick in deinem Leben rechtmäßig gehört." / "Natürlich gehört es mir. Ich hab's bezahlt."

If men are the traditional heirs of property and history in the *Heimat* ideal, *The Same Old Song* departs from that convention sharply, as history has rendered the male characters largely ineffectual. Katharina's husband fell in the war, placing her in the position of family matriarch. Her son Karl, once a brilliant lawyer who advocated for the underprivileged and who, the film hints, had been aligned ideologically with the '68 movement, suffers from severe brain damage and paralysis resulting from an automobile accident. Because Karl is unable to manage property, the family inheritance goes to Sophie. Moreover, Katharina's brother Rudolf resigned from his teaching position years ago to care for Karl, and Alf, who remained in the GDR to build a career as a doctor, now sees his position threatened by the restructuring of the hospital system. Only Stefan, Alf's grandson who is in college, still harbors some potential for a fulfilling career.

While men in the film are rendered passive, women's memory and perspectives are foregrounded. The audience has access to Katharina's reflections through voiceover, and the film thematizes women's participation in the creation of cultural artifacts through Sophie and Johanna's artistic endeavors. As the matriarch, Katharina is the most empowered member of her family. She is also the most problematic figure, and the film seems to have a conflicted view of her. On the one hand, she profited from Nazi crimes and disavows any responsibility for that past in the present. On the other hand, she is the beloved matriarch who has sacrificed time and again for her family. At moments, the film suggests that perhaps Katharina does deserve some happiness after struggling for so many decades. In the end, however, *The Same Old Song* is much less forgiving of the Nazi generation than is *Our House*. While Kurt Wrede's father is excused, to a certain degree, for his party involvement because he was not a "convinced Nazi," Katharina is more severely condemned when two more secrets from her past are revealed.

Katharina admits the first secret to her family during the celebration of her seventieth birthday: Karl is not her son, but rather, the son of Ilse and Alf. Katharina does not reveal the circumstances under which she adopted Karl, though presumably the adoption was connected to Ilse's detainment. The information is polarizing to the family: Alf, Rudolf, and Stefan find the revelation of the secret to be heartless. In her attempt to clarify the family lineage, Katharina has effectively taken Karl from Rudolf, who has sacrificed his career to care for his nephew. Moreover, Alf feels that Katharina is assigning him responsibility for Karl, even though he has just met his biological son for the first time and is unprepared to take on the responsibility of caring for him. Sophie, on the other hand, supports her grandmother for having the courage to divulge this long-held secret and believes she has learned something about herself in discovering the truth about her family. What presents itself as stronger than inheritance, *Hei-*

mat, or even blood lineage is female solidarity. Sophie stands by her grandmother through every tough decision, even after learning condemning information about the way in which Katharina acquired the house and the truth of Karl's parentage. At the same time, Sophie does not question Katharina's motivations for divulging this secret, and the audience is left to wonder whether this is Katharina's strategy for bringing the two families together, forcing the *Heimat* that she wishes to create.

We learn Katharina's darkest secret in a voiceover of her thoughts. It was she who denounced Ilse out of jealousy over Alf's affections and was responsible for her arrest. The family does not know this fact. Although Ilse was never heard from again, the film raises the question of whether her spirit might still be present in Dresden. As audience members, we see her navigating the waterways of the Elbe. She haunts Katharina in her dreams, and Alf hears her laughter from time to time. Is she a ghost? Is she still alive? Or does she exist only in the film negatives and painting that Alf keeps in his home? Like the national anthem sung in voiceover at the beginning and end of the film and the ruins that remain standing throughout the city, the specter Ilse represents the past that continues to haunt the present as two Germanys – and perhaps two families – unify.

Heimat as Material Engagement, Not Family History

Both *Our House* and *The Same Old Song* posit *Heimat*, particularly as it relates to property in the former East Germany, as a place in which one is forced to face one's relationship to Germany's difficult history. Houses in dispute no longer conceal family secrets, but become the sites where problematic histories are unearthed and made public. As such, they are the material-discursive catalysts of memory. The *Heimat* trope, however, serves as a palliative to mitigate the pain, shame, and defensive feelings aroused with the exposure of long-repressed family-national histories. Employing *Heimat* prompts the audience to consider the perspectives of all parties involved, even those with nefarious acts in their pasts.

Ultimately, both films depict the institution of property inheritance, a bedrock of *Heimat*, as incompatible with Germany's history in the twentieth century. National history necessarily encroaches on the insularity of the local. War has caused ruptures in family lines, people have been displaced for political reasons, and property has been confiscated and reappointed, all of which rend the lines of inheritance required to maintain the conventional concept of *Heimat*. The two films suggest that *Heimat* as a construction that imagines continuity without such rupture is necessarily utopian, and an amended concept of *Heimat* is necessary to account for the ever-changing materiality of home.

When Barad talks about the self-organizing, exclusionary practice of matter, the agential cut as a practice of differentiation and self-articulation, her discussion of the physical world sounds very similar to the social construct of *Heimat*, which delineates a space, landscape, and population in order to differentiate itself from that which surrounds it. However, as Barad has pointed out, agential cuts are never stable and actually lead to open-endedness, a universe of new possibilities and reconfigurations: "[...] agency is the space of possibilities opened up by the indeterminacies entailed in exclusions. [...] The reworking of exclusions entails possibilities for (discontinuous) changes in the topology of the world's becoming."[23] This is instructive for conceiving of a *Heimat* that makes sense in the real world. The two films discussed in this chapter reveal that the material-discursive configurations that constitute *Heimat* are open-ended and ever changing. The dynamic nature of *Heimat* becomes most evident in those moments when its materiality is brought to the fore – in the houses that require maintenance, the rubble and ruins, the construction sites – when we see human agency not as part of an interaction, but rather as part of an intra-action through which *Heimat* and the subject emerge as co-constitutive. By focusing on the way in which people interact with, and intra-act within, the materiality of the place conceived of as *Heimat*, we move away from an essentialist and exclusionary notion of *Heimat* based on place of birth and lines of inheritance. Instead, this concept of *Heimat* invites a more performative concept of belonging.

While both films sympathize, to a point, with the perspectives of Westerners who have returned to the East to claim a home as part of their *Heimat* ideal, they ultimately side with Easterners. To do so, the films take the same three approaches. First, both films appeal to audiences' consciences about the socio-economic disparities of the time, depicting Easterners who stand to lose far more than their Western counterparts stand to gain in the property disputes. In both *Our House* and *The Same Old Song*, Eastern families indicate that they face homelessness if the courts were to decide in Westerners' favor. While the Westerners in both films have sentimental attachment to the houses in question, this does not outweigh the hardship they would inflict if their claims were successful.

Both films also bolster their arguments in favor of Easterners by associating West Germans with the legacy of National Socialism. This is, of course, a problematic revision of history, as it disavows any engagement with National Socialism on the part of East Germans prior to the Soviet occupation and formation of the GDR. This revision effects an economy of morality that allows both films to

---

23 Karen Barad, *Meeting the Universe Halfway*, 182.

take sides with Easterners more easily by not muddying the waters of culpability. Yet they do so in different ways. While *The Same Old Song* strongly refutes Katharina's claim to the house in Dresden based on her actions during the Nazi era, *Our House* treats involvement in National Socialism much more gingerly, attempting to create an equivalent with nefarious actions of Communist party members during the formation of the GDR.

Finally, both films employ the trope of intra-activity with the land and home to argue for Easterners' claim to the *Heimat*. While *The Same Old Song* undercuts Katharina's claim based on her activities during the Nazi era, it is telling that she confronts Frau Schiller while the Schillers are engaged in yardwork, that is, the work of maintaining the home that undergirds so many cultural productions' arguments for rightful ownership of a property. The film thereby employs the trope of intra-activity that the viewing audience of the time would have understood. *Our House* is much more explicit in its argument that the Eastern family has the stronger claim to the *Heimat* because of its intra-activity with the materiality of the house and land. The *Heimat* – and thus the houses in dispute – rightfully belongs to those who have maintained it, because they and the material environment have been mutually reconfigured through their intra-actions. The Gleiniches belong to the *Heimat* because they have reshaped it as theirs, and been reshaped by it, whereas the Wredes, who left, no longer do. Ultimately, both films argue that the *Heimat* is no a priori or materially stable place, but rather, the relational and performed space of those who intra-act with and within it, in all its socio-economic, historical, and material complexity.

Chapter 3
Home in the East as a Capitalist Battlefield: *The Brocken* (Glowna, 1992) and *No More Mr. Nice Guy* (Buck, 1993)

In choosing to prioritize historical concerns when awarding property in the former East Germany, the German government framed the determination of private property as an issue of social justice and historical redress. While on its face this priority seems commendable, the analyses of news media reports and fictional productions so far in this monograph have shown that the government's decision, in practice, justified administrative policies that favored Westerners over East Germans when it came to property claims and acquisitions. What is more, by casting Communism as a historical aberration and the restoration of private property as its corrective, this rhetoric obscured the fact that neoliberalism, not the ostensible inevitabilities of history, was the real driving force behind these decisions. By treating the determination of home ownership separately from that of commercial property ownership in official discourses and bureaucratic channels, the government could avoid a narrative of neoliberalism where houses were concerned.

The films discussed so far in this monograph, *Taxi to Rathenow*, *Our House*, and *The Same Old Song* address the historical circumstances that led Westerners to claim property in the East, their moral concerns in doing so, and Easterners' vulnerability in the new capitalist system. They show how the privatization of businesses, which led to widespread unemployment, and the determination of home ownership, which led to widespread displacement, were two dimensions of the same problem. The films I will treat in this chapter, Vadim Glowna's 1992 made-for-television film *The Brocken* (*Der Brocken*) and Detlev Buck's 1993 cinematic release *No More Mr. Nice Guy* (*Wir können auch anders*), take the discussion a step further, making the links between housing issues and neoliberalism explicit. What is astonishingly different about these two films, however, is that at only one year's remove (or less) from the other films discussed, they do away with historical concerns about property rights altogether. In the scenarios these films put forth, capitalism, not national history, is in the foreground since houses belong to the broad capitalist landscape with which Easterners must now contend.[1] Perhaps even more surprisingly, Easterners in *The Brocken*

---

[1] This is not to say that the GDR disappears completely from these films. In a subplot of *The*

and *No More Mr. Nice Guy* are no longer framed as victims of Western aggression. Rather than expressing fears about an uncertain future, the Easterners in these films quickly become adept at navigating the capitalist system, winning out over Westerners in the end.

The Brocken is the success story of Ada Fenske, an elderly woman who has led a quiet life up until this point tending her house, property, and flock of geese on the island of Rügen. At the outset of the film, the German military sends an undercover intelligence agent to negotiate the purchase of her property because of its proximity to a closing Russian military camp that it plans to acquire. Ada is accustomed to the physical labor of maintaining her property but untrained in the tactics of business negotiation. She quickly realizes, however, that in the new capitalist system she must see her home and domestic skills as financial assets. With the help of a friendly Westerner, a man named Naujok, Ada employs her friends and neighbors to transform her home into a business that produces jams and knitted goods, thereby securing not only her house, but also the community's financial autonomy. In the end, Ada wins out against the military, engaging with capitalism on her own terms.

Whereas Ada in *The Brocken* succeeds in the capitalist system while also maintaining the solidarity of community fostered in the GDR, *No More Mr. Nice Guy* is less optimistic about market-based solutions to capitalism's problems. In this film, a pair of West German brothers, Morst and Kipp, have long inhabited the social margins. They hail from the lowest rungs of society, cannot read, have poor social skills, and are most likely (the film is unclear about this) homeless. However, the brothers have just received news that they stand to inherit a house from their late grandmother in the former East Germany. The capitalist dream of striking it rich appears to be a reality for them, as they embark on a road trip to claim the house, and along with it, their new future as wealthy men of leisure. Ultimately, however, the acquisition of property in the former East Germany leads only to disappointment and further financial ruin, as the brothers are swindled repeatedly by Easterners who have already internalized the rules of the capitalist game. In the end, the brothers must relinquish their claim to the home and the few other objects they possess in order to be happy. They flee the capitalist system rather than embracing it, starting a new life in an area of rural Russia not yet saturated by consumerism and competition.

Brocken, Ada threatens to expose a former Stasi member if he does not help her, and in the end, she is trying to create a style of capitalism that draws on the collectivism of the GDR. Nevertheless, the history of the GDR does not play into legal considerations about property ownership.

Upon first consideration, these films appear to have little in common. Their protagonists hail from the two different Germanys and are on opposite sides of a potential property transaction. However, several similarities bring them into conversation. First, both films portray Easterners as having enough capitalist knowledge to win out over Westerners. Capitalism is already so pervasive that Easterners are learning – or have already learned – how to manipulate the system and are engaging in market competition. Second, both films depict alienation as an effect of neoliberalism, as the protagonists must face the ways in which capitalism is changing their social and material environments. Finally, both films end by imagining somewhat utopian spaces that provide relief from the protagonists' sense of alienation. To be sure, the utopian endings that the two films propose are quite different. *The Brocken* ends with the protagonist, Ada Fenske, having created a hybrid capitalist-communist way of "doing" capitalism by recruiting her neighborhood to enter into business with her and thus privatizing collectively. *No More Mr. Nice Guy*, on the other hand, finds hope for the protagonist brothers, who cannot live comfortably within capitalist society, in a rural Russia as yet untouched by capitalism. Whereas *The Brocken* sees within neoliberalism an opportunity to shape the system for Easterners' benefit, *No More Mr. Nice Guy* sees conventional property relations as ultimately disappointing and the escape from capitalism's reach the only way to be free and happy. Both of these films enter into these discourses through the question of home ownership.

Commodifying Community in *The Brocken*

Considering *The Brocken* decades after its initial release, the film offers an incisive exposé on the ways in which neoliberal sensibilities took root in the former East Germany. It illustrates David Harvey's argument that the insidious power of neoliberalism, particularly as it spread throughout Europe, lie in the fact that the free market came to be associated with individual freedom rather than an overt display of power by any particular institution.[2] While discourses on neoliberal-

---

[2] The term "neoliberalism" refers to the capitalist ideology that the free market is the best measure for the needs of the populace and that government regulation of the market only impedes growth and should be kept at a minimum. Neoliberalism has its intellectual roots in the late 1940s and spread first in the 1970s in Latin America through brutal military coup. However, its emergence as a global phenomenon was brought on by the Reagan-Thatcherism of the 1980s, which instrumentalized the concept of "individual freedom" to garner consent to deregulate industries and markets, bust up unions, and withdraw federal funding from many social institutions, thereby leading to bankruptcies and privatization. For an excellent overview of the

ism typically address the deregulation of the market, the turn from an industrial-based economy to finance capitalism in the West, globalization, and the erosion of labor union power, rarely is the privatization of homes taken into account.[3] However, in *The Brocken*, Ada's home becomes a battleground for market forces: when a hegemonic military power masquerading as a private interest puts pressure on Ada to sell her house, a free-market solution to that problem presents itself. While the two forces seem at odds with one another, they ultimately work in tandem to bring Ada's house onto the marketplace. That is to say, in her fight against the more overtly felt, hegemonic military force, Ada consents to privatizing her home and community, introducing the market into areas of her life previously considered outside the commercial sphere.

The strong-arm approach of militarism is established in the film's opening sequence, as a military helicopter circles the island of Rügen. Through panning shots of the landscape below, the audience shares the gaze of two men in the helicopter, one in military fatigues and another in business attire. While initially the military and the corporate world appear to be working in cooperation with one another, we soon learn that they are actually one and the same. The man in the business suit is no civilian, but an intelligence officer named Albert Zwirner. Thus, military power will not make itself perceived as such to Ada, but will present itself as an overt market force. Music befitting an adventure film plays over the sequence, as does the sound of the helicopter blades chopping the air, both of which drown out any other sound, an aural metaphor of the military's hegemonic power. Zwirner holds a binder in his lap that contains maps and images of community members below. Our first introduction to Ada is her picture in the binder, to which the soldier in fatigues points, indicating that she is the target of their mission. As the officer identifies a parcel of land below with a house on it, we see that it borders on a Russian military base that is being vacated as a result of German unification. Herein lies the value of Ada's property: the German military wishes to establish its own base on the newly available premises and its adjacent plot.

The opening sequence sets up its David-and-Goliath storyline, intercutting shots from the loud, circling helicopter with a quiet sequence that introduces

---

way neoliberalism has spread historically, see David Harvey, *A Brief History of Neoliberalism* (Oxford and New York: Oxford University Press, 2005), particularly the introduction, 1–4; Chapter 1 "Freedom's Just Another Word," 5–38; and Chapter 2 "The Construction of Consent," 39–63. See also Raewyn Connell, "Understanding Neoliberalism," in *Neoliberalism and Everyday Life*, ed. Susan Braedley and Meg Luxton (Montréal and Ithaca: McGill-Queen's University Press, 2010).
[3] A notable exception is the privatization of public housing works. See Raewyn Connell, "Understanding Neoliberalism," 24.

Ada and her humble life below. As viewers, we are positioned just inside her house, watching through lace curtains and flower boxes in her window as she hangs laundry outside. As though guests in her home, we gaze out on a peaceful blue sea in the background (see fig. 3.1). This montage of quiet domestic routine intercut with the loud and dynamic sequence of the men in the helicopter signals an impending disruption to Ada's peace. When the helicopter drops low, causing Ada's laundry to whip wildly in the wind, her reaction reveals a rather unexpected character trait. Shaking her fist and yelling "What do you want here?,"[4] Ada shows that she is not as meek as she appears. She is prepared to defend her lifestyle fiercely (see fig. 3.2).

Fig. 3.1: Ada's home, a picture of *Gemütlichkeit*   **Fig. 3.2:** Ada defending her property

We soon learn that the military is not the only party interested in Ada's property. A veritable parade of private speculators will approach her throughout the film (and likely already has), even though she has not listed her house for sale. The film thereby introduces the true mechanism of neoliberalism's expansion, the market's tendency to spread to areas of life previously thought to be non-commercial. This aspect of neoliberalism is much more insidious than overt military power since it is more subtle and less visible as a foe. Soon after Ada meets Zwirner for the first time, and (mis)recognizes him as part of the business world, a friendly Westerner named Naujok appears on her property to inquire about the house. Nauojok's approach is less aggressive, but will turn out to be more effective in leading Ada onto the market. Naujok discloses that he is not interested in acquiring Ada's property, but must pose as though he were doing so in order to appease his wife, who wishes to purchase property in the East

---

4 "Was wollen Sie hier?" All translations from *The Brocken* and *No More Mr. Nice Guy* are my own, except the title of the latter.

to enhance her social status at home. Naujok, however, fears that as Westerners take over the island of Rügen, the local communities will lose their charm. For this reason, he wants to help Ada find a way to retain her house in the face of financial pressure to sell.

In order to support his vision of an unchanged Rügen, and to make a convincing case to his wife that Ada is not willing to sell cheaply, Naujok equips Ada with the knowledge she needs to refuse his wife's offer and hold other private interests at bay until she is ready to sell on her own terms. During this conversation with Naujok, Ada realizes that home has a new meaning in the capitalist system. She must think of it as a financial asset rather than a retreat from the outside world. He tells her that, for example, she should wait at least three years, at which time she could likely get double, maybe even triple, the price of her house. He also suggests that she take out a mortgage on the house in order to finance modernizing it, updating the heating for example, so that she can maximize her profits later.

Not only does Naujok bring a bit of friendly advice for Ada; he also proposes an idea for a business that she can run out of her home. And, thus, the film presents a final step in the development of neoliberalism locally: once market-based thinking entrenches itself, new markets can be created anywhere. Ada has been knitting while listening to Naujok's advice. Seeing a market for her handiwork, he suggests that she employ her friends to knit sweaters and sell them to Westerners: "Eco is in. People go crazy for it. Handmade sweaters, homemade honey, homemade juice, homemade bread, just nobody wants to make anything themselves."[5] In the age of globally mass produced commodities, people crave the unique quality of a product that has been made by hand through an individual's intra-actions within the local material environment. At the same time, consumers are too lazy or lack the knowledge to produce them themselves. To help Ada fend off financial pressure to sell her home, Naujok espouses the neoliberal rhetoric that the market can provide solutions to life's problems if one is entrepreneurial enough.

Ada's home, which had previously stood outside the realm of the marketplace, now enters it as both Zwerner and Naujok weigh in on its value. Ada is left only to choose what role her home will play on the market, either as real estate if she were to sell it to Zwirner or a business if she follows Naujok's advice. Figures 3.3 and 3.4 illustrate Ada's receptivity relative to their proposals. In figure 3.3, we see the first encounter between Ada and Zwirner, when he appears on her

---

5 "Ökozeit, die Leute sind ja verrückt nach sowas. Selbstgemachte Pullover, selbstgemachter Honig, selbstgemachter Saft, selbstgemachtes Brot, nur selber machen will es keiner."

property. As Zwirner attempts to smooth-talk his way into a good deal for his boss, Ada goes about the labor of tending to her property and only halfway pays attention to him. The two could not be more dissimilar in this scene, and their appearances underscore the difference. Zwirner appears on the property in a shiny black Mercedes with a sun roof, wearing a suit, tie, and sunglasses, his hair slicked back, the stereotypical habitus of a crooked business person from the West. Ada, by contrast, wears her hair in a neat bun behind her head, a long skirt, a sensible cardigan, and boots as she goes about her chores. In figure 3.3, we see her back turned on Zwirner, as she puts her focus on the material work in front of her. Zwirner trails behind in his attempts to get her attention. In figure 3.4, a much different dynamic is evident between Ada and Naujok in their first conversation. Naujok has gained Ada's trust through his friendlier approach, and the mutual respect between the two is recognizable in the eye contact they hold in this frame. Ada accepts Naujok's authority, and his influence over her is visible in his stance above Ada as he speaks. In the new capitalist system, Ada must face the fact that her house is attractive to potential buyers. She can either submit to a more overt market power by selling her house to Zwirner or she can retain her house by making it a business and consenting to produce commodities for the free market, as Naujok suggests. Either way, her house can no longer be considered separate from the world of capitalism, competition, and consumption.

Fig. 3.3: Zwirner the wheeler and dealer, Ada the worker **Fig. 3.4:** Ada and Naujok in friendly conversation

When proposing his idea that Ada create a business to meet Westerners' demand for authentic homemade products, Naujok introduces another important theme in the film. Here, he touches on the idea that alienation is one of the main byproducts of capitalism. In his philosophical papers on economics from 1844, Karl

Marx posited that workers become alienated from themselves and their creativity through the commodification of their labor and from each other through the competitive nature of capitalism.[6] Theorists have since built on Marx's ideas, even developing a theory of alienation that extends to the local environment and culture.[7] As Lauren Langman has written, "alienation can be found not only in the production of commodities, but also in the commodifications of culture and reification of subjectivity."[8] Indeed, Naujok supports the preservation of local cultures in the East because of their imagined quality of being as yet untarnished by the alienating effects of global capitalism. For him, the East is a place where West German tourists might reconnect with a more authentic "Germanness." Yet Naujok's market-based solution to globalization's effects is illogical. If Ada and her local community attempt to preserve the "authenticity" of their culture by commodifying it and selling it to Westerners, this will eventually result in the alienation of culture of which Langman speaks.

However, neither Naujok nor Ada recognizes this inevitability, as the film shows a number of more immediately felt ways in which global capitalism is alienating the community from their physical environment and way of life. For example, when Ada visits the local fishermen for her weekly purchase, she learns that they are no longer allowed to sell to the locals, since their catch must now be shipped to Hamburg for export. One fisherman gives her a fish under the table, but Ada will soon lose access to local fish to eat. This scene illustrates what Harvey calls neoliberalism's "creative destruction" of the earth, one aspect of which is the diversion of resources. Under capitalism, certain places become

---

[6] Alienation is a theme throughout many of Karl Marx's works. In his *Ökonomisch-philosophische Manuskripte aus dem Jahre 1844* (*Economic and Philosophic Manuscripts of 1844*), Marx describes four major forms of alienation in capitalism: the alienation of the worker from himself, from the process of producing, from his potential as a human, and from other workers. See, in particular, Karl Marx, "Die entfremdete Arbeit," in *Ökonomisch-philosophische Manuskripte aus dem Jahre 1844* (Berlin: Hofenberg, 2019): 51–65.

[7] For discussions of Marx and alienation, see the volume *The Evolution of Alienation: Trauma, Promise, and the Millennium,* ed. Lauren Langman and Devorah Kalekin-Fishman (Rowman & Littlefield Publishers, 2005), particularly the introduction 1–20; Lauren Langman, "Globalization, Alienation, and Identity," 180–183; and Roger A. Salerno, "Alienated Communities: Between Aloneness and Connectedness," 254–257; as well as John Murphy, "Philosophical Reflection, Self-Management, and the Disappearance of the Market," in *Toward a Post-Market Society,* ed. J. W. Murphy and Karen A. Callaghan (Hauppauge: Nova Science Publishers, 2011): 163. See David Harvey, "The Creative Destructive on the Land" in *The Enigma of Capital and the Crises of Capitalism* (Oxford: Oxford University Press, 2010): 184–214 for a discussion of the ways in which capitalism affects geographies.

[8] Lauren Langman, "Globalization, Alienation, and Identity," 181. She sites Jean Baudrillard, *For a Critique of the Political Economy of the Sign* (St. Louis: Telos Press, 1981).

centers of production or distribution, the "agglomerations of activity in particular places," and natural resources are diverted there, leaving locals alienated from the raw materials they previously relied upon.⁹ At the same time, *The Brocken* shows how other resources are destroyed completely when they do not serve a global scale of production. For example, the local shepherd's humble business of tending sheep and selling wool is no longer sustainable in the new market economy that has global priorities rather than local ones, so he considers sending his flock to the slaughterhouse. Later, a different neighbor marvels when telling Ada of his recent trip to Hannover, where one can buy sweaters cheaply that have been mass produced abroad.

In this new and changing system, in which Ada experiences the alienation of global capitalism and an aggressive pressure to sell her property – from both the military and private interests – there is an allure to selling out, forsaking the local way of life, and traveling now that the borders are open. In a scene in which she speaks with a local pastor, Herr Seidel, he asks her about her dreams:

> Ada: I have one [wish]. I've always wanted, even as a child, to see a real mountain, a gigantic, proper mountain.
>
> Seidel: You can have that! Next week we are making a trip to the Brocken. We can go there again, and you'll come with us.
>
> Ada: The Brocken, that's no real mountain!
>
> Seidel: No mountain? What do you mean then?
>
> Ada: Mont Blanc, that is a mountain. Nanga Parbat, Mount Everest, those are mountains. The Brocken!¹⁰

Ada is aware of a larger world than the one she has experienced and has ambitions to see it now that travel outside of East Germany is permitted. The Brocken in the former West Germany is no satisfactory travel goal when more exotic places exist. Playing devil's advocate, she makes a similar argument to Naujok during his visit, asking him why she shouldn't sell out now and travel:

> Ada: Should I [sell]? I could travel then.

---

9 David Harvey, *The Enigma of Capital*, 195.
10 Ada: Einen [Wunsch] habe ich. Ich wollte schon immer, schon als Kind, einen richtigen Berg sehen, so einen riesengroßen richtigen Berg. / Seidel: Das kannst du haben! Nächste Woche machen wir einen Ausflug zum Brocken. Da darf man nämlich wieder hin, und du kommst mit. / Ada: Der Brocken, das ist doch kein Berg! / Seidel: Kein Berg, was dann? / Ada: Der Mont Blanc, das ist ein Berg, der Nanga Parbat, der Mount Everest, das sind Berge. Der Brocken!

Naujok: Yes, but to where? It's not worth it. You either end up ripped off in some dump for tourists or shot to death by some terrorists. Go to the movies. It's all much nicer than in reality.[11]

Naujok's intentions are transparent: he wields his superior knowledge of traveling as a Westerner to scare Ada into remaining on Rügen and maintaining the image of local culture that he desires.

Now that Ada is armed with the information she has learned from Naujok, she proves to be no easy foe when Zwirner attempts to persuade her to sell. However, he also enjoys the competition and sees in Ada a worthy adversary, coaching her on the basic tactics of negotiation. For example, when he makes a low offer based on the run-down condition of the house, and she agrees that it needs a lot of work, he jokes: "Yes, but *I* have to be the one to say that. You have to say 'this gorgeous ocean view, yeah, pristine, unobstructed, classic island style.' You have to list all the positive features, Frau Fenske!"[12] She soon reveals that admitting the amount of work needed to update the property was also a tactic, meant to induce him to rescind his offer because of the undesirability of the property. She will not sell if the need for repairs brings down the sales price. She can make the repairs herself, she tells him proudly, showing off her new business savvy by stating that she could mortgage the house to finance the updates if necessary.

By introducing Ada to the more obvious tactics of negotiation, Zwirner has manipulated her into divulging her plan to take out a mortgage on the house, information that can help him in his attempt to acquire it. As discussed in chapter 1, securing a mortgage was often difficult in the former East Germany in the 1990s because of the vast number of competing property claims in the area. According to the Property Law, there must be proof that no other claimants on the house existed before a bank could legally lend a mortgage. Ada learns this in a later scene when attempting to apply for one. As the bank associate tells her, "That is our biggest problem these days: what actually belongs to whom."[13] Ada is given the burden of proof to show, through an entry in the property registry and an *Unbedenklichkeitserklärung* (declaration of no objection) from the courts that no one else could potentially claim her house. In the meantime,

---

[11] Ada: Soll ich [verkaufen]? Ich könnte dann mal verreisen. / Naujok: Ja aber wohin denn? Lohnt sich alles nicht. Entweder werden Sie geneppt in irgendeinem Touristenkaff oder von irgendwelchen Terroristen erschossen. Gehen Sie ins Kino, ist alles viel schöner als in Wirklichkeit.
[12] "Ja, aber das muss *ich* sagen. Sie müssen sagen 'dieser herrliche Meeresblick, ja, unverdorben, unverbaubar, klassischer Inselstil.' Sie müssen alle Vorzüge aufzählen, Frau Fenske!"
[13] "Das ist doch heutzutage unser allergrößtes Problem: was gehört wem wirklich."

Zwirner initiates machinations behind her back, digging up a nephew that Ada never knew she had, Karl Funke, the son of her late sister who had fled to West Berlin decades ago. Karl may also stand to inherit the house, and the competing claim will halt Ada's application for a mortgage. Moreover, Karl is a starving artist in Berlin and a squatter. With no sentimental attachment to the house, and a need for liquid assets, Karl may be motivated to convince Ada to sell out.

However, Zwirner's tactic of pitting individual interests against one another backfires. When meeting her nephew, a potential adversary in her fight for her home, Ada displays the defining character trait that will eventually defeat Zwirner and the military: she does not see things in adversarial terms. Rather than perceiving Karl as a competitor for her property, she accepts him as family, recognizes the possible validity of his claim, and hopes to work in a way that will be mutually beneficial.

Ada will greet the new economic system in a similar manner, quite literally inviting it into her home. She soon learns that she cannot turn a profit on knitting alone, because the costs of raw materials and distribution, as well as the time it takes to produce each sweater, are far too high. After receiving a shipment of wool from Naujok as an initial investment in her business, she approaches other women in the neighborhood who are talented knitters and negotiates the terms of their production. She tests out different marmalade recipes, consults with Naujok on marketing strategies and labels, employs the local taxi driver to make her deliveries, and sources the wool for her sweaters from the aforementioned local shepherd who would otherwise lose his flock. Perhaps most importantly, Ada's house becomes the business headquarters and the sheep's new home. She even capitalizes on potential buyers' interest in her house as real estate, placing an ad for an open house, even though she has no intention of selling, and then using the event to make business contacts and hand out samples of her wares.

By the end of the film, Ada has created a business that sources its own raw materials, manufactures its own products, and oversees distribution, all from her house and through the labor of her friends and neighbors. Thus, the film envisions a form of collective privatization that fends off the aggressive individualism inherent in capitalism, preserves locals' access to the land and livestock, and can face down hegemonic institutions like the military. Indeed, she makes this point explicit at the end of the film when she gives a speech at a party to celebrate the new business: "We are all a company" and then, laughing at her own joke, "a mini-multi, so to speak."[14] The crowd laughs at the fancy capitalist term used

---

14 "Wir alle hier sind eine Firma" / "ein Mini-multi, so zu sagen"

to describe their modest business built on solidarity among neighbors. But Ada's joke is incisive. The way for the community to preserve its way of life and for her to maintain ownership of her home is to corporatize her property and relationships.

In attempting to retain control of their local environment and ward off the alienation caused by globalization, Ada and her community have internalized a neoliberal mindset and contributed to its spread in the East. By commodifying their own local culture and capitalizing on the alienation Westerners feel, Ada has created a new market where none existed before. As Raewyn Connell has written:

> Neoliberalism is a missionary faith: it seeks to make existing markets wider and to create new markets where they did not exist before. [...] Needs formerly met by public agencies on the principle of citizen rights, or through personal relationships in communities and families, are now to be met by companies selling services in a market.[15]

Indeed, we see Ada restructuring her home, relationships, and skills along market lines. She creates a new market by performing the labor of knitting and making jam for profit, creating commodities rather than the handicrafts that were previously an expression of love for her friends and family. What is more, her form of collective privatization, bringing the resources, talents, and services of her friends together under one corporate umbrella shows a great deal of business savvy. It resembles what we would now call "vertical integration," a corporate strategy for keeping costs low and maximizing profits by owning the chain of supply, production, and distribution. Moreover, Ada's use of her house as corporate headquarters is at once a throwback to an earlier age when much production took place in homes and at the same time visionary, foreseeing companies like AirBnB and Uber.

This is not to say that Ada exhibits all aspects of neoliberalism to come. She does not rely on contingent, "flexible," or contract labor nor does she engage in other neoliberal labor practices that keep employees in precarious positions. Nor is her "vertical integration" meant to amass wealth at the upper echelons of the company. Rather, her form of capitalism requires mutual care of one another in the community. Beyond building her own business, she employs her new way of thinking to help a local artist negotiate a fair deal with a distributor and pitches an idea to a local fisherman for starting his own business. Still, her faith in the ability of the market to care for the community seems, from a twenty-first century

---

15 Raewyn Connell, "Understanding Neoliberalism," 23.

perspective, somewhat naïve. As her speech continues, she preaches the importance of investment:

> I've been asked: what are we actually doing with the money we are earning here? And then I can only say: investing. Because I've learned one thing in the meantime: without investment, there is no future. And everyone, believe me, will become rich. Rich in, I hope at least, fortune, rich in emotion, and rich in luck. It's up to us.[16]

In order to care for one another, Ada states, she and her friends must rely on the market. This speech, made by the protagonist in a made-for-television movie in 1992, is an address not only to Ada's employees in the film, but to a German viewing audience that was facing the transition to a market economy. At the center of neoliberal philosophy is the belief that investment in the market will bring stability and wealth.

The film ends on a triumphant note, neighbors having gathered at this party to celebrate the success of the new company. As Ada gives her toast, her change in appearance exhibits her hybrid vision of success. She still wears her knit cardigan and her hair tied back in a bun. But she also wears a silk scarf and carries a purse, and pumps have replaced her boots. These small additions to her wardrobe signal the compatibility of her new business sense with the lifestyle she wishes to preserve. Both Naujok and Zwirner are in attendance, showing their respect for Ada's success. As the military helicopter passes over her property one last time, the group waves goodbye to it in triumph. The military has given up its bid on her house.

In the final dialog of the film, Ada speaks to Pastor Seidel at the party about her future travel plans.

> Seidel: So, Ada, are you happy? Now you can fulfill your great wish and go to Mount Everest.
>
> Ada: Hmpf, when? I don't have any time [...] I have another idea. Let's make a nice weekend trip with all the staff into the Harz Mountains to the Brocken.[17]

---

16 "Ich bin [...] immer gefragt worden, was machen wir eigentlich mit dem Geld, was wir hier verdienen? Und dann kann ich nur sagen: investieren. Denn eins hab ich inzwischen gelernt: ohne Investition, keine Zukunft. Und alle, glaubt mir, werden reich werden. Reich an, so hoffe ich jedenfalls, Vermögen, reich an Empfindung und reich an Glück. Es liegt an uns."
17 Seidel: "Na, Ada, glücklich? Jetzt kannst du dir bald deinen großen Wunsch erfüllen und zu Mount Everest fahren." / Ada: "Hmpf, wann denn? Ich hab' doch gar keine Zeit. [...] ich habe eine andere Idee. Wir machen einen schönen Wochenendausflug mit allen Mitarbeitern in den Harz auf den Brocken."

Now that Ada is running a business, she no longer has time to travel to exotic places like Mount Everest. The title of the film, *The Brocken*, thus points to Ada's decision to stay close to home, defend her property, and deal with capitalism on her own terms. Or perhaps read more cynically, Ada no longer has time to fulfill her dreams of seeing a "real mountain" now that she is under the neoliberal pressure to mass produce commodities for the market.

The Cruelty of Capitalism in *No More Mr. Nice Guy*

Whereas *The Brocken* proposes a market-based solution for the alienation that commodification causes, Detlev Buck's 1993 road comedy *No More Mr. Nice Guy* has much less faith in capitalism to cure the maladies it creates. The optimistic neoliberal rhetoric of entrepreneurship and corporatization espoused in *The Brocken* gives way in this film to a depiction of capitalism as a relentlessly competitive system that has brought an ethos of greed to every corner of the former East Germany. In this film, two poor, uneducated, socially marginalized brothers from West Germany, Kipp and Morst, see the opportunity to start a new life for themselves when their late grandmother leaves them a house in the former East Germany. Ultimately, though, the capitalist myth of striking it rich proves to be what Lauren Berlant calls a "cruel optimism," as the brothers are encouraged to be optimistic about life, to desire and expect upward mobility, but capitalism fails cruelly to follow through.[18] Swindled time and again in the newly capitalist East, the brothers soon own even less than they did before they embarked on their road trip. After they suffer a final blow, finding the house they have inherited in ruins, they relinquish their claim to it and the few objects they own, relying instead on one another and the friends they make along the way to escape the capitalist system altogether.

Buck's film draws on the typical storylines that had been established to discuss property relations in the former East, yet its innovations lie in breaking with those conventions. For example, although the film features Westerners coming to the East to claim a property, the fact that there is no actual dispute on the property (in contrast to *Taxi to Rathenow*, *Our House*, and *The Same Old Song*) means that neither GDR nor family history arises as a topic. As such, the film can focus its critical gaze on the contemporary capitalist landscape. Moreover, when the brothers are outsmarted by savvier Easterners (like in *Taxi to Rathenow* and *The Brocken*), the Easterners' triumphs

---

18 See Lauren Berlant, *Cruel Optimism* (Durham: Duke UP, 2011).

are not emotionally satisfying for the viewing audience, since the brothers are neither arrogant nor speculative. Rather, Easterners' willingness to swindle the unwitting brothers throws into sharp relief just how cruel capitalist greed can be.

Perhaps the most important departure of this film, and what constitutes its contribution to the filmic discourse on property relations in the former East Germany, is the revelation that the happiness and stability that property ownership promises are merely a fantasy. Unlike in *The Brocken*, neither home ownership nor commodities help Kipp and Morst find their footing in the new capitalist system, and personal relationships do not serve the market. Rather, Kipp and Morst can only escape the alienation capitalism causes by relinquishing their claim on the house they've inherited, giving up their few material possessions, and investing instead in the personal relationships that help them to identify capitalism's borders. Indirectly, then, the inheritance has given them something much more valuable than material stability. The autonomy they had wished for turns out to be far less desirable than their intimate dependence on one another and their friends, and so they find a sense of belonging they never had in the capitalist society.

The film traces this journey, beginning with the brothers' first meeting in what appears to have been a long while. It opens with a wide shot of a non-descript gate and guard house of fenced-in premises. The camera rests there for a few seconds before our protagonist, Kipp, appears, exiting what turns out to be a mental institution. The gate slowly creaks closed behind him and he stands on the edge of the walking path in front of it, holding a bag and an oversized wreath adorned with flowers and a long ribbon (see fig. 3.5). Standing silently and rather deep in the frame, as though not quite ready to enter the world outside the gate, Kipp listens as a coockoo bird sounds loudly off-screen – an aural joke. We soon learn that Kipp has been discharged from the institution upon receiving the news that he and his brother Morst have inherited a house in the former East Germany. Now that he owns property, Kipp is deemed fit to function normally in society.

Fig. 3.5: Kipp exiting the mental institution with a wreath

Fig. 3.6: Kipp and Morst, wreath and truck

Morst, every bit the opposite of Kipp, soon arrives to pick him up. While Kipp is a dreamer and boaster who wears a suit that is too formal for most occasions, Morst is taciturn and cantankerous and prefers pragmatic work clothes (see fig. 3.6). Initially in the film, each brother is also associated with a particular object that further supports his characterization. While the audience will never see Kipp's bag again, the wreath is a continuous reminder of his penchant for formalities. Morst, by contrast, is much more practical, and his main object of attachment is his pick-up truck. Both objects are featured prominently in the frame as the brothers speak to one another for the first time (see fig. 3.6). In this intial meeting, the two brothers' habitus signal to the viewing audience that they stand little chance of integrating into the conventional property relations. Neither has a middle class sensibility, as Kipp overshoots in his attempts at social formalities and Morst disregards formality altogether.

Because of the dearth of possessions represented on-screen, the few objects the brothers do own and acquire along the way are charged with meaning for the viewing audience. In addition to serving the characterization of the two brothers, both the wreath and the pick-up truck end up playing other, often tragicomical, functions in the film. For example, when the brothers are carjacked by a Russian soldier, and they annoy him with their incessant bumbling, the soldier uses the silk ribbon from the wreath to tie them up. The wreath is subsequently forgotten on the side of the road. For the audience, the wreath functions as a visual reminder of the grandmother, the promise of a stable home in the East, and thus of the politics of inheritance that have brought the brothers on this road adventure. At the same time, the brothers' neglect of the wreath indicates that they do not claim their inheritance based on sentimental attachment to their grandmother or her property. Their sense of duty to their grandmother's grave is purely formal, a socially prescribed gesture that they perform only clumsily. Later, when the brothers come across another wreath, abandoned and tattered as it is, they find it to be an adequate replacement for the first one and load it blithely into the truck. "A wreath is a wreath," Morst says. However, the inscription on the wreath's ribbon reads "You should have seen her," which suggests a more romantic or sexually intimate sentiment than would be appropriate for the brothers to have toward their grandmother.[19] The joke, of couse, is that because the brothers cannot read, they do not recognize why this wreath is an inappropriate replacement for the previous one.

Whereas the wreath represents an empty formal gesture, the pick-up truck provides a much more solid material condition for connectedness. When the truck breaks down, and Kipp presumes to be an expert, directing Morst on the likely problem, the brothers are carjacked by the aforementioned Russian soldier. The soldier repairs the truck but, perhaps fearful that the brothers will report him to the police, does not steal it. Rather, he forces them to take him along. The soldier does not speak German, but we eventually learn that his name is Viktor and that he hopes to make it to Russia. Viktor is much more capable than the brothers and becomes a foil to them. Nevertheless, in the close proximity of the truck, the three men develop a bond and become friends. By refusing to submit to human will, the rickety truck has asserted its own agency, inviting, so to speak, Viktor's intervention and entrance into the group.

While the wreath(s) and the truck provide important clues to the human relationships that the brothers maintain, the dilapidation of a third significant object, a boat, and then eventually the house, are much more representative of Berlant's assessment that capitalism inflicts a "cruel optimism." In a scene in which the men stop at a Biergarten, Kipp feels generous, inviting two women for a drink. The women gather that the men must be Westerners and gladly accept. To entertain the women, Kipp boasts about the house they have inherited, the lifestyle they plan to lead, and the countries they want to visit by water. He explains:

> It's near the Baltic. You have to take advantage of what's available once in a while. Go to the beach and fish from time to time, take off your shoes, the whole family, and go barefoot or, if you want, you can go out on a boat, set sail, and then you go out on the boat, and then the sails and the flags flap in the wind and you can, if you want, you can go to Scandinavia, Sweden, Norway, Denmark, Romania, Denmark, as you like. They are all beautiful countries and it doesn't take any effort, and my brother and I, we are looking for such a boat. Money is no concern.[20]

---

19 "Kranz ist Kranz" / "Man muss sie gesehen haben."
20 "Das liegt in der Nähe der Ostsee. Da muss man die Gegebenheiten ja auch mal nutzen. Mal an den Strand gehen und angeln, mal die Schuhe ausziehen, die ganze Familie, und barfuß

As Kipp enthusiastically lists the countries he plans to sail to, he loses control of both syntax and logic. Realizing that the men are delusional, the women stifle laughs and steal knowing glances at one another before excusing themselves. However, another patron has overheard the conversation and approaches them. We then cut to the men standing in the parking lot of *Manni's Gebraucht-Shop* (Manni's Second-Hand Shop), unknowingly spending their last bit of money on a shabby plastic dinghy – certainly a far cry from the sailboat Kipp must have envisioned taking him to faraway places.

Kipp's optimism in these two scenes, followed ultimately by disappointment, illustrates capitalism's cruelty. The comedy of the scene in the Biergarten invites the audience to laugh along with the women at Kipp's grandiose delusions. Manni then sees Kipp's inability to align his fantasy with reality as an opportunity for profit and pressures him into a purchase that does not actually support his desired lifestyle. In fact, this purchase takes Kipp further away from it by draining his last financial resources. This scene also indicates, in a similar fashion to *The Brocken*, certain tendencies of globalization. Manni speaks with an accent that marks him as a foreigner, and the name of the business "Manni's Gebraucht-Shop" makes use of both an apostrophe to designate the possessive and the word "Shop" instead of the German "Laden," thereby pointing to a saturation of Anglophone commercialism in the German capitalist landscape.

In this scene and others, Easterners are not defending themselves against the onslaught of capitalist Westerners (as in *The Brocken* and *Taxi nach Rathenow*), as much as they are demonstrating how adept they have become at the capitalist game. The brothers immediately realize they have been suckered into buying a boat they cannot use, and to make matters worse, their remaining money is worthless. They now have only the East German Marks that they received as change when Morst was forced to buy overpriced tools at a gas station to repair his truck earlier. While they suspected at the time that they were being made to overpay, they are only now learning that they were given worthless currency as change. In need of their money back, the men return to the shop, but Manni closes his door to them. All sales are final. The purchase of the boat has made them victims of a cruel capitalist system, one that encourages them to dream big and then punishes them for it.

---

gehen oder wenn man will, kann man mit einem Boot rausfahren und, die Segel gesetzt, und dann fährt man mit dem Boot raus und dann knattern die Segel und die Wimpel im Wind und man kann auch, wenn man will, kann man nach Skandinavien, Schweden, Norwegen, Dänemark, Rumänien, Dänemark, wie man will. Das sind alles schöne Länder und das geht wie Nix und mein Bruder und ich wir sind auf der Suche nach einem geeigneten Boot. Gelder sind vorhanden."

The cruelest source of Kipp and Morst's optimism is the house. When the men finally reach the house they expect to inherit, the Gut Wendelohe, they find a stately mansion with a grand foyer, a banquet room, and a veranda with a view over the countryside. The men envision parties and peaceful breakfasts with a view, and their dreams appear to be materializing. However, while discussing whether one room would serve better as a dining room or a bedroom, a woman with coiffed hair and riding pants interrupts them, asking for their certificate of deed. Inspecting it, she informs them that there has been a misunderstanding: their inheritance is not the Gut Wendelohe, but rather the workers' quarters nearby. Unable to read the deed themselves, they have misunderstood what they were actually inheriting. What is more, they discover upon reaching the correct house that it is in ruins. The men's initial pride and hope upon approaching the Gut Wendelohe, pictured in figure 3.7 and scored with triumphant orchestra music, is paralleled by the disappointment of their gaze on their actual inheritance, pictured in figure 3.8. The audience hears a humble xylophone tune and the men hear only sheep bleeting. We see that the roof has caved in and a looter is scavenging for metal in the structure. The dilapidation is far beyond repair, and the brothers do not have the wealth to rebuild. Even in this moment, as their dreams of a new life are being dashed, capitalism is relentless. On a tree near the driveway, they find the phone number of a real estate agent posted. The land on which the house sits may be worth something, and an agent is waiting to make a commission on its sale.

Fig. 3.7: The Gut Wendelohe

Fig. 3.8: The inheritance

The fact that the house is in utter disrepair highlights the film's final contribution to the filmic discourse on houses, that is, the way in which it presents dilapidation as a theme. While all of the other films discussed so far depict houses that require renovation or repair, most of them do so to portray one party in a housing dispute as being more deserving of the property than the other. As seen in chapters 1 and 2, those films foreground the value German society places on property maintenance: if one maintains the home, putting labor and capital into it and intra-acting within its material environment, one must certainly have the stronger claim to it. While those films pose the question "who has a right to property," and then answer that question at least in part by pointing to those who have done the labor of maintenance, Buck's film sidesteps the question of property rights altogether, asking instead whether property, and its maintenance, as the source of happiness is anything more than a cruel illusion. By pointing our attention to the very instability of the material world as it dilapidates, the film hints at the inherent mistake in pinning our hopes for happiness on property.

The brothers have had an astonishingly commoditiless existence over the course of the film, as the objects they own and acquire have little or no trade-in value. Instead, they have willingly interacted with shabby and dilapidated objects during the first two-thirds of the film – the disheveled wreaths, the rattling pickup truck, and the cheap plastic dinghy – because those objects are part of a journey that promised the brothers a better life. The wreath represented their inheritance, the truck their way there, and the boat the worldliness they wish to achieve. The extreme dilapidation of the house, however, signals the very destruction of their dream and the illusory nature of its promise to begin with. Without already having the wealth to invest in renovation, this house is worthless to them as a home and a basis of social stability.

Morst and Kipp have always stood outside the system that regulates property, as their habitus and their attachment to certain objects indicate. They soon learn that they stand outside the law as well. Upon entering a local bar to contact the real estate agent about the lot, they see themselves on the news and learn they are wanted criminals. Earlier in the film, when highway robbers attempted to rob the three men, Viktor used his military-issued machine gun to force the robbers into driving their car backwards into a lake. Unbeknownst to the brothers and Viktor, some of the robbers did not survive, and when a local detective discovers the crime scene, the three become wanted for murder. Up to this point in the film, the brothers and Viktor have been oblivious to the fact that they are wanted by the police, and many of the comedic scenes center on their unwitting flight from the law as they befuddle the detectives they leave in their wake. A funeral home director turns out to be much more adept at following crime than the police, given his motivation for profit. In a gag that runs through the film, he intuitively reaches crime scenes just before the detectives do, prepared to offer his services to those affected at a reasonable price.

The sequence that follows the men's discovery of their outlaw status is important for understanding their relationship to the objects discussed so far. When police cars pull up, the three men take a waitress hostage and make their escape. First, they drive by the house without giving it another glance, having relinquished any hope of happiness they had formerly pinned to it. They then abandon the truck, which is loaded down with the wreath and the boat. Their property no longer supports the lifestyle they had envisioned for themselves and has become instead a liability. They then steal a pair of horses, making their way through the woods to keep the police off their trail. After being robbed, swindled repeatedly, and finding their inheritance a ruin, they easily take on the identity of criminals on the run.

The entrance of Nadine, their hostage, into the group provides the film's occasion to explore the brothers' masculinities and sexuality, additional unspoken reasons why they have inhabited a marginalized position in the capitalist society. As the group makes its way through the woods, Nadine and Viktor share one horse and the brothers another. Viktor effortlessly exhibits a heteronormative masculinity atop the horse with Nadine holding onto him for stability. Once again, he serves as a foil to the brothers who share one horse uncomfortably. When Nadine begins to ask questions, "Is he the boss?" nodding toward Morst, Kipp chats with her, freely giving answers. Morst, however, becomes increasingly irritated that a woman has entered their circle: "The woman is breaking up the group. She's an outsider. I've said so from the beginning."[21] When the group must stop so that Nadine can relieve herself in the woods, Morst accuses Kipp of being overly accommodating to Nadine out of sexual aspirations that are clouding his reason: "You're a skirt chaser!"[22] Kipp responds by pointing out his brother's apparent lack of desire for Nadine, "That's at least normal. You, um, you're gay. [...] You're not normal, not a real man."[23] As the two brothers take swings at each other and begin to wrestle, Viktor stands to the side, amused at the spectacle. He and Nadine then take advantage of the brothers' distraction, retreating into the forest to have sex. Once Morst finally overpowers Kipp and thereby rehabilitates his masculinity in a show of superior strength, Kipp relents. Nadine and Viktor emerge from the forest to join the two brothers who appear oblivious to the sexual encounter. The group can continue to move forward, with Nadine and Viktor's heterosexuality firmly established and the brothers' masculinities sorted out.

Eventually, the group finds its happiness based on their relationships with one another in a rural Russia outside the capitalist system. Once there, Viktor introduces Nadine to his mother, Morst works with his hands selling beer, and

---

21 "Ist er der Boss?" / "Das Weib sprengt die Gruppe. Die ist 'n Fremdkörper. Hab' ich immer gesagt."
22 "Bist ja 'n Schürzenjäger!"
23 "Das ist wenigstens normal. Du bist, ja, schwul bist du ja. [...] Du bist unnormal. Kein richtiger Mann."

Kipp holds ill-informed lectures to the locals on a variety of topics, including carp farming and how mail order catalogs work. (The locals cannot understand him but are entertained by him nonetheless.) The men have escaped the reach of capitalism, a system that kept them on the margins of society in West Germany and aggressively robbed them of all promise of property in the former East Germany. By relying on one another through brotherhood, friendship, romantic love, and the support that comes from being part of a community, they find and subvert the boundaries of neoliberalism's reach.

While most films that depict property issues focus on the relative property rights of competing parties, *No More Mr. Nice Guy* asks whether a system of private property can be anything other than cruel. Indeed, the title can be understood as a commentary on the way property issues were being discussed in the mainstream at the time. While the commercial translation of the film's title from *Wir können auch anders* to *No More Mr. Nice Guy* is true to the scene from which it originates (Kipp is trying, albeit feebly, to threaten the highway robbers), a more direct translation would be *We Can Do Things Differently*. The film shows how aggressive the capitalism being "done" is, as practically everyone in the film is trying to profit from the three men: the gas station attendant who charges too much for tools and gives worthless East German Marks as change, the second-hand wares salesman who pressures the men into buying a cheap boat and refuses to refund their money after seeing them in need, the profiteering funeral home director who quickly shows up at a crime scene when the men accidentally kill someone, and the real estate agent who has discovered the dilapidated house and is waiting to turn a profit on its lot. Having accidentally murdered men who wished to rob them and facing incarceration, Kipp, Morst, and Victor must leave town to escape being trapped in a system in which they are perpetual victims.

The film ends on a hopeful note, however, as Morst and Kipp find a happy life in Russia. And yet this, too, may be a cruel optimism. *No More Mr. Nice Guy* proposes an alternative to the neoliberal society where Morst and Kipp can live alongside a couple like Nadine and Viktor. Nevertheless, one has to wonder whether the film mitigates the cruelties of the neoliberal society for the viewing audience in order to forgive us for our complicity in that system. After all, we are left secure in the knowledge that Kipp and Morst will be okay since another space exists for those who do not fit within our society. At the same time, one wonders just how long the Russia depicted at the end of the film will remain outside capitalism's reach. When Kipp explains to his new neighbors how catalog shopping works, does he introduce commodification and alienation into the community, thus contributing to their eventual dooming, or are we to understand that since the locals do not speak his language, this worldview that he has internalized is contained?

Spaces of Resistance?

The Brocken and *No More Mr. Nice Guy* are, in some respects, more ambitious in scope than the other films discussed in this monograph. Rather than centering closely on a dispute over, or inheritance of, a property, these films engage issues of property ownership as a way to examine larger mechanisms in the spread of neoliberalism. Both films achieve a way for their protagonists to be happy based on their ability to find or create spaces where they can overcome alienation. Ada finds a market-based solution to her problem, building a business and corperatizing her home and personal relationships in order to retain access to local raw materials and maintain the solidarity among neighbors that she was accustomed to in the GDR. In *No More Mr. Nice Guy*, the brothers escape the capitalist system that has marginalized them all along, finding their happiness in rural Russia, where community is more important than individualism and competition. Both films imagine a space, either within or outside of the neoliberal society, where connectedness to the land and others is still possible. Nevertheless, the question arises with some historical distance whether either of these happy endings are realistic. Can spaces emerge that foster community and connectedness within a system that has been overtaken by capitalist competition? Or must one escape capitalism altogether to find belonging? If so, are there accessible spaces outside of neoliberalism's reach?

In their writings on neoliberalism, Wendy Brown, Raewyn Connell, Jonathan Crary, and David Harvey characterize it as an all-encompassing mindset that has, as Harvey states, "become incorporated into the common-sense way many of us interpret, live in, and understand the world."[24] The cycle of consumption and production pervades all aspects of our lives, including work, home, leisure, personal relationships, and even sleep cycles.[25] Neoliberalism has achieved this by eroding the distinctions between work and private life and by imbuing all aspects of life with commodification. Roger A. Salerno has gone so far as to write that the market makes community itself impossible: "Community in capitalistic

---

24 David Harvey, *A Brief History of Neoliberalism*, 3.
25 For a discussion of sleep as the last place of resistance to neoliberalism, as well as the war neoliberalism wages on sleep, see Jonathan Crary, *24/7: Late Capitalism and the Ends of Sleep*, (London and New York: Verso, 2013).

societies is illusionary at best because it is forever controlled by market forces, which are alien to its residents."²⁶ *The Brocken* seems to support that assessment since the activities that Ada once performed for family and friends, making them hand-knit sweaters and homemade jam, are no longer performed out of love and connectedness, but rather, to produce commodities for the market. Ada makes her place in the new capitalist system by putting everything – her personal relationships, local resources, even home – in the service of the market and gives a speech at the end of the film exalting the market as the site of care for the community.

Yet some theorists also point to certain limits of neoliberalism. Connell disagrees with Salerno, arguing that love relationships between people can create a space within the neoliberal society that withstands utter commodification and thus alienation:

> The relationships between lovers and between parents and children are penetrated by commodification but they also powerfully resist the alienation that commodification requires. The claims of mutual care and mutual responsibility, and the fundamental requirement of cooperation in human institutions (including, of course, economic production) are perhaps irreducible barriers to the expansion of competitive individualism.²⁷

Indeed, the brotherhood, friendship, and romantic love in *No More Mr. Nice Guy* support this idea that relationships can be powerful sites of resistance to neoliberalism's individualism, alienation, and obsession with private ownership.²⁸ Moreover, both Wendy Brown and David Harvey suggest that the uneven history of neoliberalism's implementation globally is evidence that it may not be as "common sense" as it is perceived to be.²⁹ As Brown writes, "Alertness to neoliberalism's inconstancy and plasticity cautions against identifying its current iteration as its essential and global truth [...]"³⁰

---

26 Roger A. Salerno, "Alienated Communities: Between Aloneness and Connectedness," 265.
27 Raewyn Connell, "Understanding Neoliberalism," 36.
28 Recent scholarship in German Studies examines the limits of neoliberalism along similar lines. For example, Hester Baer, Maria Stehle, and Carrie Smith locate the spaces of resistance that emerge within neoliberal societies through performance art and installation in their article "Digital Feminisms and the Impasse: Time, Disappearance, and Delay in Neoliberalism." At the same time, Roland Vegso and Marco Abel identify spaces of the "imminent outside" in their article "Biopolitical Education: The Edukators and the Politics of the Immanent Outside." Both articles appear in the special issue of *Studies in Twentieth and Twenty-First Century Literature* titled *Neoliberalism and the Undoing of Time*, 40.2 (2016).
29 Wendy Brown, *Undoing the Demos: Neoliberalism's Stealth Revolution* (New York: Zone Books, 2015): 21. David Harvey, *A Brief History of Neoliberalism*, 13
30 Wendy Brown, *Undoing the Demos*, 21.

If the theorists who critically examine neoliberalism seem ambivalent about its scope – some arguing that it pervades all areas of individuals' lives globally and others pointing to areas of resistance and escape – the pairing of the two films discussed in this chapter points to that same uncertainty. Whereas *The Brocken* concludes with the spread of the market into every facet of life on the island of Rügen while simultaneously positing that personal relationships and a peaceful home life can thrive there, Buck's road comedy imagines a rather utopian space at its conclusion that lies outside of capitalism's reach. And yet, one wonders whether Ada's loving relationships with her friends will withstand the pressure to grow profits that businesses face, or likewise, whether the brothers' very presence in rural Russia at the end of the film already indicates a slow spread of western thinking eastward. In both films, uncertainty about the permanence of the utopian space undercuts a straightforward optimism about the characters' future as the former East Germany privatizes and neoliberalism continues to spread.

Chapter 4
Home in the East as an Instrument of the Patriarchy: Judith Hermann's "Summerhouse, Later" (1998) and *Where Love Begins* (2014)

As we saw in the previous three chapters, the earliest fictional productions to depict the new property relations in the former East Germany were films.[1] As early as 1991, films produced for television or cinematic release addressed the motivations of both Easterners and Westerners when claiming or defending property, offering a more complex view on the new property relations than was presented in the news media reporting. By the late 1990s, prose fiction began to take up the topic as well. However, as we will see in this and the following chapters, literary texts have had somewhat different priorities when depicting property issues in the former East Germany. In prose fiction, actual face-to-face confrontations between Easterners and Westerners become briefer and less frequent, less the central motivating factor in the narrative and more often background information or side plot. Instead, protagonists face increasingly abstract threats to the security of their property or property claims, and the acquisition of a house serves as the text's starting point for addressing other widespread concerns in the newly unified country.

The first notable piece of prose fiction to depict Westerners acquiring residential property in the former East Germany was Judith Hermann's short story "Summerhouse, Later" ("Sommerhaus, später," 1998), although scholars have rarely focused their discussions of this work on the property relations it depicts.[2]

---

[1] A notable is exception is Rolf Hochhuth's play *Wessis in Weimar: Szenen aus einem besetzten Land*, which premiered at the Berliner Ensemble under the direction of Einar Schleef on February 10, 1993. It enjoyed a brief run at the Berliner Ensemble before traveling to some ninety German cities over the course of the decade. Because this theater production focuses on the privatization of businesses rather than homes, it will not be discussed further in this study.

[2] This is not to say that scholars have completely ignored the socio-political background of Hermann's story. For mentions of this context, see Peter J. Graves, "Karen Duve, Kathrin Schmidt, Judith Hermann: 'Ein Literarisches Fräuleinwunder'?" *German Life and Letters* 55, no. 2 (2002): 204; Claudia Gremler, "Country Escapes and Designs for Living: Christa Wolf, Sarah Kirsch and Judith Hermann," in *Women's Writing in Western Europe: Gender, Generation and Legacy*, ed. Adalgisa Giorgio and Julia Water (Newcastle upon Tyne: Cambridge Scholars Publishing, 2007), 535; Claudia Gremler, "Intertextualität und Vergangenheitsarbeit in Judith Herman *Sommerhaus, später*," *Text & Kontext: Zeitschrift für Germanistische Literaturforschung in Skandina-*

It appeared in Hermann's debut collection of the same title, which was a veritable literary phenomenon. Critics hailed Hermann as a leading voice among the new generation of young writers who gave expression to the world-weariness and boredom of West Germans coming of age in the era following unification. The critics characterized these writers' prose was more narrative-driven, more accessible and entertaining in style, and (even if laconic) less burdened by the historical and aesthetic encumbrances that had lent their predecessors' writing density. In evaluating Hermann's and her contemporaries' styles and content matter, these critics largely overlooked the historical weight behind many of their works.[3] "Summerhouse, Later," for example, depicts a young West Berliner who has purchased property cheaply in the former East Germany in the hope of establishing a new life for himself and his former lover. As we have seen in previous chapters in this monograph, the property relations in the former East Germany were anything but unencumbered by Germany's past.

Not only does "Summerhouse, Later" set its characters in motion within the context of the new property relations; it enriches the discourse by introducing a new premise: that the house a Westerner acquired in the East might pose a threat to its new inhabitant(s). Certainly, Hermann was not unique in depicting Westerners who perceive the East as threatening. As we saw in chapter 3, the film *No More Mr. Nice Guy* presents the East as an already fiercely competitive capitalist landscape. Rather, Hermann's contribution was in framing the house itself as a source of threat. In "Summerhouse, Later" the narrator fears that she will be coerced into a heteronormative lifestyle and conventional femininity after her former lover purchases a property in Brandenburg and proposes that they live

---

vien 37 (2015): 11–12; and Karen Leeder, "'Another Piece of the Past': 'Stories' of a New German Identity," *Oxford German Studies* 33 (2004): 138.

3 A body of scholarship on Hermann has since grown that devotes itself to explicating Hermann's references to German national history through literary history and intertextuality. For more on Hermann's intertextual allusions to German history, see, for example, Biendarra "Gen(d)eration Next" (discussing Kleist), Borgstedt "Wunschwelten" (discussing the Undine figure and Romanticism more generally), Ganeva "Female Flâneurs" (the flâneur figure of the early twentieth century), Gremler "Diesseits" and "Intertextuality" (Fontante, East German writers Sarah Kirsch and Christa Wolf, and the Undine figure), Andrea Köhler "Is That All There Is?" (Kleist), Nobile "A Ring of Keys" (Romanticism, East German writers Sarah Kirsch and Christa Wolf, and Trümmerliteratur, especially Wolfgang Borchert), Shafi *Housebound* (Romanticism and Fontane), and Stephan, "Undina an der Newa" (the Undine figure). At the same time, scholars have also noted her international influences, especially the American short story author Raymond Carver (see Leeder, "Another Piece of the Past," 140–141, Vollmer "Die sprachlose Nähe und das ferne Glück, 75–76, and Wehdeking *Generationenwechsel*) and Russian playwright Anton Chekhov (see Andrea Köhler, "Is That All There Is?" 88 and Leeder, "Another Piece of the Past," 140).

there together.⁴ The house is instrumental in fulfilling his dreams but also threatens to put an end to the non-committal lifestyle that she enjoys.

In chapter 5, I will discuss two other literary works that appeared just one year after "Summerhouse, Later" that have similarly menacing houses at their premises. In *Eduard's Homecoming* (*Eduards Heimkehr*, 1999) by Peter Schneider, the protagonist fears that his inheritance of a tenement building in the former East Berlin will ruin him financially and emotionally, as it obligates him not only to expensive maintenance costs but also to an investigation into his family's involvement in National Socialism. In Karen Duve's *Rain* (*Regenroman*, 1999), the house that a couple from Hamburg has purchased in the former East Germany threatens to fall in on them and seems to conspire with the marshy landscape to consume them. The house and the landscape have an eerie agency of their own, as though comprising an organism that wishes to expel the new inhabitants. As we will see in this chapter and the next, houses in Hermann's, Schneider's, and Duve's works reject their new Westerner owners, putting them in jeopardy in the very property system that was designed for their benefit.

The current chapter will focus on Judith Hermann's two major works that center on houses: the title story of her debut collection *Summerhouse, Later* and the novel that would follow it some sixteen years later, *Where Love Begins* (*Aller Liebe Anfang*, 2014). While "Summerhouse, Later" depicts the generation that was coming of age in the post-unification era and centers on the vital issue of property relations, *Where Love Begins* takes place long after the dust of privatization has settled. The characters are older, married, already own a house, enjoy the material comforts of middle-class existence, and live in a location that may or may not be the former East Germany. Although *Where Love Begins* is no stated sequel to "Summerhouse, Later," many of the concerns established in "Summerhouse, Later" are continued and expanded in it. While the protagonist in "Summerhouse, Later" fears that settling for a heteronormative identity will lead to social isolation and limitations on her freedom, the protagonist's troubles in *Where Love Begins* stem from those very conditions of her comfortable suburban life.

In reading these texts in tandem, we see that they present a picture of home and private life at different stages of the privatization process. "Summerhouse, Later" depicts face-to-face interactions and tensions between Easterners and Westerners as a means of addressing the characters' more deeply held insecur-

---

4 The geographical location of Hermann's Canitz is unclear. While a Canitz does exist in Saxony, Hermann's Canitz lies in close proximity to both Angermünde and the Oder River, suggesting that it is a fictional village in Brandenburg.

ities and, in this way, resembles the films discussed in this monograph. Sixteen years later, *Where Love Begins* has moved far away from East-West social relations, centering instead on the home life of its protagonist in a nondescript location. The dissolving binaries of place as thematized in "Summerhouse, Later" have thus resulted in an unsettling sense of dislocation in *Where Love Begins*, and the sexual and gender fluidity at stake in "Summerhouse, Later" has given way in *Where Love Begins* to heteronormative gender relations and reproductive sex.[5] As the female protagonists' identities in Hermann's works become increasingly untethered from place and are instead based on conventional gender roles, the existential threats posed to these women escalate, thereby revealing in Hermann's work an underlying exploration of gender, place, and patriarchy in the age of neoliberalism.

Home as an Overdetermined Place in "Summerhouse, Later"

"Summerhouse, Later" opens as the first person narrator receives a phone call from her friend and former lover, a man named Stein, asking her to accompany him into Brandenburg to visit the house that he has purchased. It has long been Stein's dream to buy a house of his own, and after several years of saving and searching, he has finally found the perfect one. He can hardly contain his excitement over the phone, and while the narrator feels trepidation, she agrees to the excursion anyway. As the two drive from Berlin into the Brandenburg countryside, the narrator recounts memories of Stein, both during their relationship together a few years prior and at other moments, as members of the same circle of friends. Once she and Stein arrive at the house, a run-down eighteenth-century estate, the narrator is both awed and frightened by it, as it becomes apparent that Stein wants to rekindle their relationship and establish a life together there, far away from Berlin. Back in the city, she refuses to give Stein an answer about moving in with him, delaying her decision time and again until one day word arrives that Stein has burned down the house and eliminated that possibility for them both.

Throughout the story, the narrator is characterized by her passivity and indecisiveness, and Berlin is presented as the blank slate that allows her to avoid committing to a conventional life path or identity. As Mila Ganeva has de-

---

[5] See Necia Chronister, "Judith Hermann's 'Sommerhaus, später': Gender Ambiguity and Smooth versus Striated Spaces," in *German Women Authors and the Spatial Turn: New Perspectives*, ed. Carola Daffner and Beth Ann Muellner (Berlin and Boston: De Gruyter, 2015), 149–165.

scribed it, Berlin in Hermann's story is "a place that is 'hollowed out,' unexciting, cold and yet immensely, inexplicably attractive with the multiplicity and ambiguity it embodies."[6] Seen through the narrator's eyes, Berlin is bereft of cultural signifiers, free of identity or meaning. The streets are rainy and deserted, and while Stalin-era buildings line the streets, they hail from another era and a wholly different country, appearing to her only as "huge and strange and beautiful."[7] In this ambiguous and multiplicitious Berlin, in which the distinguishing characteristics of the city are unrecognizable to the narrator, she is similarly able to avoid being identified through conventionally distinguishing personal characteristics like gender, sexual orientation, or professional identity. We never learn the narrator's name, and while conventions of authorship might lead one to assume a female narrator, there is nothing in the text itself to establish that as a fact.[8] The narrator has no apparent schedule, obligations, or fixed relationships. She can sleep with whomever she pleases, and the narrator's friends all sleep with one another, sometimes casually, sometimes in monogamous relationships, so that sexuality and relationships are fluid as well.

German Studies scholars have pointed out that the characters' lack of commitment to identity in Hermann's story reflects her generation's experience of young adulthood more generally in Germany, coming of age in a society changing swiftly because of unification, globalization, privatization in the former East, and a fully realized neoliberalism. As Hartmut Vollmer has pointed out, the large-scale shifts towards privatization, neoliberal work models, and political apathy in the 1990s led to the instability of many institutions that had shaped previous generations' life paths, which resulted in a dizzying multivalence of possibilities and choices for young adults.[9] Anke Biendarra has similarly read the aesthetic presentation of Berlin in "Sommerhouse, Later" as representing an unmooring of traditional identity anchors from place. In her reading, Berlin

---

[6] Mila Ganeva, "Female Flâneurs: Judith Hermann's *Sommerhaus, später* and *Nichts als Gespenster*," *Gegenwartsliteratur: A German Studies Yearbook* 3 (2004): 267.

[7] Judith Hermann, "Summerhouse, Later," in *Summerhouse, Later* (New York: Ecco, 2001), 188. Originally: "riesig und fremd und schön," Judith Hermann, "Sommerhaus, später," in *Sommerhouse, Later* (Frankfurt am Main: S. Fischer, 1998), 141.

[8] See Necia Chronister, "Judith Hermann's 'Sommerhaus, später': Gender Ambiguity."

[9] As Vollmer points out, the various terms used in the popular media and among scholars to characterize German society of that era – "'information society,' 'global society,' 'consumer society,' 'labor-' and 'unemployment society,' 'fun society,' 'ego society,' 'multi-option society'" among others – indicate the dizzying multivalence of possibilities and choices young adults faced. See Hartmut Vollmer, "Die sprachlose Nähe und das ferne Glück. Sehnsuchtsbilder und erzählerische Leerstellen in der Prosa von Judith Hermann und Peter Stamm," *Literatur für Leser* 29, no. 1 (2006): 62–63.

has become "deterritorialized" as part of globalization. Here, she draws on John Tomlinson's definition of the term: "the simultaneous penetration of local worlds by distant forces, and the dislodging of everyday meanings from their 'anchors' in the local environment."[10] For Biendarra, the Berlin in Hermann's story has been emptied of its cultural signifiers through processes of globalization, in which places become interchangeable and signifiers specific to place become free-floating.[11]

While the latter might be true in Hermann's world, the Berlin of "Summerhouse, Later" is hardly penetrated by cultural signifiers from other places. The few recognizable city spaces presented in the story, such as the Stalin-era buildings lining the Frankfurter Allee, have been emptied of their signification, but no Starbucks or McDonald's has moved in to lend them new identity. I maintain that Hermann's Berlin, as a city emptied of signifiers, instead resembles the deterritorialization conceived of by Gilles Deleuze and Félix Guattari, who distinguish between de- and reterritorialization. In this version of the concept, the cultural signifiers of a place disappear when outside forces impose themselves, such as in colonialism or globalization. This deterritorialization is then typically accompanied, or closely followed, by reterritorialization, as new cultural signifiers imported from the dominating culture replace them.[12] In Hermann's post-unification Berlin, a deterritorialization has taken place because of the absence of East-West tensions that formerly dominated the city. However, a neoliberal reterritorialization has not yet occurred, as the spaces of Berlin remain devoid of meaning in the eyes of the (Western) narrator. Rather, the only imports from abroad in Hermann's story are the American and European musical artists that the narrator and Stein listen to when cruising the streets of Berlin, the highways, and the rural roads in the surrounding area. David Bowie, Maria Callas, Paolo Conte, Massive Attack, and Trans-AM – but also Bach – lend meaning to movement rather than to any particular place for the narrator.

---

[10] Anke Biendarra, "Globalization, Travel, and Identity: Judith Hermann and Gregor Hens," *Gegenwartsliteratur: A German Studies Yearbook* 5 (2006): 234. Here she quotes John Tomlinson, *Globalization and Culture* (Chicago: University of Chicago Press, 1999), 29.
[11] Anke Biendarra, "Globalization," 234–235. Since Biendarra is one of the few people to have commented on both "Summerhouse, Later" and *Where Love Begins*, she will be an important interlocutor in my analysis.
[12] Gilles Deleuze and Félix Guattari, *A Thousand Plateaus: Capitalism and Schizophrenia*, trans. Brian Massoumi (Minneapolis: University of Minnesota Press, 1987), 143. While de- and reterritorialization appear throughout *A Thousand Plateaus*, page 143 provides the most concise indication of what Deleuze and Guattari mean by those terms.

When Stein purchases a property in the former East Germany, and thus commits to settling into a place, he introduces the main conflict of the story. Just as the narrator fears, Stein's invitation to see the house turns into an invitation to live there with him. In the narrator's view, though, Brandenburg is for recreation, a place where her circle of friends' uprootedness allows for certain destructive freedoms precisely because they do not live there:

> We hung out with [Stein], there in the gardens and houses of people we really had nothing to do with. Workers had lived there, small farmers, and amateur gardeners who hated us and whom we despised. We avoided the locals; just thinking about them ruined everything for us. It didn't feel right. We robbed them of their feeling of exclusivity, and we disfigured the villages, the fields, even the sky; it was in the way we strode around with our Easy Rider gait, flicked our joint butts into the flower beds in their front yards, the way we nudged each other self-importantly. But regardless, we wanted to be there.[13]

Brandenburg is the place where the group identities of Berliners and Brandenburgers – and perhaps correlatively Westerners and Easterners – are mutually reaffirmed. The narrator shares the behaviors and postures of her friends in their collective affronts to the homes, objects, and landscapes of the area. They traverse areas where they know they are unwanted, disregarding signs with "Berliners out!" posted on front lawns.[14] "Berliners" here stands certainly for city dwellers, but most likely also for Westerners more generally, who were categorically feared to be property speculators.[15]

Although Brandenburg is a place for the group to affirm its identity as Berliners, Stein has always disrupted the group's coherence. As the narrator states, "Stein was always there with us, and yet, somehow, he wasn't. He didn't really

---

13 Judith Hermann, "Summerhouse, Later," 189–190; originally: "Wir saßen mit ihm da rum, in den Gärten und Häusern von Leuten, mit denen wir nichts zu tun hatten. Arbeiter hatten da gelebt, Kleinbauern, Hobbygärtner, die uns haßten und die wir haßten. Den Einheimischen gingen wir aus dem Weg, schon an sie zu denken machte alles kaputt. Es paßte nicht. Wir klauten ihnen das "Unter-uns-Sein", enstellten die Dörfer, Felder und noch den Himmel, das kriegten sie mit, an der Art und Weise, wie wir da umhergingen im Easy-Rider-Schritt, die abgebrannten Jointstummel in die Blumenrabatten ihrer Vorgärten schnippten, uns anstießen, echauffiert. Aber wir wollten da sein, trotz allem." Judith Hermann, "Sommerhaus, später," 143.
14 Judith Hermann, "Sommerhaus, später," 142. My translation. Margot Bettauer Dembo leaves the original "Berliner raus!" in her translation.
15 See chapter 1 for a discussion of a similar sign spotted in Brandenburg, as reported in *Die Zeit*.

belong, but for one reason or another he stayed."[16] Unlike the others, he is capable of engaging with the places and people of the former East Germany, and as such, is able to lend the group access to properties outside of Berlin when he works there renovating homes. In the block quote above, the narrator implies that Stein's labor serves new (Western) owners since workers and small farmers no longer live there. While Stein tears down wallpaper and replaces plaster, the rest of the group sits in the gardens, drinking alcohol, doing LSD, and engaging in intellectual discussion about theater directors Frank Castorf and Heiner Müller. Whereas Stein has the skills and knowledge of working-class laborers and is attuned to the material and economic realities of the new political situation, the rest of the group appropriates the intellectual contributions of the former East Germany that have since gained cachet in Berlin. After his work is finished, Stein joins them; he is both part of the group and apart from it.

Since the friends typically venture into Brandenburg as a pack, it is unusual that Stein wishes to introduce the house to the narrator alone, and the narrative tension grows as she realizes that his intentions are romantic. Their brief relationship two years prior began in a car, his taxi, when she hired him to take her to a party. In the weeks that followed, Stein moved in with her and they spent their time together driving around Berlin and the countryside. For the narrator a romantic (or at least sexual) relationship with Stein entails movement through space rather than stasis; it means being two people in a car. Stein's drive with her through Brandenburg, just the two of them, is a signal of his desire to reconnect in a monogamous way.

Indeed, whereas the rest of the group enjoys excursing into the former East Germany, Stein wishes to achieve stability there. In Berlin he lives out of his taxi, and as Helga Meise has pointed out, Stein's homelessness casts a somber shadow on the self-stylized itinerancy that the others perform when they sleep over with each other interchangeably.[17] For Stein, flight from the city into the country means leaving an itinerant and polyamorous existence to establish a more lasting connection to home and place.[18] This attempt at stability, however, is de-

---

16 Judith Hermann, "Summerhouse, Later," 189. Originally: "Er war dabei. Und auch nicht. Er gehörte nicht dazu, aber aus irgendeinem Grund blieb er." Judith Hermann, "Sommerhaus, später," 142.
17 Helga Meise, "Mythos Berlin: Orte und Nicht-Orte bei Julia Franck, Inka Parei und Judith Hermann," in *Fräuleinwunder literarisch. Literatur von Frauen zu Beginn des 21. Jahrhunderts*, ed. Christiane Caemmerer, Walter Delabar, and Helga Meise (Frankfurt am Main: Lang, 2005), 129 and 136.
18 See also Claudia Gremler, "Country Escapes," 127; Helga Meise, "Mythos Berlin,"127; and Natasha Gordinsky, "Das Draußen im Eigenen entdecken: Judith Hermanns *Sommerhaus, später*,"

pendent upon an antiquated ideal. His description of the home he has purchased – "a country house, a manor house, an estate house, linden trees in front, chestnuts at the back, sky above, a Brandenburg lake, at least two and a half acres of land"[19] – evokes strong associations with the *Heimat* ideal, a concept that conventionally relies on heteronormative gender relations and which contrasts with the gender and sexual fluidity that Berlin offers in Hermann's story.

While the narrator conveys most of her memories and observations in a sleepy, impressionistic style, two events shake her out of her detachedness. The first is when Stein collects the keys from the previous tenants and thereby forces her to face the political reality of the present. As they pull up to a building in Angermünde, a woman with a sickly child answers the door, hands Stein the keys, and gives him some curtly worded information about the house. The narrator watches the exchange with disgust: "I always hated the way he dealt with these kinds of people."[20] Back in the car, Stein explains that the woman and child had lived in the house but were evicted when he purchased it from a man who lives in Dortmund. Stein owns the home because a Westerner had acquired it – through inheritance, a successful claim, or an investment purchase – and sold it to him cheaply, resulting in the current inhabitants' displacement. The narrator's rather elitist response, "But they're disgusting,"[21] voices her sense of abjection in the Kristevan sense, her repulsion that marks a line of distinction between herself and the woman and child in order to reaffirm her sense of integrity and difference from them.[22] While Stein may be comfortable interact-

---

Gegenwartsliteratur: A German Studies Yearbook 11 (2012): 319. Critics have read Stein's name as signifying his desire for stability. See, for example, Georg Mein, *Erzählungen der Gegenwart: von Judith Hermann zu Bernhard Schlink* (Munich: Oldenbourg, 2005): 73; and Christian Rink, "'Nichts als Gespenster': Zur Identitätsproblematik in den Erzählungen Judith Hermanns," in *Autobiographisches Schreiben in der deutschsprachigen Gegenwartsliteratur, Band 1: Grenzen der Identität und der Fiktionalität*, ed. Ulrich Breuer and Beatrice Sandberg (Munich: Iudicium, 2006), 117.
19 Judith Hermann, "Summerhouse, Later," 185. Originally: "Landhaus, Herrenhaus, Gutshaus, Linden davor, Kastanien dahinter, Himmel darüber, See märksich, drei Morgen Land mindestens." Judith Hermann, "Sommerhaus, später," 139.
20 Judith Hermann, "Summerhouse, Later," 193. Originally: "ich hatte seine Art, mit Leuten dieses Schlags umzugehen, schon immer gehaßt." Judith Hermann, "Sommerhaus, später," 146.
21 Judith Hermann, "Summerhouse, Later," 194. Originally: "Die sind doch ekelhaft." Judith Hermann, "Sommerhaus, später," 147.
22 Julia Kristeva, *The Powers of Horror: An Essay on Abjection*, trans. Leon S. Roudiez (New York: Columbia University Press, 1982).

ing with "these kinds of people" (a category the narrator fails to explicate) and can accept their fate, she does not want to become like them.

The second scene in which the narrator appears to be acutely awake (and fearful) is when they arrive at the house itself. The house is simultaneously lovely and terrifying: "The house was beautiful. It was *the* house. And it was a ruin."[23] The narrator's detailed description of the eighteenth-century estate, and the damage it has sustained, stands out in contrast to her minimalist place descriptions so far, primarily of Berlin:

> It was a large, two-story country manor house of red brick; its skeletonized gable roof had two wooden horse's heads, one at each end. Most of the windows had lost their glass panes, the crooked veranda was held together only by a dense tangle of ivy, and cracks as wide as a thumb ran through the brickwork.[24]

Just like Berlin, this eighteenth-century estate in the former East Germany would have seen the regimes of modern Germany, from the Prussian monarchy to the first German unification and age of the Kaisers, the Weimar Republic, the Nazi era, Allied occupation, the GDR, and now the Berlin Republic. However, not yet deterritorialized, it evokes this history in a way that Berlin does not for the narrator. The missing glass and thick cracks in the outer walls speak to its experience and history in a way that the narrator does not describe seeing in Berlin.

The narrator feels this historical weight balanced precariously within and on the dilapidating structure, "as if every tremor might be too much."[25] (This is perhaps the closest Hermann comes to expressing her own hesitation to address the German past directly in her works. It is so tricky, so overwhelmingly dangerous, that any false move could be disastrous.) At the same time, the narrator calls the house "a proud vessel beached in times long gone."[26] While the reader might interpret this remark as an allegory of the nation, the narrator is more likely ex-

---

[23] Judith Hermann, "Summerhouse, Later," 196. Originally: "Das Haus war schön. Es war *das* Haus. Und es war eine Ruine." Judith Hermann, "Sommerhaus, später," 148.
[24] Judith Hermann, "Summerhouse, Later," 196. Originally: "Es war ein großes, zweistöckiges Gutshaus aus rotem Ziegelstein, es hatte ein skelettiertes Giebelach mit zwei hölzernen Pferdeköpfen zu beiden Seiten, in den meisten Fenstern waren keine Scheiben mehr. Die windschiefe Veranda wurde nur noch vom dichten Efeu zusammengehalten, und durchs Mauerwerk liefen daumendicke Risse." Judith Hermann, "Sommerhaus, später," 148.
[25] Judith Hermann, "Summerhouse, Later," 196. Originally: "als könne jede Erschütterung eine zuviel sein [...]" Judith Hermann, "Sommerhaus, später," 148.
[26] Judith Hermann, "Summerhouse, Later," 196. Originally: "ein in lange vergangener Zeit gestrandetes, stolzes Schiff." Judith Hermann, "Sommerhaus, später," 148.

pressing her fear that a move from Berlin to Canitz would put an end to her own freedom and mobility; a life here would be marked by the passage of time, not the passing through space.

Stein does not share the narrator's view. He sees the house only as his proud purchase, and a brief exchange between them illustrates their gendered difference in perspective: "'Stein!' I called up. 'Get out of there! It's going to collapse!' / 'Come in!' he yelled back. It's *my* house!"[27] The narrator fears entering the structure, as she could be physically injured if it were to collapse on her. But she is also afraid of the house metaphorically, afraid of being trapped in the lifestyle that she sees herself having to assume if she were to enter into a life with Stein there. Stein is not afraid of it; after all, it belongs to him. He can move freely in a structure that he has ownership of (as a symbol of the patriarchy) and cannot recognize the threat it poses to her.

While Hermann's narrator can perhaps be faulted for her myopic, selfish view of the situation, seeing herself as the party most burdened by Stein's purchase (instead of the woman and child who were actually displaced as a result of it),[28] Hermann legitimizes her narrator's fears somewhat by projecting them onto a house. In doing so, she taps into a long literary history in which houses, as tools of patriarchal control, are sites of women's confinement. Dwellings in works by Charlotte Brontë, Emily Dickinson, Edith Wharton, and Virginia Woolf from the Anglophone tradition, as well as Henrik Ibsen, G. E. Lessing, and Theodor Fontane from continental European traditions, come to mind.[29] In such narratives, marriage and houses are deeply entwined, as they reflect women's centuries-long experiences in Western culture of being displaced as part of marriage, conventionally from the house of adolescence to the house of the husband.[30] Sigrid Weigel has argued in her broad study of femininity in modern European philosophy and literature that the socialization of girls to be-

---

27 Judith Hermann, "Summerhouse, Later," 196. "'Stein!' rief ich. 'Komm da raus! Es stürzt zusammen!' / 'Komm rein!' rief er zurück. 'Es ist doch mein Haus!'" Judith Hermann, "Sommerhaus, später, 149.
28 This myopic view is common to many of Hermann's and her contemporaries' characters. See Mila Ganeva, "Female Flâneurs," 251.
29 Claudia Gremler ("Country Escapes) and Nancy Nobile ("A Ring of Keys) have argued the opposite, citing *Allerlei-Rauh* (1988) by Sarah Kirsch and *Sommerstück* (1989) by Christa Wolf as the intertexts. In these works by East German authors, countryside homes in the GDR were sites of communal living, not hetero-patriarchal control. However, the narrator in Hermann's text fails to recognize this possibility and instead appears to associate the house with a more conventional domesticity.
30 For an excellent discussion of this topic, see Ann Jacobsen, "Edith Wharton's Houses Full of Rooms," *Women's Studies* 44 (2015): 516–536.

come wives and move from the house of the father to the house of the husband constitutes a colonization of women. Indeed, houses serve in this capacity as key tools of the patriarchy, the space in which to contain the "excesses" of femininity, including female sexuality, and to instill in women a sense of morality and modesty.[31]

While Hermann's characters in "Summerhouse, Later" do not follow conventional models of gender in most respects, her writing style is nevertheless infused with anachronistic characterizations of gender. Biendarra describes women in Hermann's work as having an "almost ethereal frailty" that is "bothersome because it stands in sharp contrast to the experience of a modern female reader."[32] Similarly, Ganeva has argued that Hermann's female characters "are essentially dependent on and submissive to their inert, disinclined male friends. [...] When summoned, they travel to Prague, Wurzburg, Karlovy Vary, or wherever their male friends ask them to go."[33] Indeed, the narrator of "Summerhouse, Later" comes when Stein beckons and visits the house despite her desire not to. Even when Stein describes plans for the house that would not uphold a conventional, heteronormative, and patriarchal gender dynamic between them – he says he will renovate the house to accommodate the group's communal living arrangements and sexual fluidity – the narrator cannot believe him. The opposing evidence is too strong. When the child from the previous scene in Angermünde reappears mysteriously while the two are visiting the house, the narrator is unsettled by the triangulated vision of husband, wife, and child.

Although Hermann paints a somewhat anachronistic picture of gender relations in her stories, she also reveals this dynamic to be fragile, as the men in her stories are largely ineffectual in their pursuits.[34] Stein's illusion of sharing a life with the narrator in which he provides security for her in a patriarchal fashion proves foolish when they discover that the house is fully penetrable. Doors and windows are missing, and the locks on the remaining doors no longer function. The ring of keys the characters have retrieved from the woman in Angermünde has no functional purpose and, for all intents and purposes, is now

---

31 Sigrid Weigel, *Topographien der Geschlechter* (Reinbek bei Hamburg: Rowohlt Taschenbuch Verlag, 1990), 128–131. For an in-depth investigation of the concept of the feminine, particularly discourses of the feminine and domesticization, in European intellectual history, see Sigrid Weigel, *Topographien der Geschlechter*, part 2 "Wildnis und Stadt."
32 Anke Biendarra, "Gen(d)eration Next," 228.
33 Mila Ganeva, "Female Flâneurs," 269.
34 See also Esther K. Bauer, "Narratives of Femninity in Judith Hermann's *Summerhouse, Later*," *Women in German Yearbook* 25 (2009): 61–63; Anke Biendarra, "Gen(d)eration Next," 225.

only a beautiful antique.[35] The house cannot be the instrument by which Stein secures stability for the narrator; his dream is based on an antiquated way of life that may be romanticized but is no longer available or even desirable in the era of globalization and deterritorialization.[36]

The narrator, while anxious, has moments of ambivalence that stem from this romanticized view. The house itself, while a "ruin" is also "beautiful," and the narrator harbors tender feelings toward Stein at times. After she disappoints him by expressing her disdain for the house, she has a sudden moment of longing to return to their prior relationship: "I thought of last summer, of that hour in Heinze's garden in Lunow, I wished Stein would look at me one more time the way he looked at me then, and I hated myself for thinking it."[37] Once back in Berlin, the narrator returns to her life of free love, kissing Anna and Christiane and Falk, but she must also look away out of jealousy when Stein kisses another girl. Once he begins sending her postcards from Canitz updating her on his progress with the renovations, she is paralyzed by her own ambivalence and the possibility that Stein has provided her. The house is both a utopian space and a stifling one, and the narrator feels "somewhere between everything-is-possible and it-makes-no-difference," as Andrea Köhler puts it.[38] As long as the narrator makes no choice, the house can mean everything and nothing all at once, and she appears to enjoy the empty space between those two thoughts. The narrator thus contributes to the deterritorialization of the house, further emptying it of any distinct meaning as long as she makes no choice.

In the end, deterritorialization wins out. Stein burns the house down, destroying the historical identity that it held, driven most likely by the realization that the narrator will never share his dream.[39] Indeed, with each of his major ac-

---

35 Monika Shafi offers a beautiful reading of the keyring in *Housebound*, *Housebound: Selfhood and Domestic Space in Contemporary German Fiction* (Rochester: Camden House, 2012), 118.
36 See Monika Shafi, *Housebound*, 118 and Claudia Gremler, "Country Escapes," 129.
37 Judith Hermann, "Summerhouse, Later," 199–200. Originally: "ich dachte an den Sommer, an die Stunde in Heinzes Garten in Lunow, ich wünschte mir, daß mich Stein noch einmal so ansehen würde, wie er mich damals angesehen hatte, und ich haßte mich dafür." Judith Hermann, "Sommerhaus, später," 152.
38 Andrea Köhler, "'Is That All There Is?' Judith Hermann oder Die Geschichte eines Erfolgs," in *Aufgerissen. Zur Literatur der 90er*, ed. Thomas Kraft (Munich and Zurich: Piper, 2000), 84. My translation. Originally: "Kein angenehmes Gefühl, doch richtig schlimm ist es auch wieder nicht, so irgendwas zwischen Alles-ist-möglich und Es-ist-alles-egal."
39 While it is commonly assumed in the secondary literature that Stein has burned the house down, Nancy Nobile suggests that the evicted child might be the culprit. See Nancy Nobile, "A Ring of Keys: Thresholds to the Past in Judith Hermann's *Sommerhaus, später*." *Gegenwartsliteratur* 9 (2010): 311.

tions, he has participated in the deterritorialization of the former East Germany. By purchasing this property with an identity anchored in a long German tradition and seeking to renovate it, Stein has participated in the processes of putting property in the former East Germany into Westerners' hands, which would inevitably lead to the blurring of distinctions between East and West. He has displaced a family and, in the end, destroyed an historic building. At the same time, the narrator remains free to lead a life without commitments in Berlin, but not without having to face her own responsibility in the processes of privatization and deterritorialization. When Stein sends her a newspaper clipping about the Gutshaus in Canitz that has burned down, she places it in a drawer and thinks "later." While scholars have often read this response as a disavowel of her responsibility or a deferral of thinking about the possibility that Stein has destroyed, I understand it differently. It could be a realization: that right now, Berlin is where she wants to be, but later she will participate in the conventional, heteronormative order of home and property ownership in whatever form that may take as the deterritorialization of the region progresses.

Deterritorialized Home as a Nightmare in *Where Love Begins*

If "later" is the last word we are left with in Hermann's short story, the novel that would come sixteen years later, *Where Love Begins* (*Aller Liebe Anfang*), seems to fulfill that promise. *Where Love Begins* is no stated sequel to "Summerhouse, Later." However, it takes up its main concerns – private property ownership, withdrawl from a community into a heteronormative family structure, isolation, and deterritorialization – by depicting a woman's vulnerability inside a house. The protagonist, Stella, lives with her husband, Jason, and daughter, Ava, in a non-descript suburban neighborhood on the edge of a town and a wood. She works only part-time outside of her home, spending most of her time alone behind locked doors and a gated fence. She is not acquainted with her neighbors, preferring instead to read books and write letters to her only close friend, Clara, who lives far away. Stella lives in material comfort in a single-family house that she and her husband own, is largely isolated from others in her community, and has settled into her identity as a wife and a mother – the realized fear of the narrator in "Summerhouse, Later." Stella's suburban life seems secure, if perhaps a bit boring, until a man appears at her door, demands to talk with her, and quickly becomes her stalker. The safety Stella feels in her house soon proves to be fragile, as the stalker finds ways to threaten its integrity. Having not built relationships with her neighbors and having settled into a marriage in which she relies on her husband to protect her, Stella finds herself incapable of defending herself when she is alone. She is fully ensnared in a patriarchal trap that is built on conventional gender roles and extreme individualism.

Where Love Begins is a pscyhological thriller, and the third person narration focalized closely through Stella's perspective heightens the tension for the reader. True to the genre, we are limited to the knowledge that Stella has about her stalker, are held in anticipation of encounters with him, and wonder how, or even whether, she will escape his advances. The close focalization through her perspective gives us access to her thoughts, fears, and reactions, and as such, Stella's state of mind is in the foreground. At the same time, the third person narration replaces Stella's own voice, contributing to an overall feeling that she is not in control of her story. Indeed, Stella does not have much control, and the nightmarish scenario that she is subjected to in the novel results from the very same isolation and gender normativity that the narrator in "Summerhouse, Later" associates with living in a privately owned, single-family home. Jason, like Stein, works in construction, and his way of protecting Stella ultimately contributes to her insecurity. Stella also appears to be the adult version of the protagonist of "Summerhouse, Later," having given up a life with friends in the city to marry, have a child, and move into a house.

Not only do the main characters support the continuity of themes between the two texts; the presentation of space and place does as well, as the dissolution of binaries between East and West in "Summerhouse, Later" leads to a much more fully realized deterritorialization in *Where Love Begins*. Whereas Stein's house in "Summerhouse, Later" has an architectural style with flourishes hailing from another era that lend it identity and historical weight for the narrator, Stella and Jason's house has no such features. It is one house among several that all have the same floor plan, picture window, and sunroom in a newer, non-descript neighborhood, a suburban in-between place that exhibits the characteristics of neither city nor countryside. The narrator never discloses where the house and neighborhood are even located. The family could be living in the former East Germany, in the former West Germany, or somewhere abroad. The main characters' names – Stella, Jason, and their daughter Ava (not the Germanic "Eva") – may indicate that they live in an Anglophone culture or may be of no consequence at all, given the penetration of the English language globally in the era of neoliberalism.[40]

Stella's vulnerability thus stems, in part, from the same paired themes of deterritorialization and displacement presented in "Summerhouse, Later." It also results from the fact that Jason, not she, determines the conditions of her life

---

[40] See this point in chapter 3 pertaining to *No More Mr. Nice Guy*.

there. Just as in "Summerhouse, Later," men in this novel handle the business of purchasing homes, while women and children are the primary inhabitants of them.[41] Jason bought the house on the occasion of Stella's pregnancy, and thus it is explicitly linked with heteronormative sexuality and patriarchal gender roles. Jason is rarely at home, his job requiring him to be away for long stretches of time, and so Stella and Ava's presence in the house are evocative of the woman and child in the house in Angermünde that is so repugnant to the narrator of "Summerhouse, Later." Also like that woman and child, who are displaced by men's decisions about property, Stella and Ava will one day be separated from this house. As the narrator tells us, "This is Stella's and Jason's house; it's the house Jason buys when Stella is pregnant with Ava. A house for a family. Not a house for always. We'll move from here someday, Jason says. We'll move on."[42] Jason wields control over the connection between home, place, and time for the family. Stella's life resembles what many women have experienced in patriarchal society: not quite themselves someone else's property, yet living a life that they have little say in directing.

This gendered way of practicing home also extends into the work lives of Stella and Jason, which, curiously enough, center on houses. Jason is a construction worker and spends long stretches of time away from home building houses that other families will occupy. After visiting one of Jason's construction sites, Stella describes it as "a house like an idea, a vision of a distant future."[43] Jason is in the business of shaping the material futures of others, just as he has done, albeit in a different way, with Stella. While Jason engages in the stereotypically masculine work of construction, Stella engages in more conventionally female work as a caregiver in the homes of her elderly patients. In contrast to Jason, whose work offers others the promise of starting in a new house, Stella works with people who are inhabiting their homes at the end of their lives. For them, home is mostly about memories, and in the case of some patients, the painful loss of memory. Home is essentially a thing of the past for them.

---

41 In "Summerhouse, Later" Stein, the male "owner from Dortmund" (German makes the distinction between the masculine "Eigentümer" and the female "Eigentümerin"), and Heinz buy and sell homes, whereas the narrator and the woman and child are faced with the circumstances of habitation chosen by those men.
42 Judith Hermann, *Where Love Begins* (London: The Clerkenwell Press, 2016), 4–5. Originally: "Das ist Stellas und Jasons Haus, das ist das Haus, das Jason kauft, als Stella mit Ava schwanger ist. Ein Haus für eine Familie. Kein Haus für immer. Wir werden hier auch wieder wegziehen, sagt Jason, wir werden weiterziehen." Judith Hermann, *Aller Liebe Anfang* (Frankfurt am Main: S. Fischer Verlag, 2014), 12.
43 Judith Hermann, *Where Love Begins*, 89. Originally: "ein Haus wie eine Idee, eine Vorstellung von einer fernen Zukunft." Judith Hermann, *Aller Liebe Anfang*, 118.

Unlike her patients, Stella has not been able to invest her emotions into her home. Nor is she able to connect emotionally with Jason or their daughter Ava. Instead, she relates more closely with the items within the house, developing an affection for her family members' possessions.[44] "Standing in Ava's room, she regards the still life on Ava's table, an apple with a bite taken out of it, a memory card, thin, coloured-pencil shavings, a juice glass. She'd like to clean it up; she'd like it to stay exactly as it is."[45] The objects' proximity to one another serves as a stand-in for connectedness: "Stella's books pile up around the armchair. For some time now Ava's books have also been piling up around the chair," and "Jason's shirt, Stella's book" lie together on the floor, sharing an apparent intimacy that they do not.[46] Stella finds herself seeking contact to Jason when he is away by engaging with his belongings: "she is straightening up the bureau, sorting Jason's shirts, extending his presence that way; she doesn't want to lose touch [...]."[47] The proximity of the family members' personal items that have amassed themselves in the house is the closest thing that Stella has to an emotional connection with them.

Whereas in "Summerhouse, Later" the overall dearth of objects described results in a few objects being charged with meaning – the house, the keys, the postcards – there is an overabundance of meaning attached to objects in *Where Love Begins*. It is perhaps because objects hold so much meaning for Stella that her first encounter with her eventual stalker, a man named Mister Pfister, is so upsetting to her. When he rings at her front gate for the first time, he is not wearing or holding anything that identifies him: "a man without any gear, no bag, no backpack, not carrying a bouquet of flowers – a man wearing light-col-

---

44 For a discussion of the way in which Hermann places her characters within constellations of items rather than in connected relationships, see Necia Chronister, "The Poetics of the Surface as a Critical Aesthetic in Judith Hermann's *Alice* (2009) and *Aller Liebe Anfang* (2014)," *Gegenwartsliteratur: A German Studies Yearbook* 14 (2015): 265–289.
45 Judith Hermann, *Where Love Begins*, 12. Originally: "Steht in Avas Zimmer und sieht sich das Stillleben auf Avas Tisch an, ein angebissener Apfel, eine Memorykarte, feine Buntstiftspäne, ein Saftglas. Sie möchte das aufräumen; sie möchte, dass das genau so bleibt." Judith Hermann, *Aller Liebe Anfang*, 21.
46 Judith Hermann, *Where Love Begins*, 6–7. Originally: "Stellas Bücher stapeln sich um den Sessel herum. Seit einiger Zeit stapeln sich auch Avas Bücher um den Sessel herum." Judith Hermann, *Aller Liebe Anfang*, 14. / Judith Hermann, *Where Love Begins*, 8. Originally: "Jasons Hemd, Stellas Buch." Judith Hermann, *Aller Liebe Anfang*, 16.
47 Judith Hermann, *Where Love Begins*, 139. Originally: "sie räumt die Wäschekommode auf, sortiert Jasons Hemden und verlängert damit seine Anwesenheit, sie will den Kontakt nicht verlieren [...]" Judith Hermann, *Aller Liebe Anfang*, 181.

oured trousers, a dark jacket, no identifiable characteristics. An apparition."[48] Hardly able to register him as a person because he bears no identifying objects, she perceives him instead as otherworldly. Much less can she fathom his intentions to establish contact with her.

When Stella refuses to speak with Mister Pfister, and he nevertheless returns repeatedly over the ensuing weeks to insist on having contact, the house and the objects Stella and her family own fail to provide her a sense of security. At times, the house becomes a trap, a place she cannot leave because Mister Pfister might be outside. At other times, it is a place to avoid altogether. She changes her work schedule and spends more time in public in order to evade him. When at home, she must think of the rooms in the house in terms of their relative protection from, or exposure to, the outside. With repeated visits from Mister Pfister, Stella learns which rooms and windows provide her the best view for detecting him before he rings. She also learns which rooms violate the division of interiority and exteriority. For example, Stella realizes with some horror that her habit of reading in front of the picture window in the living room had put her on display and might be what attracted Mister Pfister initially. Even the objects in the house become liabilities. Stella feels apprehension when Ava leaves her toys and rain boots in the sunroom and lawn, as though Ava herself were visible to others in these semi-private extensions of the house. After the first encounter with Mister Pfister, the presence of Jason's possessions feels like a rebuke to her: "Jason's shirt is draped over the back of the chair, and Stella straightens it as if Jason had surprised her at something."[49] The immediacy Jason's clothing evokes feelings of guilt, as though he has caught her betraying him.

Like the house in Canitz in "Summerhouse, Later," whose locks and doors only provide the illusion of security, this house too proves to be permeable. There is a sense throughout the novel that things enter and leave the house without Stella's control. Heat penetrates it in the summer, as do occasional breezes and sounds through windows that are left open to combat the heat. The house is equipped with a telecommunication system connected to the front gate, which Mister Pfister uses to make himself known to Stella. He rings each day and in the middle of the night, startling her awake when she is home alone. Mister Pfister does not enter the house, but leaves messages for Stella in the mailbox that

---

[48] Judith Hermann, *Where Love Begins*, 13. Originally: "ein Mann ohne eine Ausrüstung, ohne Tasche, ohne Rucksack, ohne einen Blumenstrauß, ein Mann in einer hellen Hose, dunklen Jacke, durch nichts zu identifizieren. Eine Erscheinung." Judith Hermann, *Aller Liebe Anfang*, 23.
[49] Judith Hermann, *Where Love Begins*, 16. Originally: "über der Lehne des Stuhls hängt Jasons Hemd, und Stella zieht es glatt, als hätte Jason sie bei etwas ertappt." Judith Hermann, *Aller Liebe Anfang*, 26.

she feels compelled to bring inside and store until she can show them to Jason. The messages themselves escalate in format, from notes and postcards to letters to photographs, burned CDs, and eventually a USB stick. Because Stella is accustomed to viewing Ava's and Jason's objects as stand-ins for their persons, the items Mister Pfister leaves also become stand-ins for him in the home. Worst of all, Mister Pfister has entered her house through her awareness of him: "She tries [...] to get him out of her house by not thinking about him. It's impossible."[50] Through his obsessive habit of ringing, he has made himself into an ever-present entity in her thoughts. The interiority of the house parallels the interiority of the mind.[51]

Only after a chance encounter with Mister Pfister at a grocery store does Stella understand that his fascination with her is limited to her material home environment. In this scene, Stella spots him as she enters the store. They lock eyes, and Stella hurries toward the exit in order to confront him once and for all in public. However, upon exiting, she finds that he has not waited for her, and she leaves the grocery store confounded. Once she reaches her house, she sees him again, ringing her doorbell. This act makes no logical sense, as he has just seen her outside of the house. It then occurs to her that even though Mister Pfister saw her in public, she was not the version of Stella, in that environment, that he is fixated on:

> The Stella Mister Pfister has in mind doesn't exist; in any case, *she* has nothing to do with that Stella. Mister Pfister recognised her, but that's not who he's interested in – this Stella who goes shopping after work in flat-heeled sandals and with a tired face without make-up, tense, harried, and obviously needy, this Stella doesn't interest him. Mister Pfister is interested in Stella in her locked house. In her face behind the small windowpane next to the door, her distant figure in the chair at the edge of the lawn far back in the garden, in the Stella waiting at her desk upstairs in her room. That Stella is the one Mister Pfister is interested in. An imagined Stella. *His* Stella.[52]

---

50 Judith Hermann, *Where Love Begins*, 116. Originally: "Sie versucht, [...] ihn aus ihrem Haus rauszukriegen, indem sie nicht an ihn denkt. Es ist unmöglich." Judith Hermann, *Aller Liebe Anfang*, 151.
51 For a discussion of this symbolism in literary history, see Ann Jacobsen, "Edith Wharton's Houses," 530–531.
52 Judith Hermann, *Where Love Begins*, 108. Originally: "Die Stella, die Mister Pfister meint, gibt es nicht, sie hat jedenfalls mit Stella nichts zu tun. Mister Pfister hat sie erkannt, aber er meint sie gar nicht – diese Stella, die nach Feierabend in flachen Sandalen und mit einem müden, ungeschminkten Gesicht einkaufen geht, angespannt, hektisch und offenbar bedürftig, diese Stella interessiert ihn nicht. Mister Pfister interessiert sich für Stella in ihrem verschlossenen Haus. Für ihr Gesicht hinter der kleinen Scheibe neben der Tür, ihre entfernte Gestalt im Stuhl am Rand der Wiese weit weg hinter im Garten, für die wartende Stella am Schreibtisch oben in ihrem

Mister Pfister is fixated on the version of Stella that exists within the constellation of objects in her house. He wants her alone and locked in, or perhaps he is unable to interpret her outside of this context.

While it surprises Stella to learn that Mister Pfister can only perceive her within the configuration of her material possessions, she has already demonstrated that she sees him in a similar way, unable to interpret him without the context of material signifiers. What is more, she will continue with this practice. Upon reading the return address on one of his letters, she discovers that he lives in her neighborhood. When curiosity finally gets the best of her and she visits his address, she perceives the outside of the house as blank and nondescript, just as Mister Pfister had appeared to her on their first encounter: "Mister Pfister's house is white. A grapevine grows skyward next to the front door. The grass is bleached. No flowerbeds, no garden chairs, no clay pots, no table, no umbrella. Nothing."[53] The property has been neglected: the lawn is brown, grass is growing between cracks in the steps leading up to the house, and the mailbox is overflowing. Looking at the overstuffed mailbox, Stella imagines the interiority of the house as that of a hoarder:

> Stella has a sudden inkling about the inside of his house: mountains of paper, piles of newspapers, garbage bags, the kitchen half dark, the table full of things [...]. A bizarre, glowing, toxic wave of chaos sloshes from the house over the doorsill out into the garden, flowing towards Stella, and Stella lets the cover of the mailbox drop and backs away.[54]

Stella believes the house to be a reflection of Mister Pfister's personality – blank and nondescript on the outside, but with a chaotic interior state that threatens to spill out and engulf her.

While both Stella and Mister Pfister see each other in relationship to their material contexts, there is a subtle but key difference. Whereas Mister Pfister (and, as it turns out, Jason) sees Stella as part of the world of objects, Stella

---

Zimmer. Diese Stella meint Mister Pfister. Eine imaginierte Stella. Seine." Judith Hermann, *Aller Liebe Anfang*, 142.

53 Judith Hermann, *Where Love Begins*, 71. Originally: "Mister Pfisters Haus ist weiß. Neben der Haustür wächst ein Weinstock hoch. Der Rasen ist verblichen. Keine Beete, keine Gartenstühle, keine Tontöpfe, kein Tisch, kein Sonnenschirm. Nichts." Judith Hermann, *Aller Liebe Anfang*, 95.

54 Judith Hermann, *Where Love Begins*, 72. Originally: "Stella hat eine jähe Ahnung vom Inneren seines Hauses, Papierberge, Zeitungsstapel, Müllsäcke, Halbdunkel in der Küche, Tisch voller Gegenstände [...]. Aus dem Haus heraus schappt eine bizarre, leuchtende, toxische Woge von Chaos, schwappt über die Türschwelle hinaus in den Garten und läuft auf Stella zu, und Stella lässt die Klappe vom Briefkasten herunterfallen und weicht zurück." Judith Hermann, *Aller Liebe Anfang*, 97.

sees objects as representative of people. Both attitudes are flawed. As a woman, Stella is objectified by the men around her, which means that they do not perceive her feelings, thoughts, and agency. The perception of women as part of the world of objects, and particularly as one's property, can lead to violence. Stella's mistake, however, is that she replaces relationships with objects, which leaves her isolated, vulnerable, and incapable of understanding Mister Pfister's desire to have a personal connection with her.

With Jason away from home and no one else to turn to, Stella approaches the only person who is consistently visible in the neighborhood, a retired bicycle mechanic who spends his days on his lawn. They talk about how insulating the neighborhood is by its very design: "There is a time warp here, have you noticed that already? Time has stood still here, and everyone who lives here keeps to himself. I've seen you for years, yet this is the first time we're talking to each other."[55] There is no sense of community in the neighborhood, and single-family houses guide their inhabitants' focus inward. In describing the neighborhood as a time loop, the bicycle mechanic refers to the residents' tendency to organize their time around their works schedules rather than events that would bring a neighborhood together: they get up in the morning, leave for work, and return in the evening only to prepare food for themselves and go to bed. Stella has also practiced this individualism, structuring her life around her personal concerns and isolating herself from those around her.

While the bike mechanic is sympathetic to Stella, he nevertheless upholds the patriarchal system that traps her: "If you've never spoken to him, then maybe you ought to do it sometime. Tell him, talk to him. One can talk to him; I'm sure one can."[56] This advice is not only contrary to the advice Stella has received from Jason, Clara, and in her internet research on stalking; it exposes the patriarchal underpinnings of the situation. By encouraging Stella to speak with Mister Pfister, the neighbor implies that she has caused the problem and owes it to Mister Pfister to give him what he wants – ostensibly a conversation. The bike mechanic does not recognize this as dangerous, sexist advice because he himself can talk with Mister Pfister without consequence, without coming out of the conversation "owing" him anything further. With this scenario, Hermann

---

[55] Judith Hermann, *Where Love Begins*, 126. Originally: "Hier gibt es eine Zeitschleife, ist dir das schon aufgefallen? Hier ist die Zeit stehengeblieben, und jeder, der hier lebt, bleibt für sich. Ich sehe dich seit Jahren, wir sprechen zum ersten Mal miteinander." Judith Hermann, *Aller Liebe Anfang*, 164.

[56] Judith Hermann, *Where Love Begins*, 129. Originally: "Wenn du nie mit ihm gesprochen hast, dann solltest du's vielleicht mal tun. Sag ihm das, rede mit ihm. Man kann mit ihm reden, da bin ich sicher, das kann man." Judith Hermann, *Aller Liebe Anfang*, 168.

brings to light the ways in which long-existing patriarchal strategies of control continue in insidious forms: even though women have achieved a more equal status in the liberal society and are able to realize their dreams and potentials in many ways that are unprecedented in Western society, the unspoken assumption persists that women owe men what they want.

Mister Pfister's threat comes to a head when Stella does finally confront him, that is, when she follows the bike mechanic's advice, but on her own terms. After finding a note in her mailbox that reads "*Hello, so what does it feel like to be stalked,*"[57] Stella marches to his house, rings at the gate, and confronts him about the psychological terror he has inflicted. After she emphasizes that she will not be someone he can talk to, he responds by appearing at her house later that day and threatening her with escalated violence: "I'll not only kick in your garden gate, I'll also kick in the door to your house. I'll trample your entire life to pieces; it's something I can do. You'll lie under the bedcovers and bite your fingernails; your teeth will chatter."[58] Stella's marriage, the house, and the locked gate will be insufficient to protect her from Mister Pfister. He already has control over her because he can scare her, make her chew her nails and tremble inside her house. He has power over Stella because she is in a patriarchal trap.

If, in "Summerhouse, Later" the narrator fears being an accessory to another person's fantasized life, this kind of patriarchal fantasy turns into a pathology in *Where Love Begins*. Stella belongs to the world of objects inside Jason's house, and there she has become the fantasized object of Mister Pfister. She realizes only too late that she has always relied on and obeyed Jason rather than using her own faculties: "When haven't I listened to you, Stella thinks. [...] Were there ever any moments when I should have listened to you, done what you said and instead did something else? What?"[59] She also realizes only too late that Jason likely sees her as part of his property. The next time Mister Pfister shows up at the house and does attempt to kick in the front door, Jason meets him there and beats him viciously. The violent act of "stand your ground" prop-

---

57 Judith Hermann, *Where Love Begins*, 140, emphasis in the original. Originally: "*Hallo, wie ist es denn so, gestalkt zu werden.*" Judith Hermann, *Aller Liebe Anfang*, 182.
58 Judith Hermann, *Where Love Begins*, 146. Originally: "Ich trete dir nicht nur dein Gartentor ein, ich trete dir auch deine Haustür ein. Ich trete dir dein ganzes Leben zusammen, ich bin in der Lage dazu. Du wirst unter der Bettdecke liegen und an den Nägeln kauen, du wirst mit den Zähnen klappern." Judith Hermann, *Aller Liebe Anfang*, 190.
59 Judith Hermann, *Where Love Begins*, 149. Originally: "Wann habe ich denn nicht auf dich gehört, denkt Stella. [...] Gab es Momente, in denen ich auf dich hätte hören sollen, tun sollen, was du sagst, und stattdessen was anderes getan habe? Was denn?" Judith Hermann, *Aller Liebe Anfang*, 194.

erty defense unnerves Stella: "Later, Stella sometimes thinks about how powerful Jason's blows must have been. What these blows were really all about. [...] wondering whether, while he was hitting Mister Pfister with the stick, Jason was thinking of her, whether Jason as he was landing all those blows was thinking of Stella."[60] It is unclear what, precisely, Stella fears: the violence that Jason is capable of, that he could beat her as well, or that he defended her merely as part of his property.

Where "Summerhouse, Later" casts gender relations at the end of the twentieth century as still bound to antiquated models and behaviors, the premise of stalking in *Where Love Begins* brings the threats inherent in patriarchy into the twenty-first century. The scenario of a man demanding that a woman owes him something and then reacting violently when she refuses is all too familiar: numerous news stories recently, especially in the United States, have covered men committing public acts of violence and attributing their motivations to a rejection by a woman.[61] This aspect of the hetero-patriarchy has deep roots in conventional gender relations, in which men have traditionally made decisions about women's lives, displaced them as a result of those decisions, and rendered them into objects in the home. All these things add up to men not being able to accept women's agency and their right to refuse men. Stella's moment of taking action – confronting Mister Pfister – is met with violent retaliation. Ultimately, though, the conflict is not between Mister Pfister and Stella, but between Mister

---

[60] Judith Hermann, *Where Love Begins*, 165–166. Originally: "Später denkt Stella manchmal darüber nach, wie viel Kraft in Jasons Schlägen gelegen haben muss. Worum es in diesen Schlägen eigentlich gegangen ist. [...] fragt sich, ob Jason an sie gedacht hat, während er zuschlug, ob Jason schlagend an Stella gedacht hat." Judith Hermann, *Aller Liebe Anfang*, 215–216.

[61] May 2014: Elliot Rodger, a man in his twenties, killed six people, injured fourteen others, and then killed himself near the UC Santa Barbara campus after posting a video on Youtube in which he stated that wanted to punish women for rejecting him. November 2015: Charles McKinney shot and killed a woman in a bar in Pittsburgh after she rejected him. June 2017: Davion D. Brown shot and killed a woman in Fort Wayne after she refused to date him. He also shot and wounded two others, then killed himself. February 2018: Nikolas Cruz reportedly stalked a girl at Stoneman Douglas High School in Parkland, Florida before committing a mass shooting there that left seventeen dead. He had also been abusive to his ex-girlfriend and had been expelled from school for fighting her boyfriend. April 2018: Alek Minassian wrote a Facebook post detailing his aggressive behavior toward women before striking and killing ten pedestrians with a van in Toronto. May 2018: Dimitrios Pagourtzis, a teen, killed ten people in an El Paso, Texas school after a girl rejected him, according to the girl's mother. August 2018: Jarrod Ramos committed a mass shooting at an Annapolis, Maryland newspaper that had written about Ramos's criminal conviction of harassing women. November 2018: Scott Beierle, who had a history of harassing young women and recorded misogynistic videos about women online, entered a yoga studio, shot six women, killing two, and beat a man.

Pfister and Jason, revealing that the stakes of their confrontation are about patriarchal rights pertaining to women as/and property.

Is There a Reterritorialization?

In both "Summerhouse, Later" and *Where Love Begins*, the belief that a house will provide stability and comfort gives way to women's fears of isolation, restrictions on identity, and vulnerability. The house becomes the material structure that upholds the patriarchy, limiting women's movement inside and out of it and ultimately leaving women vulnerable to the power differential that men hold. In her oeuvre, Hermann harkens back to reactionary gender norms that, in my reading, continue to thrive in the present, at times through the romantic desires of her characters and at others through the characters' interactions in their home life. Stein's fantasy of a heteronormative lifestyle in the country, if realized, would put an end to the narrator's fluid sexuality and gender expression in "Summerhouse, Later." In *Where Love Begins*, the main characters' conventional gender expression promises security but ultimately leaves Stella vulnerable to violent threats.

In Hermann's narratives, the dissolution of community and the increased individualism in the globalized, neoliberal society result in an alienation that plays out on an interpersonal level. The characters in "Summerhouse, Later" are capable of only fleeting moments of sexual connection and affection. The minimalist presentation of Berlin underscores this sense of detachment, which Stein seeks to overcome by establishing a life in the countryside with the narrator. In the end, though, detachment and deterritorialization win out when the narrator passively refuses to move there and Stein destroys the house. *Where Love Begins* demonstrates that home ownership and private property do not overcome alienation and detachment, as Stein would have it. Rather, Stella's life in the single-family home that Jason purchased for her has furthered her alienation in her marriage and placed her in a neighborhood in which people lead lives isolated from one another. Mister Pfister represents the extreme version of that alienation, having a pathological need for connection for which he has no outlet.

The question then arises: has the deterritorialization, the emptying of spaces of their signifiers and functioning social networks, left a vacuum for violence like that between Jason and Mister Pfister to take place? Or is the violence itself the reterritorialization that Deleuze and Guattari argue follows (or takes place simultaneously with) deterritorialization? While issues of alienation, individualism, and patriarchal gender relations are presented in understated forms in "Summerhouse, Later," they come to the fore as particular US-American afflictions in *Where Love Begins*. Not only is stalking a decidedly US-American concept, but so are hoarding and violent "stand your ground" attitudes about the protection of individual property. These extreme symptoms of individualistic, materialistic, and patriarchal society are key contributors to the danger Stella faces in the novel.

While these larger social issues might point to the United States being the undisclosed setting of *Where Love Begins*, it is important that Hermann does not name a setting, and thereby does not make the novel a commentary on the US specifically. The fact remains that this novel could take place anywhere that is attuned to US-American cultural behaviors and standards, which could be nearly anywhere in the era of globalization. The reterritorialization in Hermann's novel is not, as one might expect, the appearance of McDonald's or Starbucks in the empty spaces of the former East Berlin. Rather, uniquely US-American forms of patriarchal and materialistic violence have entered the European consciousness, and therein lies the nature of reterritorialization. In Hermann's works, these reterritorializations play out on the interpersonal level, meaning that the geography is rather irrelevant.

Finally, it is of note that these two houses, the most important houses in Hermann's oeuvre, represent two stages in the process of privatization and globalization in the post-unification era. The privatization of East Germany was an important step in the spread of neoliberalism in the 1990s. Stein's purchase of the eighteenth-century estate in "Summerhouse, Later," the subsequent displacement of a family, and the home's eventual destruction represent the threats many Easterners faced of losing their property and identity. With that historical structure gone, Stein has been an active participant in the deterritorialization of the former East Germany. The non-descript, cookie cutter houses situated on the edge of nowhere in *Where Love Begins* exemplify that loss of identity.

Chapter 5
Home in the East as a Threat to Men's Control: Peter Schneider's *Eduard's Homecoming* (1999) and Karen Duve's *Rain* (1999)

One of the most enduring images from the post-unification era in the collective imagination of East Germans is that of Mercedes appearing on their roads and in their neighborhoods. As Knut Böser, the screenwriter of *The Brocken*, described to me in a conversation, "You could see the lines of Mercedes driving up and down the country roads in those first years."[1] Perhaps a bit embellished, this statement nonetheless captures the fear many Easterners felt that Westerners were coming for their property. In the films and texts depicting the property relations of the time, the Mercedes serves as a metonymy of the faceless invaders from the West, a seemingly unstoppable force coming to snap up properties at cheap prices or by historical claim. Because this image has left its trace in film and literature, its association with masculinity has been preserved. To take examples already discussed in this monograph, one might recall Georg's pride in his Mercedes taxi, coupled with his espoused views of superiority to Easterners, in *Taxi to Rathenow* or Albert Zwirner's Mercedes as part of his overall habitus as a wheeler and dealer from the West in *The Brocken*. To be sure, the image of the Mercedes entering the East implied a driver who was not only economically independent and unrestricted in his movement, but also, and with only few exceptions, male.

The Mercedes as a metonymy of Western male hegemony supports the assessment of gender and property discussed in chapter 4 of this monograph. In Judith Hermann's short story "Summerhouse, Later" and novel *Where Love Begins*, male characters have a relatively high decision-making power over women in the conventional property relations, and women are often made vulnerable by the decisions that men make. However, in the two novels discussed in this chapter, *Eduard's Homecoming* (*Eduards Heimkehr*, 1999) by Peter Schneider and *Rain* (*Regenroman*, 1999) by Karen Duve, the image of the Mercedes-driving Western profiteer gives way to that of helpless men who have lost control of the situation.[2] Inheriting or purchasing a property in the former East Germany seems

---

[1] Knut Böser, in-person conversation, June 17, 2014. Quoted with permission.
[2] In *Eduard's Homecoming*, Eduard refutes association with the Mercedes-driving army of Westerners coming into the East to purchase property. He does not want to see himself as a profiteer.

like a fortuitous undertaking for both novels' protagonists until it goes woefully wrong for them. By acquiring property in the former East, both protagonists become subjected to powers higher than themselves – whether political, financial, or natural.

Eduard's Homecoming and *Rain* appeared at the end of the milleneum as property disputes continued to be a ubiquitous issue, but also at a time when scholars and the popular media were identifying a "crisis of masculinity" taking place at large in German culture. In 2001, for example, an issue of *Der Spiegel* titled "Das zerbrechliche Geschlecht" ("The Fragile Sex") was devoted to questions of men's health, sexuality, mental well-being, virility, and the costs and benefits of testosterone treatments.[3] In 2002, the feature article of the magazine *Focus*, "Das benachteiligte Geschlecht. Arme Jungs!" ("The Disadvantaged Sex. Poor Boys!") espoused fears that modern parenting trends in Germany had effectively weakened boys' masculinity.[4] Scholarly monographs and edited volumes on the topic soon followed in German Studies. Special issues of the scholarly journals *Seminar* (2008), the *Edinburgh German Yearbook* (2008), and *Colloquia Germanica* (2013) took critical approaches to examining Germany's so-called "masculinity crisis" at the turn of the millennium.[5] In his introduction to that special issue of *Seminar*, Michael Boehringer explains that the term "masculinity crisis" actually indicated a "crisis of masculine hegemony" in German culture at that time.[6] Claudia Breger situated it as a "broad configuration of 'identity long-

---

Peter Schneider, *Eduards Heimkehr* (Reinbek bei Hamburg: Rowohlt Taschenbuch Verlag, 2005), 36. The role of the Mercedes in characterizing Leon in *Rain* is much more sustained and will be touched upon in the second half of this chapter.

3 *Der Spiegel* 36 (2001), https://www.spiegel.de/spiegel/print/index-2001–36.html

4 *Focus* 32 (2002), https://www.focus.de/magazin/archiv/jahrgang_2002/ausgabe_32/

5 Michael Boerhringer, editor, *Discourses on Masculinity in German Literature and Film*, special issue of *Seminar: A Journal of Germanic Studies* 44, no.1 (2008); Sarah Colvin and Peter Davies, editors, *Masculinities in German Culture*, special issue of *Edinburgh German Yearbook* 2 (2008); Muriel Cormican and Gary Schmidt, editors, *Masculinity in Contemporary German Culture*, special issue of *Colloquia Germanica* 46, no. 1 (2013).

6 Michael Boehringer, "Introduction," *Discourses on Masculinity in German Literature and Film*, special issue of *Seminar: A Journal of Germanic Studies* 44, no.1 (2008): 1. Here he points to the destabilization of what R. W. Connell calls "hegemonic masculinity," the version of masculinity that comes to be idealized among many simultaneously existing masculinities in any given culture at any given time. The hegemonic form of masculinity is typically the one that situates men above women and thus reinforces the patriarchal society, and part of its function is to marginalize other masculinities. See R. W. Connell, *Masculinities* (Berkeley and Los Angeles: University of California Press, 1995), especially 37. Work by Klaus-Michael Bogdal and Wolfgang Schmale, two scholars working at the intersections of Masculinity Studies and German Studies, support Boehringer's claim, arguing that the hegemonic form of masculinity had lost legitimacy in the

ing' in contemporary Germany,"[7] spurred on by Germany's renewed push to reckon with its past after unification.

Both *Eduard's Homecoming* and *Rain* present property ownership as a part of their respective male characters' ideals about masculinity, and in both novels, the protagonist's inability to manage his property effectively is coupled with a personal masculinity crisis. In *Eduard's Homecoming*, after the eponymous Eduard accepts his inheritance of a tenement building in the East Berlin district of Friedrichshain, he becomes aware of both the potentially ruinous financial burden he has taken on and the possibility that his family may have acquired the building from a Jewish family through a coerced sale during the Nazi period. Eduard's feelings of anxiety brought on by these discoveries are compounded when his wife, Jenny, admits that she has never achieved orgasm during sex with him. While on the surface, Eduard's sexual troubles appear to be separate from the problems of financial strain and family history, a closer look yields that all three problems become entwined when they challenge Eduard's security in his masculinity.

In the second novel discussed in this chapter, *Rain*, the protagonist Leon Ulbricht also experiences a masculinity crisis connected to his acquisition of property in the former East Germany. Leon, a writer, has bought a house in the countryside on a marsh for himself and his new wife Martina. It is an ideal picture of *Heimat* that Leon believes will inspire his talents as a writer. However, the house and the marsh prove to be more than Leon can manage, as he fights to keep the house upright and avoid drowning in the swampy landscape. Injured and incapacitated by the labor of maintaining the house, Leon eventually becomes defeated by it. The more time Leon spends sedentary in the house, allowing the walls to saturate with water, the more his body morphs from the slim, hardened body that he associates with manliness to the robust, curvy, and permeable body associated with femininity and the Eastern landscape in the text.

---

second half of the twentieth century as it came to be identified as a root cause of the World Wars, racism, sexism, homophobia, and genocide. As cultural acceptance of the hegemonic form of masculinity waned, other masculinities proliferated. Klaus-Michael Bogdal, "Hard-Cold-Fast: Imagining Masculinity in the German Academy, Literature, and the Media," in *Conceptions of Postwar German Masculinity*, edited by Roy Jerome (Albany: State University of New York Press, 2001), 35–38. See also Wolfgang Schmale, *Geschichte der Männlichkeit in Europa (1450–2000)* (Vienna, Cologne, and Weimar: Böhlau Verlag, 2003), 238–240.

7 Claudia Breger, "Hegemony, Marginalization, and Feminine Masculinity: Antje Rávic Strubel's *Unter Schnee*," *Discourses on Masculinity in German Literature and Film*, special issue of *Seminar: A Journal of Germanic Studies* 44, no. 1 (2008): 154.

The intersections of property, helplessness, and masculinity crises in both *Eduard's Homecoming* and *Rain* evoke questions that complicate our discussion of property relations so far. What do we gain from these novels that depict vulnerable men from the West rather than the East? How are these vulnerabilities different from those already depicted in relation to East German men, and how are they different from the vulnerabilities of women, East or West? What is at stake for Western men, and what does this mean for German society, which was still in the process of unifying? The fact that these two novels propose very different outcomes for their protagonists suggests that while the "masculinity crisis" in the Berlin Republic provoked anxiety in some, for others, it presented an opportunity to gain power.

Property, History, and Emasculation in *Eduard's Homecoming*

Eduard's Homecoming has been lauded in the scholarship as an exemplary piece of post-unification fiction. Carol Anne Costabile-Heming has called Schneider's novel a *"Zeitdokument* [documentation of the time] that gives voice to the changes in the New Berlin as they occur," and Paul Michael Lützeler has called it "one of the best novelistic parables about the complicated process of unification of the two German states."[8] As these scholars point out, Schneider's novel serves, in many ways, as an archive of the era, addressing a breadth of unification-induced ills, including the widespread unemployment Easterners faced, feelings of enmity that many Easterners harbored toward Westerners, changing property relations, the newly opened Stasi files, memory contests centered on architecture and the changing topography of Berlin, xenophobia and neo-Nazism, and the revival of discourses on collective guilt brought on by unification.[9] The

---

[8] Carol Anne Costabile-Heming, "Peter Schneider's *Eduards Heimkehr* and the Image of the 'New Berlin,'" *German Studies Review* 25, no. 3 (2002): 498. Paul Michael Lützeler, "'Postmetropolis': Peter Schneiders Berlin-Trilogie," *Gegenwartsliteratur: A German Studies Yearbook* 4 (2005): 103. Originally: "eine der gelungensten romanhaften Parabeln auf den komplikationsreichen Prozeß der Wiedervereinigung der beiden deutschen Staaten." At the same time, Astrid Köhler has criticized Schneider for his evident plagiarism, demonstrating that Schneider used the life and work of a lesser known author, Klaus Schlesinger, as the inspiration for his own novels, particularly *Eduard's Homecoming*, without acknowledgement. Astrid Köhler, "Plagiat oder Intertextualität? Zur literarischen Beziehung zwischen Klaus Schlesinger und Peter Schneider," in *Justitiabilität und Rechtmäßigkeit: Verrechtlichungsprozesse von Literatur und Film in der Moderne*, ed. Claude D. Conter (Amsterdam: Rodopi, 2010), 97–108.

[9] See also Viana Guarda, "Gedächtnis, Raum und Identität in Peter Schneiders Postwenderoman," *Estudios Filológicos Alemanes* 22 (2011): 410. As Paul Michael Lützeler and others point

novel achieves this breadth by tying these themes to the trials and tribulations of its protagonist's, Eduard's, inheritance of a tenement building in Friedrichshain. Having left West Berlin some eight years ago to build a life with his wife and children in San Francisco, Eduard's "homecoming" upon inheriting a tenement building in the former East Berlin turns out to be a cold plunge back into the politics and troubled history of twentieth-century Germany.

Claiming an inheritance is thus the main metaphorical thrust of the book, as Eduard's property claim forces him to acknowledge his own social "inheritance" as a German two generations after World War II and the Holocaust. Ultimately, however, the novel positions Eduard as a victim of the national history, as well as a bystander to, rather than an active participant in, the current power dynamic that privileges Westerners over Easterners. As such, he is never held accountable for either. Instead, Eduard is cast as someone just as burdened by the difficulties of unification as those he sees around him. The third person narration focalized closely through Eduard's perspective supports this view on him, strengthening the sense that Eduard has been thrust into a situation over which he has little control. Since the reader has access to Eduard's thoughts and emotions, his reactions frame our understanding of the many problems he encounters with his property inheritance. Eduard suffers emotionally, even though he stands to profit handily from his inheritance, and thus the novel sympathizes with the demographic least negatively affected by unification: white West German men.

While Eduard does not consciously attach his sense of masculinity to his property inheritance, the narrator betrays the connection. The inheritance line is both paternal and fraternal, as Eduard and his brother Lothar inherit the property from their paternal grandfather,[10] and the narrator tells us that Eduard feels "admitted to a fraternity whose existence he'd never dreamed of."[11] Moreover, the conversations about property inheritance in the novel happen between men and showcase stereotypical traits of Western male privilege, including un-

---

out, *Eduard's Homecoming* is Schneider's third major novel centered in Berlin and thus serves as the final chapter in a trilogy that includes *Der Mauerspringer* (1982) and *Paarungen* (1992). Paul Michael Lützeler, "Postmetropolis," 96. For an in-depth discussion of construction, Berlin's topography, and memory debates in the Berlin Republic as presented in *Eduard's Homecoming*, see Carol Anne Costabile-Heming, "Tracing History Through Berlin's Topography: Historical Memories and Post-1989 Berlin Narratives," *German Life and Letters* 58, no. 3 (2005): 344–356.

10 Eduard and Lothar's maternal grandfather is featured in the previous novel, *Paarungen*, so the grandfather in *Eduard's Homecoming* must be paternal.

11 Peter Schneider, *Eduard's Homecoming*, trans. John Brownjohn (New York: Farrar, Straus and Giroux, 2000), 11–12. Originally: "aufgenommen in eine Bruderschaft, von deren Existenz er zuvor nichts geahnt hatte." Peter Schneider, *Eduards Heimkehr*, 20.

earned confidence in matters in which the characters have no experience or expertise. For example, during the phone conversation in which Eduard informs Lothar of their inheritance, the two men indulge themselves in an exhilarating conversation about whether to sell or rent, what kinds of prices they could get, and the costs and benefits of renovating. Although neither has any actual experience in property management or sales, they both speak as though they had expertise. In another conversation, a male friend frames his warning about property inheritance in decidedly paternalistic terms: "A bequest [...] could prove a calamity, a source of unforeseeable and unwonted tribulations, a misfortune productive of ever more misfortunes. You could always turn down a bequest, of course, but unless you did so in time [...] it would dog you throughout your life like an unwanted child."[12] To communicate to Eduard the potential perils of inheriting a house, this friend appeals to the fear he assumes every man understands: unwanted children.

Eduard enjoys the excitement of inheriting a property with his brother, his fantasized role as a landlord, and his sense of belonging to a fraternity, all of which bolster his sense of manliness. Indeed, the notion that property ownership legitimizes one's masculinity taps into a long history of Western property relations as described by Klaus-Michael Bogdal and Wolfgang Schmale. Not only has inheritance run primarily along paternal lines since the eighteenth century in Western cultures, but property itself is also a central aspect of the modern hegemonic concept of masculinity. According to Schmale, the Western hegemonic form of masculinity stems from Enlightenment-era thinking that deemed certain human traits to be "essential" or "natural," attributed them to either men or women, and then extrapolated normative gender roles from them. This gender stratification was then solidified by a broad range of social transformations: industrialization, educational reforms that grew the bourgeoisie, the changing purpose of religious confessions, widespread secularization, new career paths for men and women, the rise of political parties and unions, and public management by engineers, industries, and banks.[13] Among the most important social developments of the time was the division of public and private spaces, such that the public, or political, realm was considered to be men's domain, and one's participation in it was necessary for being perceived as a "real" man. Of course, this

---

12 Peter Schneider, *Eduard's Homecoming*, 12. Originally: "Ein Erbe [...] könne ein Verhängnis sein, ein Springquell unvorhersehbarer und ganz ungewohnter Leiden, ein Fluch, ein Unglück, das unaufhörlich neues Unglück produziere. Zwar könne man ein Erbe ausschlagen. Doch wenn dies nicht rechtzeitig [...] geschehe, begleite ein Erbe den Erben, wie ein unerwünschtes Kind den Vater, durchs ganze weitere Leben." Peter Schneider, *Eduards Heimkehr*, 21.
13 Wolfgang Schmale, *Geschichte der Männlichkeit in Europa*, 227–228.

masculinity is qualified, class- and race-based, and hegemonic: only men of the propertied class were allowed to vote and thus participate in the political sphere.[14]

In his writing about masculinity, Bogdal emphasizes the disintegration of the feudal system and its replacement with the private property system. He states that

> New demands arose out of the category of property, and consequently, men became increasingly responsible for securing and increasing assets through capitalization and inheritance. Male gender identity was constructed around and through the category of property; "real" men were identified as *producers-protectors-providers* for themselves, their families, and their communities.[15]

Although Eduard is living in a time that, by all accounts, challenges the hegemonic form of masculinity, his identity largely aligns with the conventions established in the eighteenth century as Bogdal and Schmale describe them.[16] Eduard is a scientist who has built a career at Stanford University and recently accepted a job offer in Berlin. He is a man of scientific rationality, orientation toward goals, and economic independence, thereby fulfilling the *producer-protector-provider* role within the family. Upon inheriting a property, he enters into relations that further reinforce a conventional male gender identity rooted in eighteenth-century discourses.

While Eduard's inheritance has lent him a sense of belonging to a fraternity and thus bolstered his masculinity, he soon finds that this new pillar of his identity is unsound. The inhabitants of the building neither respect him as their new landlord nor care to maintain the building itself. Windows are missing, a makeshift door of sheet metal covers the main entrance, and bullet holes and graffiti

---

14 Wolfgang Schmale, *Geschichte der Männlichkeit in Europa*, 194.
15 Klaus-Michael Bogdal, "Hard-Cold-Fast," 29. Bogdal outlines a number of challenges to the Enlightenment-era model of masculinity throughout its history, not just in the second half of the twentieth century. However, he sees no real change to the way masculinity itself is conceptualized in our society. Klaus-Michael Bogdal, "Hard-Cold-Fast," 38. This opinion contrasts with Schmale's, who sees a change from the hegemonic masculinity construction to a polymorphous masculinity at the turn of the millennium. Wolfgang Schmale, *Geschichte der Männlichkeit in Europa*, 240. For their full discussions of these topics, see Klaus-Michael Bogdal, "Hard-Cold-Fast," 29–38 and Wolfgang Schmale, *Geschichte der Männlichkeit in Europa*, 229–240. For further reading on post-war German masculinities as a response to the hegemonic masculinity of the war generation, see Roy Jerome ed., *Conceptions of Postwar German Masculinity* (Albany: State University of New York Press, 2001).
16 Klaus-Michael Bogdal, "Hard-Cold-Fast," 29–38; Wolfgang Schmale, *Geschichte der Männlichkeit in Europa*, 173–194,

reading "EAT THE RICH" and "BUILDINGS BELONG TO THEIR OCCUPANTS"[17] adorn the walls. The dilapidation of the building itself – "that it was still standing seemed miraculous"[18] – points to the precariousness of Eduard's inheritance as a bolster to his gender identity. To add injury to insult (and not the other way around), Eduard's new tenants shoot light munitions at him from the rooftop, grazing his neck and forcing him to retreat.

On the surface, the challenges the building presents to Eduard seem separate from issues of gender. However, one source of these challenges is almost immediately localized on the body of a female inhabitant. Not only has the tenement building fallen into disrepair; it is also burdened by a mortgage dating from the GDR. Eduard is now personally responsible for the costs of renovation, the mortgage, and the squatters' unbridled utility use, altogether estimated at over half a million Deutsche Mark. When Eduard tries to have utility services cancelled, however, his attorney informs him that a pregnant woman is living among the squatters, and thus the group is protected by law. The city will not discontinue utilities, and Eduard will be financially responsible for paying the costs. Thus, the pregnant body enacts the first "emasculation" of Eduard in the text, severely restricting his rights to his property and curtailing his financial independence, both of which are central to conventional Western concepts of masculinity as described by Bogdal and Schmale.

The pregnant body confounds Eduard since it disrupts the property relations that he has just entered into. The novel has coded property relations as the domain of men, and thus Eduard has difficulty accepting that a woman's body might be the deciding factor in a property issue. (To be sure, this is a different dynamic than the patriarchal connection between a pregnant body and a house in *Where Love Begins*, discussed in chapter 4, in which Jason makes a property decision for the pregnant Stella. In *Eduard's Homecoming* the pregnant woman has control over her body and her living arrangements.) What is more, this pregnancy protects a group of people who wish to undermine conventional property relations. The leadership of the squatter group is multi-generational and multi-gendered. Eduard is more accustomed to handling matters of property among men and does not know how to interact with this group, in which a pregnant woman and a young boy turn out to be the most visible representatives.

Vera Rheinland, the pregnant squatter, is only the first woman to threaten Eduard's sense of security in his masculinity. His wife Jenny is far more impact-

---

17 Peter Schneider, *Eduard's Homecoming*, 18. Originally: "EAT THE RICH" is in English; "DIE HÄUSER DENEN DIE DARIN WOHNEN." Peter Schneider, *Eduards Heimkehr*, 30.
18 Peter Schneider, *Eduard's Homecoming*, 18. Originally: "ein Wunder daß es noch stand." Peter Schneider, *Eduards Heimkehr*, 29–30.

ful. Since arriving in Berlin, Eduard cannot shake the memory of their last sexual activity before his flight, when Jenny asked him mid-coitus if he had remembered to go to his dental appointment. Eduard would have preferred that she focus on having an orgasm rather than on his dental hygiene, and the memory of that frustration lingers. Once Jenny arrives in Berlin, Eduard asks her over dinner about her sexual satisfaction, specifically, how often she has had orgasms with him. When pressed, she admits that she has only ever had one orgasm, and that it was with another man:

> I don't know, it was crazy and dangerous, that's all – very romantic, too. Picture a couple on the north face of the Eiger, and the man tells his female companion, whom he's never even touched before, that he must either take her on the edge of the precipice, here and now, or jump to his death right away. [...] Women are princesses – you know that, or you should. They may adore you, but they still want you to risk your life to conquer them.[19]

The news of Jenny's inability to orgasm during sex with him, and her one orgasm with another man, sends Eduard reeling. He becomes fixated on figuring out how to make Jenny have an orgasm so that he can repair his "male self-esteem" ("Mannesstolz"), as he puts it.[20] (Here and elsewhere in this chapter where it is important to represent Eduard's thinking, I intentionally use language that reflects his egocentric attitude that men are supposed to cause orgasms in women.) Over the course of the novel, he seeks advice from sex manuals and friends and has dreams that suggest methods for making Jenny have an orgasm, all of which fail. At one point, Jenny shuts down a conversation on the topic, exasperated by Eduard's attempts to figure out the mechanics of her sexuality. Eduard's crisis turns out to be not only financial and social, but also sexual and gendered. Schneider's novel serves thus as a *Zeitdokument* in a way that has not yet been accounted for in the scholarship: it signals the masculinity crisis at the turn of the millennium that Breger and others have described.

The chauvinism pervading Schneider's text is undeniable. Jenny is presented as an emasculating woman who, while fully competent and career-oriented, states that she, like "all women," needs a hero and wants to be conquered.

---

19 Peter Schneider, *Eduard's Homecoming*, 90. Originally: "Ich weiß nicht, es war eben verrückt, extrem und sehr romantisch. Stell dir ein Paar in der Eigernordwand vor, und der Mann eröffnet seiner bis dahin unberührten Begleiterin im Angesicht des Abgrunds, daß er sie jetzt und für immer auf diesem Felsvorsprung haben oder sich auf der Stelle in die Tiefe stürzen müsse. [...] Du weißt oder solltest wissen, daß Frauen Prinzessinnen sind. Auch wenn sie über dich promovieren, sie wollen immer, daß du dein Leben riskierst, um sie zu erobern." Peter Schneider, *Eduards Heimkehr*, 126–127.
20 Peter Schneider, *Eduard's Homecoming*, 101. Peter Schneider, *Eduards Heimkehr*, 141.

Eduard enjoys admiring her from afar or when she is asleep, attracted to her childlike face on a woman's body – an infantilizing male fantasy. Up close and awake, she is withholding, preferring to place obstacles in Eduard's way rather than work toward their mutual satisfaction. The riddle she seems to put before him on how best to achieve an orgasm for her (or, actually, an orgasm for her for himself) seems out of touch with the more liberated sexuality of the 68ers, their own generation. Perhaps even worse are the conversations between men about women's sexuality, which range from laughable to infuriating. Eduard and his friend Theo debate whether the female orgasm is biologically superfluous, "a pleasurable irrelevance,"[21] or whether it serves the purpose of loyalty, "biological proof of fidelity, a pledge that no other male is intruding into the biological chain."[22] In a bout of self-pity Eduard even asks himself: "What was the significance of his wish to induce a sensation that other cultures forcibly eliminated by means of ritual female circumcision?"[23] With that self-congratulatory question, he fails to recognize the assumption he shares with those who practice clitorectomy: that men should wield control over women's sexual satisfaction.

Marina, a second romantic interest for Eduard, serves as a counterpoint to Jenny in Eduard's sexual crisis. However, she is just as much a male fantasy as Jenny is. After Jenny returns to San Francisco, Eduard begins having an affair with his colleague Marina, who extols East German women for being freer and more satisfied with their sexuality, having evaded the traps of Western feminism: "Wouldn't [East German women] make ideal partners for West German men who'd been rattled by the women's libbers? 'Self-confident professionals but – wonder of wonders – feminine notwithstanding!'"[24] She repeats the statistic that Eduard had read earlier in the newspaper that East German women have more orgasms than West German women, attributing that finding to their less strained relationship to femininity. However, Marina is still not able to mend

---

[21] Peter Schneider, *Eduard's Homecoming*, 108. Originally: "eine schöne Nebensache." Peter Schneider, *Eduards Heimkehr*, 150.

[22] Peter Schneider, *Eduard's Homecoming*, 109. Originally: "der biologische Beweis der Treue, ein Versprechen darauf, daß sich kein anderer in die biologische Kette mischt." Peter Schneider, *Eduards Heimkehr*, 151.

[23] Peter Schneider, *Eduard's Homecoming*, 155. Originally: "Was hatte es zu bedeuten daß er eine weibliche Fähigkeit, die andere Kulturen mit dem Ritual der Klitorisbeschneidung gewalttätig beseitigten, herbeizwingen wollte?" Peter Schneider, *Eduards Heimkehr*, 213.

[24] Peter Schneider, *Eduard's Homecoming*, 250. Originally: "Seien sie nicht die idealen Partnerinnen für den von Emanzipationsdebatten verstörten westdeutschen Mann? 'Selstbewußt, berufstätig und, o Wunder, dennoch weiblich!'" Peter Schneider, *Eduards Heimkehr*, 331.

Eduard's ego. He is so defeated by his wife's inability to have an orgasm with him that when he and Marina sleep together, he cannot believe he has assisted in her sexual climax: "All that irked him was the notion that he might only be a surrogate – that Marina's explosions owed nothing at all to himself and his skill as a lover."[25] To be sure, Schneider has authored a confident, self-assured female character in order to voice the perspective that women's liberation has done lasting damage to the fragile male ego. Marina leaves the narrative after serving that purpose, falling in love with Eduard despite herself (another male fantasy), and breaking off the relationship to save herself further heartbreak.

After two sources of emasculation have been established in the text – a financial one brought on by a pregnant female body and a sexual one brought about by a sexually "frigid" and withholding wife – a third emasculation occurs when Eduard must face Germans' obligations to the Nazi past. Eduard learns through the squatters' efforts to delegitimize his property claim that his grandfather, formerly a Nazi party member, may have acquired the building from a Jewish family through a coerced sale. Eduard's lawyer informs him that his right of inheritance is binding, and, having missed the deadline to renounce his claim, it would constitute absconding if he were to leave now. These financial and historical problems are inescapable and thus overwhelming to Eduard. The tenement building has lured him into a trap: by accepting the inherited property, he is no longer able to disavow his personal responsibility to the past.

As a member of the 68 generation, Eduard believes he had already addressed Germany's past sufficiently. However, the novel evidences various ways in which members of that generation have defaulted on their ideals. Klott, Eduard's lawyer and formerly a Maoist activist during their university days, now profits from the changing property relations in the newly unified Germany. His corpulence and excessive eating habits, a stark contrast from Eduard's memory of him as a student, reflect his willingness to "feed on" others' financial fortunes (and misfortunes) in the neoliberal process of privatization. Eduard's inheritance similarly motivates him to distance himself from the person he was three decades earlier. He now faults his generation for having utilized a rhetoric of blame and self-righteousness, having condemned an entire society rather than judging individuals.[26] Now that his family history could jeopardize his inheri-

---

25 Peter Schneider, *Eduard's Homecoming*, 254. Originally: "Nur noch aus der Erinnerung steifte ihn der Gedanke, daß er vielleicht nur ein Stellvertreter war, daß es auf ihn und seine Künste gar nicht ankam, um Marinas Explosionen auszulösen." Peter Schneider, *Eduards Heimkehr*, 336.
26 See Susanne Rinner, "Intergenerational Conflicts and Intercultural Relations: Peter Schneider's *Eduards Heimkehr*," *Gegenwartsliteratur: A German Studies Yearbook* 7 (2008): 207.

tance, Eduard abandons the practice of assigning blanket blame. It is more advantageous to him to find out if his grandfather might have been innocent after all.

Furthermore, Eduard has long felt burdened by Germany's past in his marriage to Jenny, who is Jewish.[27] Eduard recalls, for example, that during her first pregnancy, she feared telling her mother that the father is German. He also recounts watching the celebrations of November 9, 1989 on television with Jenny, his own enthusiasm tempered by her mistrust of a potentially unified Germany. In these moments, German collective responsibility for the Nazi past emerges in unexpected ways in his marriage and causes tension between the two. Thus, whereas Marina blames feminism for the reportedly low sexual satisfaction of Western women relative to Eastern women, the novel seems to indicate that a stronger factor in Eduard's marriage is Germany's responsibility for National Socialism and the Holocaust.

Not only does Eduard experience a sexual crisis at the same time as he is learning about his family's possible involvement in Nazi crimes; it turns out that he will need to rehabilitate his grandfather as a "good German" before he can solve his problem with Jenny. Eduard becomes embroiled in a media controversy on a national scale when the squatters identify another possible claimant on the property, a Jewish woman named Edita Schlandt whose family was reportedly coerced into selling their property in an Aryanization process in 1933. The squatters see Eduard as an opportunist, ready to profit from the crimes of his family, and they stage a protest in front of the Palace of the Republic. In doing so, they elegantly tie Eduard's property inheritance to a larger debate on identity and Western colonization in the unifying Berlin. However, when he visits Edita Schlandt, Eduard learns that the squatters are mistaken. His grandfather, Egon Hoffmann, was close friends with Edita's father, Kasimir Marwitz. Egon not only used his position within the Nazi party to slow the Aryanization of Kasimir's business, but he also saved the family by buying the apartment building that Kasimir owned, paying 25% above market value so that the family could emigrate. Eduard returns to Berlin relieved of his guilt, secure that his inheritance of the building is rightful, and lamenting the fact that Germany does not celebrate heroes like his grandfather.

The most troublesome aspect of Schneider's novel is his willingness to create characters for the purpose of excusing Eduard (read as an average West German man) of any real responsibility. Thus while Eduard does a great deal of soul

---

27 See also Susanne Rinner, *The German Student Movement and the Literary Imagination: Transnational Memories of Protest and Dissent* (New York and Oxford: Berghahn, 2013), 46–47.

searching in the novel, he does not actually grow as a person. Marina exists in Schneider's novel to lambast feminism for being emasculating rather than to assist Eduard in developing more equitable thinking about sex. Edita's role is even more problematic, as she exists to absolve Eduard of his guilt about the past and to suggest a different, less burdensome way to deal with it. First, Edita scoffs at the idea of donating the building or its proceeds to an organization like the Jewish Claims Conference. It's "just goyish nonsense,"[28] she says, that Eduard should feel guilty about inheriting the building and profiting from it. Second, she says she does not understand why Germany has forgotten the good citizens of the Nazi era: "Why is it always us, the rescued, who plant trees for the few Germans who helped us and pin medals on their chests? Why don't you do that? Any German third-grader can spell the names of Hitler, Goebbels, and Eichmann, but he's never heard of the Egons."[29] By using Egon's first name after listing some of the most infamous last names of the Third Reich, Edita differentiates between normal citizens and the genocidal Nazi machine, asserting that Germans should supplement the nation's official historical memory with a commemoration of the nation's forgotten everyday heroes. This thinking, of course, excuses the society at large of its responsibility for the genocidal system, and Eduard, who previously felt that he had been offered up to "the Moloch of German guilt"[30] can proceed, alleviated that his grandfather was one of the good guys. With this conscience cleared, he can profit from the sale of the tenement building, regardless of the fact that it came into his family through the tragedy that Edita's family experienced.[31]

---

28 Peter Schneider, *Eduard's Homecoming*, 275. Originally: "so ein gojischer Krampf." Peter Schneider, *Eduards Heimkehr*, 366.
29 Peter Schneider, *Eduard's Homecoming*, 275. Originally: "Warum sind es immer nur wir, die Geretteten, die für die paar Deutschen, die geholfen haben, Bäume pflanzen und ihnen Orden an die Brust heften? Warum macht ihr das nicht? Jeder Volksschüler bei euch kann die Namen Hitler, Goebbels, Eichmann buchstabieren, aber er weiß nichts von den Egons." Peter Schneider, *Eduards Heimkehr*, 366.
30 Peter Schneider, *Eduard's Homecoming*, 236. Originally: "das Ungeheuer der deutschen Schuld." Peter Schneider, *Eduards Heimkehr*, 314.
31 A number of scholars have addressed Edita as Schneider's mouthpiece in this scene. Susanne Rinner sees her character as Schneider's attempt to bring a Jewish perspective into a discourse that otherwise makes no room for it. See Susan Rinner, "Intergenerational Conflicts," 207, 216. Colin Riordan applauds Schneider for trying to approximate a Jewish perspective, albeit with qualifications. Colin Riordan, "German-Jewish Relations in the Works of Peter Schneider," in *Jews in German Literature since 1945: German-Jewish Literature?*, ed. Pól O'Dochartaigh (Amsterdam: Rodopi, 2000), 634. Ulrich Baer is much less forgiving, arguing that Schneider "presumes to have written himself 'free,' transcended these struggles, and killed off the previous generation's troubles in his novels." Ulrich Baer, "The Hubris of Humility: Günter Grass, Peter

Now that Eduard no longer feels burdened by collective guilt, he can set his other affairs right. The squatters unexpectedly decide to purchase the building, realizing that the only way to preserve their collective way of life is to become property owners themselves. They negotiate Eduard down to 850,000 Deutsche Mark, a third of the originally stated worth, but the deal also relieves him of his financial burden to the city. The conventional property relations, and thus the foundation of the hegemonic construction of masculinity, have been restored to an acceptable degree. With renewed confidence, Eduard is then able to confront Jenny in the novel's final scene. After a session of attempted love making, in which she becomes distracted, Eduard accuses her of not loving him and leaves. However, Eduard inadvertently chooses the wrong door out of the room and, because of construction work underway on the building where they are staying in Berlin, he falls a floor down into a swimming pool below. Once he is back in their apartment, bruised but not terribly injured, Jenny manipulates his penis, crawls on top of him, and has her first orgasm with him. He has risked his life for her, which is all she ever wanted from him, or as she puts it: "a man who would risk his life for the woman of a lifetime – risk his neck to conquer me."[32]

While Jenny's newfound ability to orgasm is mysterious – "When you disappeared into space like that, something snapped inside me"[33] – all Eduard has done is stand up to her. With his newfound confidence rooted in having participated in, and profited from, the conventional property relations, and having unburdened himself from the guilt of Germany's past, Eduard will no longer tolerate his wife's apparent lack of sexual interest in him – and this does the trick for her. Now that his confidence is restored, his masculinity crisis is resolved and his wife can perform sexually as *he* desires.

Schneider, and German Guilt After 1989," *Germanic Review* 80, no. 1 (2005): 70. Whereas Susanne Rinner argues for the necessity of an ongoing dialogue between survivors and the descendants of perpetrators, Baer argues that this kind of dialogue can be traumatic and dehumanizing to Jewish people asked to participate in them. Susanne Rinner, *The German Student Movement and the Literary Imagination*, 47; Ulrich Baer, "The Hubris of Humility," 51–53.

32 Peter Schneider, *Eduard's Homecoming*, 307. Originally: "ein Mann, der für die Frau seines Lebens sein Leben waagt, einer, der Kopf und Kragen aufs Spiel setzt, um mich zu erobern." Peter Schneider, *Eduards Heimkehr*, 407.

33 Peter Schneider, *Eduard's Homecoming*, 307. Originally: "Als du so plötzlich vor meinen Augen über die Dächer verschwunden bist, da ist irgend etwas bei mir gerissen." Peter Schneider, *Eduards Heimkehr*, 407.

Threatening Women, Threatening Landscapes in *Rain*

Given that novels require months, if not years, of work, it seems remarkable that two novels would appear in the same year that frame the property relations in the former East Germany in the same particular way. Like Eduard in *Eduard's Homecoming*, Leon in Karen Duve's *Rain* assumes ownership of a property in the East without fully understanding the responsibilities and liabilities such an endeavor entails, becomes overwhelmed by them, and subsequently experiences a masculinity crisis. However, some important differences exists between the two men's struggles. For one, masculinity means something different to Leon than it does to Eduard. While the hegemonic masculine construct that Eduard follows requires him to manage his property, finances, historical obligations, and wife's sexual satisfaction, for Leon, masculinity has to do with maintaining control over his body and physical environment. Perpetually feeling inadequate, Leon pursues his elusive masculine ideal by driving a Mercedes, keeping his body lean, seeking out the validation of men he regards as more masculine than himself, and trying to maintain control over the physical condition of the house that he has purchased in the former East Germany. Whereas Eduard faces off against human-caused forces (historical, political, and economic) that jeopardize his financial stability and weaken his sense of self-worth, Leon in *Rain* must contend with natural and material forces that endanger him physically. The run-down house in the countryside perpetually threatens to fall in on him, and one false step on the property's marshy landscape could result in drowning. In the end, the men experience different outcomes to their masculinity crises. Whereas Eduard regains his self-confidence by profiting from his inheritance, clearing his family name, and watching his wife have an orgasm assisted by his penis, Leon loses control of both body and mind, a crisis that leads to his eventual death.

Leon's male chauvinism, his insistence on a construction of masculinity that privileges men over women and non-human nature, is established in the novel's opening scene. Leon and his wife Martina are traveling into Mecklenburg to visit the house they plan to purchase on a marshland, a beautiful rural setting that Leon is sure will inspire his talents as a writer. While on their way, they discover a corpse floating in a river by the side of the road, an inauspicious sign of Leon's fate within this Eastern countryside where water, death, and femininity prevail. The narrator's description of the corpse, focalized through Martina's perspective, presages the eventual triumph of materiality's agency over human subjectivity while foregrounding gender:

> The flesh looked crumbly, as if you could pick it off with your bare hands. Martina wondered if the woman had been young when she died. Yes, very likely. [...] She had very long hair. Black hair. Pitch-black hair which must once have fallen to her hips, and was now drifting in the slow current. [...] It had no eyes. [...] It looked so soft, that body, so vulnerable. Fine strands of green waterweed were entwined in its pubic hair.[34]

Martina notes the crumbling flesh, a body material so transformed that it now shows little connection with the human life it was once a part of. The eyes are missing, a symbol of lost subjectivity, and Martina wonders about the age of the woman when she died. In contrast to Martina, who recognizes the murdered woman's vulnerability and the loss of her lived potential, Leon impassively pokes the corpse with a stick to find out if the skin would rip. A number of scholars have attributed Leon's cruel curiosity in this moment to a male chauvinism that is sanctioned both in the scientific and the literary traditions, that is, in the objectifying eye of scientific observation and the poetic fascination with the "beautiful female corpse" in literature.[35] The female floating corpse, of course, recalls *Hamlet*'s Ophelia,[36] and, especially in a German cultural context, the "pitch-black hair" references the death-like sleep of Snow White.

---

34 Karen Duve, *Rain*, trans. Anthea Bell (New York: Bloomsbury, 2002), 6. Originally: "Das Fleisch sah mürbe aus – als ob man es mit bloßen Händen reißen könnte. Martina fragte sich, ob die Frau jung gewesen war, als sie starb. Wahrscheinlich war sie jung. [...] Sie besaß unerhört lange Haare. Schwarze Haare. Pechschwarze Haare, die ihr einmal bis auf die Hüften gefallen sein mußten. Jetzt wiegten sie sich in der trägen Strömung [...] Die Augäpfel fehlten. [...] Er sah so weich aus, dieser Leib, so verletzlich. Im Schamhaar wuchsen feine grüne Algenfäden." Karen Duve, *Regenroman* (Berlin: Eichborn, 1999), 12–13.
35 Elizabeth Boa, "Lust or Disgust? The Blurring of Boundaries in Karen Duve's *Regenroman*," in *Pushing Boundaries: Approaches to Contemporary German Women Writers from Karen Duve to Jenny Erpenbeck*, ed. Heike Bartel and Elizabeth Boa (Amsterdam: Rodopi, 2006), 63–64; Alexandra M. Hill, "The Violent Turn: West German Women as Victims of Neoliberalism," *German Quarterly* 91, no. 2 (2018): 143; Teresa Ludden, "Nature, Bodies, and Breakdowns in Anne Duden's *Das Landhaus* and Karen Duve's *Regenroman*," in *Pushing at Boundaries: Approaches to Contemporary German Women Writers from Karen Duve to Jenny Erpenbeck*, ed. Heike Bartel and Elizabeth Boa (Amsterdam: Rodopi, 2006), 49; Anna Richards, "'Ob Mädchen oder Hunde': Women and Animals in Karen Duve's *Regenroman*," *German Life and Letters* 71, no. 4 (2018): 496.
36 For a discussion of the corpse as an allusion to Ophelia, see Elizabeth Boa, "Lust or Disgust," 63, and Elisa Müller-Adams, "'De Nymphis, Sylphis, Pygmaeis et Salamandris': Zur Verwendung eines Motivkreises in Texten von Michael Fritz, Julia Schoch und Karen Duve," in *Pushing at Boundaries: Approaches to Contemporary German Women Writers from Karen Duve to Jenny Erpenbeck*, ed. Heike Bartel and Elizabeth Boa (Amsterdam: Rodopi, 2006), 81. For further discussions of intertextuality and aesthetic influence on Duve's novel, see Elizabeth Boa, "Lust or Disgust," 58, 64–66; Monika Shafi, "Spaces of Violence," 373–388; and Axel Goodbody, "Na-

In addition to Martina, who identifies or at least sympathizes, with the woman who lost her life, and Leon, who objectifies the corpse, a third agent in this scene is indifferent to both characters' associations and priorities: non-human nature. The algae growing in the pubic hair connects sexuality, materiality, and death, while also pointing to the fact that human subjectivity must eventually give way to other non-human forces. The agency of materiality – of the natural world, the house, and the human body – will stand at odds against human will in this novel, particularly against Leon's as he tries to assert control over his environment. The novel's narration supports this theme. Shifting focalization often between Martina (whose perspective we follow at the beginning and end of the novel), Leon, others in their community, and even, in one instance, the dog that they adopt, the novel emphasizes that Leon is only one of many actors within the material environment.

Leon and Martina are both Western urbanites hailing from Hamburg, yet they have different motivations, instincts, and abilities when interacting with the new home and landscape. While Martina is moving to the East with Leon to escape her controlling father, Leon seeks the quietude of the countryside in order to write "thick, weighty books of a mature, judicious man."[37] Martina's decision is thus a pragmatic act of self-preservation, whereas Leon's is ego-centric. Leon also bases his decision on somewhat misleading cultural notions about pastoral life, believing that the marsh will provide him the time and quietude to write serious books because the ideal of *Heimat* promises a natural and easy relationship to nature.

As he and Martina arrive at the property for the first time, however, the landscape mimicks the fact that Leon's judgment is clouded:

> There were the marshes. [...] Directly behind the house began a matted carpet of bright green tussocks of vegetation interspersed by circular, dark-brown pools. A meadow of tall swamp grass adjoined it, stretching a long way, up to a row of pines. The overcast sky had taken on a pastel-blue tint. Above the trees two long, diagonal rifts broke though the cloud cover, with yellow sunbeams descending from them to earth [...]. There was a purple haze over the marshes, making most of the outlines blur in psychedelic lighting effects."[38]

---

ture's Revenge: The Ecological Adaptation of Traditional Narratives in Fifty Years of German-Speaking Writing." *Tamkang Review* 37, no. 1 (2006): 20–22.

[37] Karen Duve, *Rain*, 22. Originally: "[d]icke, schwere Bücher eines abgeklärten, gereiften Mannes." Karen Duve, *Regenroman*, 32.

[38] Karen Duve, *Rain*, 26. Originally: "Da war das Moor. [...] Eine Wiese aus hohem Sumpfgras schloß sich an. Weit, weit erstreckte sie sich bis zu einer Reihe Moorkiefern. Der verhangene Himmel hatte eine blaue Pastellfarbe angenommen. Nur über die Bäumen durchbrachen zwei

Leon is dumbstruck by the vision of romantic beauty that the fog over the marsh creates. The narrative focalization then shifts to Martina to lampoon him. She has little patience for Leon's maudlin posturing, as he was "staring at the marshes with a happy grin on his face. He looked silly."[39] While Leon gapes at the landscape, Martina goes about the work of inspecting the house, noting repairs that would have to be made and envisioning improvements. In this first encounter with the house and countryside, Martina demonstrates clear-sightedness where Leon does not.

Leon soon learns that life in the countryside is more demanding than the *Heimat* ideal supposes. Rather than spending his days in intellectual pursuit, inspired by the quiet landscape, Leon's time and energy are consumed by his efforts to mitigate the damage that the never-ending rains cause to his house. He must try to repair the plumbing when the toilet, bathtub, and sinks back up; figure out how to dry the walls and foundation of the house; collect and transport the buckets full of slugs that invade and make the floors dangerously slippery; and chase away the frogs that make a cacophonous noise and further keep him from writing. The hazardous marshland that surrounds the house constantly flows inward, despite Leon and Martina's best efforts to keep it at bay. Indeed, the house and marshland resemble an organism with a will and agency, threatening to consume the new residents. As Monika Shafi has phrased it, it is "a true 'house of horrors' that offers only a lethal escape."[40]

The novel establishes early on that Leon is unaccustomed to physical labor and can only perform it clumsily, which makes him feel inadequate as a man. After discovering the corpse at the beginning of the novel, Leon and Martina stop at an auto repair shop so that Martina can report it to the police and Leon can have an attendant fix windshield wipers on his Mercedes. When the mechanic inadvertently makes Leon feel incompetent for being unable to fix the problem himself, Leon replies that he need not fill his head with "prole knowledge" ("Proletwissen")[41] when he can pay others to do that labor for

---

lange schräge Risse Wolkendecke, aus denen gelbe Sonnenstrahlen auf die Erde hinunterstießen [...]. Violetter Dunst lag über dem Moor und ließ die meisten Konturen in psychedelischen Lichteffekten verschwimmen [...]" Karen Duve, *Regenroman*, 36.

39 Karen Duve, *Rain*, 27. Originally: "starrte [...] mit glücklich vererttem Gesicht auf das Moor. Dumm sah er aus." Karen Duve, *Regenroman*, 38.

40 Monika Shafi, "Spaces of Violence: On the Role of Home, Nature and Gender in Narratives by Karen Duve and Felicitas Hoppe," in *Violence, Culture and Identity: Essays on German and Austrian Literature, Politics and Society*, ed. Helen Chambers (Oxford: Peter Lang, 2006), 383.

41 Karen Duve, *Regenroman*, 19. This is my translation. Anthea Bell's translation of this word as "proletarian skills" loses the pejorative intent of Leon's assertion.

him. This classist assertion meant to punish the attendant conceals his embarrassment for lacking what he considers to be quintessential male qualities: "A real man was someone who earned big money, had a house, fathered children, knew how to repair cars and never failed to open a jar of pickled cucumbers. A real man could always get a hard-on when it mattered, and that was that."[42] According to Leon, a man has control over his body, his family, and his material environment. His views on masculinity thus resemble the hegemonic construct outlined by Bogdal and Schmale.

Leon's fatal character flaw, that for which he will be punished in this novel, is his male chauvinism. Duve has created a version *Heimat* that insists on the kinds of intra-actions within the environment that I discussed in chapters 1 and 2 of this monograph. However, this version of *Heimat* is far more severe than those represented in the cultural productions already discussed. Whereas the characters in *Taxi to Rathenow, Our House,* and *The Same Old Song* see the labor of intra-acting within the environment positively, having earned them the right to call a place their *Heimat*, in *Rain*, Leon sees this labor as an undue burden, believing that he deserves an easy connection to *Heimat* as a Western man with purchasing power. For this kind of thinking, Leon will be punished. Nature in this novel will not be sculpted by humans who wish to maintain a *Heimat* ideal; rather, nature seeks a full enmeshment of humans and the physical environment.

Heimat in *Rain* thus resembles what Stacy Alaimo calls a "trans-corporal space," that is, a space read for the ways in which materialities and agencies interact and enmesh. According to Alaimo, the natural world and the human one are both shaped by the same forces. She writes that the "'body' and 'nature' are comprised of the same material, which has been constituted, simultaneously, by the forces of evolution, natural and human history, political inequities, cultural contestations, biological and chemical processes, and other factors too numerous to list."[43] By recognizing that we are not materially distinct entities from our physical environment or one another, we are freed from the "delusions of grandeur that place us far above a base nature."[44] This understanding allows

---

[42] Karen Duve, *Rain*, 21. Originally: "Ein Mann war jemand, der einen Haufen Geld verdiente, ein Haus besaß, Kinder zeugte, Autos reparieren konnte und jedes Gurkenglas aufbekam. Ein Mann war jemand, der einen stehen hatte, wenn es darauf ankam – und damit fertig." Karen Duve, *Regenroman*, 30.
[43] Stacy Alaimo, "Trans-Corporal Feminisms and the Ethical Space of Nature," in *Material Feminisms*, ed. Stacy Alaimo and Susan Hekman (Bloomington and Indianapolis: Indianapolis University Press), 257.
[44] Stacy Alaimo, "Trans-Corporal Feminisms," 258.

us to conceive of other agencies and organizing principles active in nature that are separate from, but on par with, human subjectivity. In *Rain*, the landscape refuses to allow Leon to see himself as separate from and superior to it, which initiates his masculinity crisis as a new homeowner in the Eastern countryside. To make matters worse for Leon, women outnumber men in the area and prove to be much more adept at living in the treacherous marsh than he is. The *Heimat* thus becomes the trans-corporal space that equalizes materialities and agencies and makes their inextricability evident.

Within the trans-corporal space, the function of the house itself must be rethought. Whereas Leon understands the house to be separate from nature, a man-made structure that should serve as a hardened extension of himself, a Theweleitian "body armor" (*Körperpanzer*) that protects him against the uncontainable threat of watery nature[45] and an indication of his success as a man, another reading of the house is much more compelling. Alaimo calls for an understanding of agency in the material world, such that "nonhuman nature or the human body can 'talk back,' resist, or otherwise affect its cultural construction."[46] I contend that if we think broadly about non-human agency in the material world, dilapidation emerges as an important form of material agency that houses assert. Dilapidation, decay, crumbling, and warping are ways that the materials composing a house "talk back" and assert their agency against human will. The constant negotiation that takes place between dilapidating houses and people forms a particular intra-action of humans, environment, and technology. In this paradigm, the house is not to be conceived of as an extension of Leon, but rather, as part of the material world that brings to light Leon's enmeshment within it.

When the watery environment threatens the integrity of Leon's house, exacerbating his overall sense of inadequacy as a man, Duve is drawing on a long literary and artistic tradition of depicting men's anxieties about being engulfed in the material world. In his foundational work *Male Fantasies*, Klaus Theweleit has famously shown that female mythical and folkloric characters like dangerous and seductive water nymphs, naiads, nixies, and mermaids have long served as an expression of men's fears of both the material world and "uncontainable" femininity.[47] Indeed, Duve has stated that she was reading *Male Fantasies* while writing *Rain*.[48] According to Theweleit, men in various historical contexts, most

---

45 Klaus Theweleit, *Male Fantasies*, trans. Stephen Conway, et al. (Minneapolis: University of Minnesota Press, 1987), 300. Theweleit's work was orignally published as *Männerphantasien* in 1977.
46 Stacy Alaimo, "Trans-corporal Feminisms," 242.
47 Klaus Theweleit, *Male Fantasies*, 236–310.
48 Teresa Ludden, "Nature, Bodies, and Breakdowns, 51.

notably during wartime, have felt obliged to undertake a "steeling up" of the male body against the "flowing" and "soft" femininity of their mothers, lovers, and even war enemies (who were often coded feminine in war propaganda).[49] To be sure, this steeled up version of masculinity is what Leon strives for. He idolizes men who are muscular, athletic, and have control of their bodies and bodily fluids, like the boxer and pimp, Benno Pfitzner, whose biography he is writing.

Parodying this literary tradition, Duve's female characters prove to be much more capable than Leon is of surviving on the watery marsh. However, the novel nimbly avoids essentialist notions about women's perceived proximity to nature by presenting a range of women who exhibit varying degrees of femininity and masculinity. Martina has already been established as fashionable and hard-bodied, practicing a femininity that represents the Western, neoliberal culture of self-optimization, self-monitoring, and self-discipline, as Alexandra Merley Hill has argued.[50] Martina and Leon's nearest neighbors, the sisters Isadora and Kay, perform gender quite differently. Isadora is a short, curvy "earth-mother" type who wears clothes and jewelry with nature motifs in watery blue and green hues. Kay, by contrast, is a tall, thin, and decidedly masculine lesbian who wears overalls and work boots.[51] Whereas Isadora is in touch with nature, the marsh, and sex, Kay understands construction and machines. In this environment, women prevail, whether more feminine or more masculine in their gender expression. The only cis-gendered man in the area aside from Leon is the village grocer, Guido Kerbel, who also exhibits an affinity with the feminine, dressing in women's clothes for his own sexual pleasure.

Leon detests the femininity associated with the watery landscape in the novel, but is also seduced by it, especially by Isadora, the marsh incarnate. In a scene of voyeurism that recalls Melusine, Leon glimpses Isadora while she is bathing in the marsh outside his window and mistakes her initially for the corpse he and Martina saw earlier:

> Suddenly he had such a shock that he felt it in his fingers like physical pain [...]. There was the drowned woman just beyond the fence – in one of the marshy pools. She was up to her belly in the mud, and her skin was so white that it shone. Long black hair fell over the

---

[49] Klaus Theweleit, *Male Fantasies*, 229–310.
[50] Alexandra M. Hill, "The Violent Turn," 142.
[51] Teresa Ludden, "Nature, Bodies, and Breakdowns," 50. Elisa Müller-Adams argues that Duve is taking a feminist approach to the woman-as-nature, woman-as-water trope in German literature, reclaiming the mermaid/nymph/siren by bringing her into the world of parody and the grotesque so that she can enact her revenge on the male-authored tradition represented here by Leon. Elisa Müller-Adams, "De Nymphis," 84. See also Elizabeth Boa, "Lust or Disgust," 63–64.

upper part of her body. [...] She was not alone. A smooth skull was moving between the rosey islands of her knees.⁵²

Not only does the corpse motif return as an evocation of sex, death, and femininity in this scene; but Isadora's actions strengthen those associations. Upon approaching her, Leon interrupts what may be a sexual encounter between Isadora and an animal, person, or the remains thereof, as she appears to be playing with a skull between her legs. Then, like a siren who lures men to their deaths, she playfully dashes away. Leon chases her, nearly meeting his own death when he steps into a hole in the marsh and narrowly avoids being sucked in completely.⁵³

In the sexual encounters between Leon and Isadora that follow, he feels engulfed by her, which foreshadows his own eventual death by consumation with the watery earth at the end of the novel. One night, after again mistaking Isadora for an otherworldly being on the marsh, he follows her to her house, where they have sex. "He lay on top of her. [...] This was the first time he'd ever slept with a fat woman. It was good. She was so [...] so soft. There was so much of her. It was like sleeping with the whole of the marshes."⁵⁴ Leon revels in sex with the marsh personified, but afterwards feels repulsed and ashamed when he observes her body. In a later, more grotesque scene, Isadora appears as the dangerous, consuming marsh when Leon is incapacitated with back pain and cannot physically resist her. She pours a bucket of slugs on his lap, eats one, and forces him to have sex with her. Leon resists, but then has the most satisfying orgasm of his life. Ultimately it is a frightening and shameful experience for Leon to be engulfed by the feminine, incapable of fending Isadora off. Afterwards, his only feeble consolation is that he had an erection, one of the traits of manliness that he had listed previously. Nevertheless, "[h]is triumph in still being able to

---

[52] Karen Duve, *Rain*, 65. Originally: "Plötzlich erschrak er so sehr, daß er den Schreck als körperlichen Schmerz in seinen Fingern spürte [...]. Direkt hinter dem Zaun saß die Wasserleiche – in einem der Moorlöcher. Sie steckte bis zum Bauch im Schlick, und ihre Haut war so weiß, daß sie leuchtete. Auf ihren Oberkörper fiel das schwarze lange Haar. [...] Sie war nicht allein. Zwischen den rosigen Inseln ihrer Knie bewegte sich ein glatter Schädel." Karen Duve, *Regenroman*, 82–83.
[53] Elisa Müller-Adams, "De Nymphis," 82.
[54] Karen Duve, *Rain*, 125. Originally: "Er legt sich auf sie. [...] Es war das erste Mal, daß er mit einer Frau schlief, die dick war. Es war gut. Es war so [...] – so weich. So viel. Als würde er mit dem ganzen Moor schlafen." Karen Duve, *Regenroman*, 152.

get an erection was clouded by the painful fact that he had just been taken against his will by a stupid, fat woman. And that he had enjoyed it too."[55]

Leon's erection is a complicated material circumstance in this scene. As Theresa Ludden has written "The whole experience is linked to a loss of boundary between self and other, where the male ego is positioned as self, and the earth-woman as other."[56] Leon's erection is a significant part of this loss of the self's boundaries, even if he tries to interpret it as the opposite. Theweleit argues that the male body "steels up" in order to delineate itself as separate from its environment and women, which allows the male ego to conceive of itself as distinct and in control.[57] In this scene, however, Leon's hardened body is a physiological response, a material manifestation that the body is, in fact, part of nature. Leon has surrendered to the material circumstance of his environment, and he must acknowledge that his "triumph" of achieving an erection cannot be attributed to his own efforts. Isadora and the marsh challenge Leon's self-concept of being distinct from, and elevated above, nature, showing that a different logic prevails in the material world.

Leon is not the only character punished for male chauvinism. When Pfitzner and his goon Harry arrive at the house and become violent, the women and the landscape render them neutral. Leon initially welcomes the possibility for male companionship when the two men arrive unexpectedly, and he shows his reverence for the masculinity that they perform by putting Martina in a servile position. He refrains from any tender gestures toward her and instead orders her to cook their guests some steaks (arguably, the most macho of all meals). Leon's behavior is confusing to Martina: "It was dawning on her that she didn't really know much about Leon or what mattered to him. The way he looked at that old brute! As if he were God Almighty!"[58] However, her adopted dog Noah understands the pack logic:

---

[55] Karen Duve, *Rain*, 182. Originally: "Sein Triumph, daß er es immer noch bringen konnte, wurde von dem peinlichen Umstand getrübt, daß er gerade von einem fetten, dummen Weib gegen seinen Willen rangenommen worden war. Und daß ihm das auch noch gefallen hatte." Karen Duve, *Regenroman*, 221.
[56] Teresa Ludden, "Nature, Bodies, and Breakdowns in Anne Duden's *Das Landhaus* and Karen Duve's *Regenroman*," in *Pushing at Boundaries: Approaches to Contemporary German Women Writers from Karen Duve to Jenny Erpenbeck*, ed. Heike Bartel and Elizabeth Boa (Amsterdam: Rodopi, 2006), 51.
[57] Klaus Theweleit, *Male Fantasies*, 300–305.
[58] Karen Duve, *Rain*, 105. Originally: "Ihr dämmerte, daß sie nicht besonders viel über Leon wußte oder über die Dinge, die ihm wichtig waren. Wie er den alten, brutalen Kerl ansah. Als wenn er der liebe Gott wäre!" Karen Duve, *Regenroman*, 129.

> Noah sensed the tall, grey-haired man's clarity of mind and overwhelming determination, the kind of determination possessed only by a male dog absolutely certain of his strength. [...] The man by the bookshelves was not to be trusted. He was the kind who would bite and attack without warning. [...] But it looked as if Leon had seen it too and was conducting himself appropriately. That reassured Noah. A respectful display of his own low rank would secure Leon's membership in the pack and spare everyone trouble."⁵⁹

Whereas Leon and Martina understand intuitively that they must perform certain roles around Pfitzner, who exhibits the hegemonic masculinity that Leon idolizes and Martina fears, Noah appears to understand the gendered hierarchy on a conscious level.

Pfitzner has arrived at Leon and Martina's house because he disapproves of Leon's attempt to author him as a psychologically complex character in his biography and wants to intimidate him into revising the manuscript. He asserts his power over Leon by repossessing the Mercedes he had given him as part of the book deal, Leon's main touchstone with his masculinity and his and Martina's only mode of transportation in the countryside. While this constitutes a symbolic emasculation, Pfitzner's second visit brings outright violence: Harry rapes Martina while Pfitzner beats Leon senseless in the next room. However, Martina's rape cannot go unpunished in this environment dominated by women. In a gruesome scene of rescue and revenge, Kay and Isadora break into the house, and Kay burns Harry and Pfitzner alive with a flamethrower. Afterwards, the two sisters know just where to dump the bodies in the marsh. Kay, Isadora, and Martina then abandon Leon in the house as a punishment for his complicity in the toxic behavior that culminated in the violent act.⁶⁰

---

59 Karen Duve, *Rain*, 106–107. Originally: "Noah spürte die Klarheit und überwältigende Entschlossenheit, die von dem großen Grauhaarigen ausging, eine Entschlossenheit, wie sie nur eine Rüde besaß, der sich seiner Macht sehr sicher war. [...] Dem Mann an der Bücherwand war nicht zu trauen. Ein Beißer, und zwar einer, der ohne Vorwarnung angriff. [...] Aber Leon hatte sie anscheinend auch bemerkt und vierhielt sich entsprechend. Das beruhigte Naoh. Ein respektvolles Zurschaustellen des eigenen niederen Ranges würde Leon die Mitgliedschaft im Rudel sichern und allen Ärger ersparen." Karen Duve, *Regenroman*, 131.

60 Scholars have debated the grotesque violence in these scenes. Monika Shafi has suggested that because Duve writes with a Gothic mode anchored in realism that elicits strong emotional response from the reader, *Rain* risks glorifying violence. Monika Shafi, "Spaces of Violence," 381–382, 388. However, as Elizabeth Boa has pointed out, the violence itself is tempered by its cartoonishness, drawing on a tradition of comic strip and pulp fiction violence, while also subverting certain tropes of female wickedness in the literary and film traditions. Elizabeth Boa, "Lust or Disgust," 67–68. Beth Linklater has argued that the violence imparted by women "is not gratuitous, it is about women attempting to wrest back a form of control." Beth Linklater, "'Philomela's Revenge': Challenges to Rape in Recent Writing in German," *Ger-*

Leon has lost all control – of his career, his marriage, his house – and the final loss of control, which builds over the course of the novel but comes to full fruition at its end, is over his body. Bodily control is an important theme in *Rain* and is associated through most of the novel with Martina, who binge eats and purges when under emotional stress. Leon's loss of bodily control begins with his back, which he strains while collecting slugs and digging a trench to dry out the foundation of the house. His back pain incapacitates him repeatedly, as in the scene described above when Isadora rapes him. Spending long stretches of time unable to move, Leon soon gains weight, taking on the curves and corpulence he associates with femininity and particularly Isadora, the watery earth. At the end of the novel, when Martina searches for her hidden stash of sweets to binge and purge, we discover that Leon has also engaged in disordered eating.

Whereas Martina's binge eating and purging can be read as a violence she inflicts upon her body in response to the neoliberal demand for perfection,[61] or perhaps as her own way to "steel up" her body (in a Theweleitian sense) in order to handle the emotional challenges of her environment, Leon's binge eating signals his further enmeshment with the material world. As Alaimo writes, "Perhaps the most palpable example of trans-corporeality is that of food, whereby plants or animals become the substance of the human."[62] Leon's material substance increases as he incorporates an excess of food into his body, and this weight gain also signals his masculinity crisis. Throughout the novel, Leon has expressed disdain for women's bodies, "Those limp extremities – nothing by comparison with men's legs and arms. That odourless body – except for the stink between their legs. And most of all the female genitals – hairy, wrinkly, a deep red hole – and the way they felt like boiled noodles afterwards."[63] Women's bodies are soft, weak, and indefinable to Leon, unlike the hardened, muscular male body that he idolizes. In the end, Leon's body is similarly round and uncontrollable, and he discovers with revulsion that he has feminine-look-

---

man Life and Letters 54, no. 3 (2001): 267. As Boa, Linklater, and Hill have pointed out, Duve's depiction of rape, focalized through Martina as she psychologically copes with the attack on her body, subverts any potential eroticism. Elizabeth Boa, "Lust or Disgust," 67–68; Beth Linklater, "Philomela's Revenge," 261, 270; Alexandra M. Hill, "The Violent Turn, 142.
61 Alexandra M. Hill, "The Violent Turn," 141.
62 Stacy Alaimo, "Trans-corporal Feminisms," 253.
63 Karen Duve, *Rain*, 127. Originally: "Diese schlaffen Extremitäten – nicht zu vergleichen mit Männerbeinen, Männerarmen. Diese duftlosen Körper – bis auf den Gestank zwischen ihren Beinen. Überhaupt das weibliche Geschlechsteil – Haare, Schrumpeliges und ein tiefes rotes Loch – und hinterher fühlte es sich an wie zerkochte Nudeln." Karen Duve, *Regenroman*, 155.

ing breasts: "Disgusting [...] at least there isn't any milk coming out of them."[64] When Martina confronts Leon about having eaten their supplies, Leon responds that he "was very hungry today [...] and what's more [...] in pain."[65] Leon is compelled by his body, its hunger and pain, the way that, according to Alaimo, the "human body can 'talk back,' resist, or otherwise affect its cultural construction."[66] Leon's hunger, his back pain, and his weight gain are all beyond his control, manifestations of his body's material agency.

At the end of the novel, Leon's masculinity crisis has reached an extreme, as he no longer recognizes himself as a man at all. When Kay attempts to rescue him from his collapsing house after a severe storm, she tries to motivate him by appealing to his sense of masculinity, "For God's sake, pull yourself together! Are you a man or aren't you?"[67] He answers "No, I don't think I am"[68] and is then frightened by the sight of his own penis, which he mistakes for a slug. After running away from Kay, he finally merges with the landscape, once and for all. In a fit of hallucination, he believes he sees Isadora, falls to the ground to submit to her, and suffocates in the muddy earth: "His hands grasped damp, warm mud, and the bog closed, gurgling, over his head. Leon sank into a world of total darkness and swelling softness. [...] How good it was to be mould beneath the mould. Leon sank back into the womb of his true mother."[69] Yet this surrender to the material world is no peaceful one; it has its own violence. "The marshes were not warm and gentle now; they were brutal, taking possession of the cavity of his chest, trickling into his bronchial tubes, mingling with the water of which he himself was made and filling him entirely, like a ship wrecked in the silt."[70] This moment recalls the corpse that Leon and Martina find at the begin-

---

[64] Karen Duve, *Rain*, 235. Originally: "Wie ekelhaft. [...] Wenigstens kommt da keine Milch raus." Karen Duve, *Regenroman*, 284.

[65] Karen Duve, *Rain*, 184. Originally: "hatte heute großen Hunger. [...] Und außerdem [...] Schmerzen." Karen Duve, *Regenroman*, 224.

[66] Stacy Alaimo, "Trans-corporal Feminisms," 242.

[67] Karen Duve, *Rain*, 239. Originally: "Herrgottnochmal, nun reiß dich doch zusammen! Bist du ein Mann oder nicht?" Karen Duve, *Regenroman*, 289.

[68] Karen Duve, *Rain*, 239. Originally: "Nein, ich glaube nicht." Karen Duve, *Regenroman*, 289.

[69] Karen Duve, *Rain*, 246. Originally: "Seine Hände griffen in feuchtwarmen Morast, glucksend schloß sich das Moor über seinem Schädel. Leon versank in eine Welt voller Dunkelheit und schwellender Weichheit. [...] Wie gut es war, Moder unter Moder zu sein. Leon sank zurück in den Schoß seiner wahren Mutter." Karen Duve, *Regenroman*, 297.

[70] Karen Duve, *Rain*, 246. Originally: "Nun war das Moor nicht mehr warm und sanft; es eroberte brutal seinen Brustraum, durchsickerte seine Bronchien, vermischte sich mit dem Wasser, aus dem er selbst bestand, und füllte ihn wie ein verschlickendes Schiffswrack." Karen Duve, *Regenroman*, 298.

ning of the novel, in which water and plant life have taken over and mingle with the material remains of a human body. Here, human subjectivity is coming to an end as material agencies take over the body that Leon once strived to have control over. Ludden has faulted Duve for not having transcended the mind/body split or the opposition of self/other as Leon surrenders to nature.[71] However, I maintain that this point is moot if the marsh is read as a trans-corporal space. Human subjectivity is not rendered wholly material in this paradigm (although its material grounding is undeniable); rather, human subjectivity is recognized as only one of many kinds of agency operating in the material world. Leon retains his subjectivity until the very end while submitting himself to material forces.

The trans-corporal space of *Heimat* has no tolerance for Leon's male chauvinism and his indulgence in the delusions that place humans over nature. Leon's feelings of superiority are punished by a landscape and society that insist on enacting their own agencies. Martina, by contrast, has shown kindness and connectedness to nature, caring for Noah, learning how to live on the marsh from Kay and Isadora, and making efforts to save the slugs who invade the house instead of killing them. While Martina does not, in the end, lead a harmonious, integrated life in the East German countryside – she leaves after Noah disappears and Kay confesses her love for her – she is the only character to show some growth through her intra-actions within the *Heimat*. At the end of the novel, Martina returns to Hamburg and enacts revenge on her father, who has shamed her repeatedly since her teenage years after he caught her having sex in a car. She sets fire to the very same car, which he keeps on display in front of his junkyard as a reminder of Martina's indiscretions. The fact that she turns to fire – not water – as the element of her revenge is reminiscent of Kay's use of the flamethrower to kill Pfitzner and Harry. (Boa aptly calls Kay the "Promethean Woman" and indeed, she has brought fire to the arsenal of female empowerment that Martina now draws from.[72]) This use of fire rather than water might also signal Duve's rejection of the literary traditions, authored and prolonged largely by men, that associate women, water, and threat and which find aesthetic pleasure in dead women as beautiful floating corpses. Martina, having learned from Kay, wields a different kind of power. Through her experiences in the *Heimat* and in solidarity with women, Martina has found her own agency.

---

71 Teresa Ludden, "Nature, Bodies, and Breakdowns," 52.
72 Elizabeth Boa, "Lust or Disgust," 60.

Gendered Anxieties, Gendered Fantasies

Read together, *Eduard's Homecoming* and *Rain* illustrate how, at the turn of the millennium, conventional property relations remained central to the hegemonic construction of masculinity: an upheaval of one meant a crisis for the other. In *Eduard's Homecoming*, the hegemonic masculine construct requires Eduard to have control over his property, finances, historical obligations, and wife's sexuality. In *Rain*, the hegemonic masculine construct has to do with managing ones physical environment, especially one's property, but also with maintaining a hardened body and knowing one's position within the hierarchy of masculinities. Though these two novels present somewhat different constructs of masculinity, property ownership is the common feature between the two. Both novels center on male characters who feel anguish about their perceived inadequacy as men when they are unable to manage the property they have acquired in the former East Germany.

Given that these two novels appeared at a time of widespread concern about masculinity in Germany, as evidenced in the media and scholarship, it seems clear that they exemplify broader fears – or perhaps hopes – about Western men losing the social control they once wielded. In both novels, men lose control over their property against a backdrop of broader societal change. *Eduard's Homecoming* situates Eduard's troubles within a social landscape that includes widespread unemployment in the East, a destabilized educational system, and the memory debates centering on Berlin's changing topography, among other issues. By framing Eduard's property claim as an inheritance, the novel makes clear that he is obligated to a social inheritance as well, specifically, responsibility for the National Socialist past. Moreover, by claiming property in the former East Germany, Eduard has become a participant in the power dynamics that shape East-West relations. Both of these responsibilities – to the past and to the social politics of the present – overwhelm him, and in conjunction with the newfound knowledge that his wife has not experienced an orgasm with him, throw him into a full-blown masculinity crisis. Eduard's masculinity becomes a central concern of the novel, as the inheritance of the tenement building puts Eduard in the position of reevaluating his relationship with his wife and is the impetus for him to interact with the other major female characters in the novel. All of these women are concerned with his masculinity, either emasculating him (Vera Rheinland and Jenny) or restoring his security in his manhood (Marina and Edita Schlandt).

While Eduard's masculinity crisis is linked to a broad number of issues in the swiftly changing German society of the 1990s, Leon's stems, at least in part, from with the shifting gender dynamics in the East. When Leon reads in the newspaper that men are leaving the area to find work in the West, he wonders if he made the wrong decision to move there.[73] In contrast to Hamburg, which is coded in the text as masculine through its associations with Pfitzner and Harry, as well as Leon's life as a bachelor before Martina, the East German countryside exhibits a range of feminities and gentler, more fluid masculinities. In the Eastern countryside, Leon's male chauvinism causes his downfall, as he fails to adapt to the proliferation of gender constructions that thrive on the marsh. He experiences a masculinity crisis when he cannot assert control over his environment, seeing this loss of power as an inadequacy.

By comparing the concerns of male protagonists in *Eduard's Homecoming* and *Rain* with those of the female protagonists in Judith Hermann's narratives, discussed in chapter 4, it is evident that men and women in fiction represented very different anxieties about the new property relations. The women in Hermann's narratives, as well as Martina in *Eduard's Homecoming* are concerned about their housing security and their safety from violent men. By contrast, men's concerns in *Eduard's Homecoming* and *Rain* are largely egocentric, as material problems trigger their identity crises. The question then emerges: why do men's vulnerabilities in these narratives lead to insecurity about having an adequate masculinity? After all, women's vulnerabilities do not threaten their security in their femininity. (Is there such a thing as a femininity crisis?) Men's crises in these texts have to do with their inability to maintain power in a social environment that no longer upholds hegemonic masculinity. Women's crises are about dealing with the fallout of the hegemonic construct of manliness.

Indeed, as *Eduard's Homecoming* and *Rain* make clear, the rapidly changing property relations in Germany in the 1990s unleashed powerful fears and fantasies about who would be in control, and who would lose power, in the unified Germany. The novels' vastly different outcomes are particularly telling, especially when the authors' genders are taken into account. Schneider, a cis-gender man, wrote a novel in which a man who exhibits traits of a conventional hegemonic masculinity regains control in the end and is able to successfully participate in a restored private property system. The status quo wins out and Western men retain some sense of control. By contrast, Duve, a cis-gender woman, wrote a novel in which Western men lose the power they once wielded, as women wrest control from the men around them. The status quo is forever al-

---

73 Karen Duve, *Rain*, 169. Originally: "Die Männer wanderten ab. Hier stand, daß es überwiegend Männer waren, die auf der Suche nach Glück und Arbeitsplätzen nach Westdeutschland übersiedelten. Die Frauen blieben in Ostdeutschland. Die Frauen und Kerbel. [...] Und er, Leon, war hierher gezogen. Wie hatte er das tun können? In die DDR zog man nicht, aus ihr lief man weg." Karen Duve, *Regenroman*, 206.

tered and a space exists where women and natural agencies rule. At the turn of the millennium the future was up for grabs, as these two novels make clear. However, one thing is certain: Western men would either profit from their participation in the property relations (like Eduard) or die trying (like Leon).

Chapter 6
Home in the East as a Thing of the Past: Jenny Erpenbeck's *Visitation* (2008) and Kathrin Gerlof's *Now That's a Story* (2014)

"Time," the East German architect in Jenny Erpenbeck's *Visitation* (*Heimsuchung*, 2008) thinks as he hides valuables on his property before fleeing to West Berlin, "[...] is now expelling him from house and home."[1] He thinks this on a Friday, or perhaps a Saturday. If he remains in the house through the weekend, he will be arrested on Monday for having imported building materials from West Germany. If he waits, it will be people, representatives of the government, who expel him. Now, as he prepares to flee, time forces him to leave.

With this thought, the architect draws attention to the power that time wields over people, impelling us to think, feel, and act in certain ways. This is indeed true of the main characters in the cultural productions discussed in this monograph. For example, in the made-for-television films *Taxi to Rathenow* and *Our House*, characters from the West wish to claim a childhood home in the East out of nostalgic longing for the past, while characters from the East feel threatened by an undecided future. Alternately, the past can become a burden in a way that the future cannot. In *Our House*, *The Same Old Song*, and *Eduard's Homecoming*, a family's past involvement in National Socialism jeopardizes the property claims of those in the present, and in Judith Hermann's short story "Summerhouse, Later," the precariously standing house in the countryside represents a long national history that the narrator, or perhaps Hermann herself, is afraid to engage with. Even the unstoppable forward motion of the present heightens anxieties for some characters. In *Eduard's Homecoming*, Eduard is defenseless against the squatters' utility costs, which increase by the minute and threaten him with ever more severe financial ruin. In all of these narratives, time – the future, the past, the present – lends urgency to the characters' problems and endeavors.

In the two novels discussed in this chapter, Jenny Erpenbeck's *Visitation* and Kathrin Gerlof's *Now That's a Story* (*Das ist eine Geschichte*, 2014), time is not merely a factor within a larger complex of problems pertaining to property rights

---

[1] Jenny Erpenbeck, *Visitation*, trans. Susan Bernofsky (New York: New Directions, 2010), 24. Originally: "die Zeit [...] jagt ihn jetzt aus seinem Gehäuse." Jenny Erpenbeck, *Heimsuchung* (Frankfurt am Main: Eichborn Verlag, 2008), 37.

https://doi.org/10.1515/9783110673975-008

and home ownership. Rather, it comes to the fore as the main antagonist in both novels. *Visitation* centers on a house and a plot of land that four families and several generations inhabit from the late nineteenth century into the post-unification era. The novel has no single protagonist, aside from perhaps the house. Instead, each of the main chapters depicts a different character or generation living there or on the neighboring property. The third person narrator relays the events that take place in and around the house, sometimes by giving the reader access to a character's thoughts through free indirect speech and at other times by relaying events as though observing from a distance. The chapter titles – "The Gardener," "The Wealthy Farmer and His Four Daughters," "The Architect," etc. – signal the shift in both focalization and habitation of the property from one chapter to the next. Decade after decade, humans perpetrate injustices against one another on the same plot of land, which result in expulsion, murder, and flight. With no consistent human antagonist, time emerges as that which ultimately removes people from the property. In *Visitation*, little memory survives from one generation of inhabitants to the next, and it is erased altogether with the demolition of the house at the end of the novel.

Kathrin Gerlof's *Now That's a Story* (2014) presents a quite different scenario, but it bears discussing alongside *Visitation* for similarly positing time as the main antagonist of its characters. *Now That's a Story* is set in the present day, as the residents of the fictional village of Warenberg in the former East Germany face losing their homes when heirs of a Jewish family petition for reparations for property lost during the Nazi era. Even though the heirs are petitioning for financial compensation rather than the restoration of property, some of the residents will be forced to sell their houses in order to pay their part in the settlement. Most of the Warenbergers see this as an undue burden, themselves working class citizens of the former GDR who can live only modestly in the newly unified Germany.

Like *Visitation*, each chapter of *Now That's a Story* is focalized through a different character, and the chapter titles signal this shift in focalization. However, instead of indicating the type of character we will now follow, each chapter title in *Now That's a Story* bears the respective character's home address. Thus the novel frames each major character as part of the community and emphasizes that any decision that a character makes will affect others. As the residents debate their responsibilities toward the national history, displaying a range of positions, it becomes clear that the main antagonist of the novel is not the heirs, but rather, the residents' relationships to the Nazi past. After engaging in research in order to build their court case, they arrive at conflicting versions of the area's history. Some of the residents have produced falsified versions of the past, and so the community's case will not hold up in court. No one can escape their place in the national history; no one can evade responsibility for violence done in the past; and those who wish to do so prove to be in the wrong.

In both *Visitation* and *Now That's a Story*, time threatens the inhabitants of homes, most markedly when it is perceived in the form of inevitability. In both novels, the past and the present bump up against one another, compete, and produce a friction that renders the characters helpless. Time conceals truths, which results, in the case of *Visitation*, in further injustices and, in the case of *Now That's a Story*, in an obligation for people today to atone for a violent past for which they have little direct personal culpability. Most devastatingly, time is indifferent to humans in both novels, and human suffering is forgotten as it moves forward. In both novels, humans have committed grave injustices against one another – displacement, exploitation, murder – and the forward march of time guarantees that no one can safely claim a space for themselves in the present day for very long.

The Erratic Linearity of Time in Jenny Erpenbeck's *Visitation*

Jenny Erpenbeck's *Visitation* is a requiem of home. It centers on a house on the Scharmützelsee in Brandenburg from the Wilhelmine period to the 1990s, covering a long twentieth century as four different families seek stability and happiness there but are each, in turn, driven from the property. The original title of the novel, *Heimsuchung*, encapsulates this longing for home in a way that the English translation "visitation" does not. While *Heimsuchung* translates to "visitation" in the sense of "haunting," one can also break the German composite noun into "Heim" (home) and "suchen" (to search). Indeed, the house represents both: the longing for a home that does not exist and also the way in which Germany is haunted by the brutal events of the twentieth century.[2] The promise of a quiet life in the *Heimat* is broken for each family that inhabits the lakeside house and property at the center of the novel, as the national and global politics of the twentieth century devastate their peace there. Indeed, *Visitation* capitalizes on the affective force of *Heimat*, drawing on and then betraying the promise that one can belong unequivocally within an innocent, unchanging, and tranquil

---

[2] I give the same explanation of the original German title in my essay "Narrating the Fault Lines: German Literature since the Fall of the Wall," *World Literature Today* online version (November 2014 issue), https://www.worldliteraturetoday.org/2014/november/narrating-fault-lines-german-literature-fall-wall-necia-chronister.

landscape. In depicting a revolving door of owners and inhabitants of the same property, *Visitation* turns the loss of *Heimat* into the characters' lived experience of home.³

The space of *Heimat* with which Erpenbeck presents us is never inviting, not even initially. The first sentence of the novel, rather than drawing the reader into a pleasant landscape, challenges us to grapple with an unfathomable geological transformation: "Approximately twenty-four thousand years ago a glacier advanced until it reached a large outcropping of rock that now is nothing more than a gentle hill above where the house stands."⁴ In the ensuing pages, the narrator describes the millennia-long process of freezes and thaws that formed the hills, lake, and shoals while displacing animals, destroying trees, and creating conditions that were utterly inhospitable to human life for thousands of years. Foregrounding natural rather than human agency and a timescale that far exceeds human lifespans, the preface introduces the novel's setting in an alienating manner that frames the presentation of home for the rest of the chapters. Time will be the engine of material change, and humans will have little agency in their own security.

While the bulk of the novel will center on the large-scale historical events of the twentieth century that ruptured people's sense of continuity, it takes some time for the novel to settle into that focus. In the first full chapter (after the prolog and an interlude about the perennial gardener figure) the third-person narrator recounts how the Wurrach family has owned the tract of land at the center of the novel since the king awarded it to them in the 1650s. Handed down from father to son over the centuries, the land has now, at the turn of the twentieth century, met the end of the family's patriarchal lineage. The large landholder Wurrach has only daughters and no sons, and rather than bequeathing the land to his daughter Klara, as promised, he instead parcels and sells it to industrialists from Berlin. With this act, Wurrach not only fragments the land that had been perceived as one tract for centuries, but he also breaks with the continuity of family inheritance. The twentieth century is thus introduced in the novel as fracturing both space and time. Klara's suicide after the sale of her inheritance signals the death of the older order as the new one arrives. However, certain aspects of the traditional property relations will remain intact. Wurrach's decisions

---

3 As Monika Shafi has pointed out, *Heimat* is necessarily a nostalgic construct, one that relies on a sense of loss. Monika Shafi, *Housebound: Selfhood and Domestic Space in Contemporary German Fiction* (Rochester: Camden House, 2012), 27.
4 Jenny Erpenbeck, *Visitation*, 1. Originally: "Bis zum Felsmassiv, das inzwischen nur noch als sanfter Hügel oberhalb des Hauses zu sehen ist, schob sich vor ungefähr vierundzwanzigtausend Jahren das Eis vor." Jenny Erpenbeck, *Heimsuchung*, 9.

about the family's property ends in tragedy for his daughter. As we saw in chapter 4, men's decisions about property will continue to have deleterious effects on women for at least the next century.

Visitation thus emphasizes loss, rather than belonging, as the primary characteristic of *Heimat*. The *Heimat* of Erpenbeck's novel is neither insulated from the political world nor unchanging, but instead is fully entangled in the events of the twentieth century.[5] It proves to be penetrable by outside forces, for example, when the woods are cleared at the beginning of the century to build lakeside vacation homes for wealthy Berliners, or later, more devastatingly, when Russian soldiers march through the area at the end of the World War II, occupy the house, and destroy the garden. In some instances, politics do not invade the home from without, but rather, originate from within it. For example, the architect who buys one of the parcels from Wurrach and builds a house on it in 1936 for his wife eventually joins the Reich Chamber of Culture. In one scene, he ponders the relationship between aesthetics and biology as he cultivates the *Heimat* landscape and garden, and this inner monologue gains resonance later when the reader learns that the architect will become part of Albert Speer's infamous Germania project to redesign Berlin under Hitler's orders.[6]

The *Heimat* serves as the site on which twentieth century politics play out and thus can offer no protection from them. At approximately the same time as the architect purchases his plot of land from Wurrach, a Jewish cloth manufacturer purchases the neighboring plot. The family will soon be forced to sell and flee, but are murdered nonetheless while waiting for an exit visa. As Axel Goodbody has pointed out, the house in this instance not only fails to protect the family, but becomes a trap for them.[7] A few years later, when the Soviet army advances through the area, occupying the house and destroying the garden, the house becomes the site of a rape. The reader occupies a ghostly position, observing the land over a superhuman timeframe. We witness the injustices that take place on it, sometimes from a distance, as the narrator relays events with scant detail, and at other times with an intimate proximity to the characters as we read their thoughts.

---

[5] See also Friederike Eigler, "Critical Approaches to Heimat and the 'Spatial Turn,'" *New German Critique* 39, no. 1 (2012): 45–48.

[6] See also Sven Kramer, "Reconsidering 'Heimat': Jenny Erpenbeck's Novel *Heimsuchung* (2008)," in *Readings in Twenty-First-Century European Literatures*, ed. Michael Gratzke, Margaret-Anne Hutton, and Claire Whitehead (Oxford: Peter Lang, 2014), 202.

[7] Axel Goodbody, "*Heimat* and the Place of Humans in the World: Jenny Erpenbeck's *Heimsuchung* in Ecocritical Perspective," *New German Critique* 43, no. 2 (2016): 141.

As the twentieth century proceeds, the *Heimat* becomes the site of legally sanctioned injustices. In the early 1950s, the architect, who managed to evade the first rounds of expropriation under SMAD despite his activity in the Nazi party a few years prior, must now flee with his wife from their home for illegally importing building materials from the West in order to compensate for shortages and meet his work requirements. Subsequently the house (but not the land, as per GDR law) is appointed to a married couple, writers returning from exile in the Soviet Union, but this too leads to loss. In the final chapters, the writers' granddaughter must relinquish the house when the heirs of the architect's wife win a restitution case on it after unification. She is forced to give up the house that she cherishes, which will then, tragically, be sold to developers and razed to make way for new buildings.

Not only does Erpenbeck show us the fallacy of relying on a depoliticized image of home; the novel also reveals *Heimat* to be both a material and emotional construct. As Goodbody has shown in his ecocritical work on *Visitation*, the constructedness of *Heimat* is evident in the "building and garden design as instances of the human attempt to make oneself at home in the world."[8] *Heimat* is thus neither natural nor given, but the result of exertive intra-actions within the material environment. The architect's intra-actions within the landscape shape the experience that others will have there for generations to come: "That's his profession: planning homes, planning a homeland [Heimat]."[9] Moreover, the architect practices the Nazi ideology of expanding the *Heimat* at a microcosmic level when he purchases the neighboring plot cheaply from the Jewish family that is forced to flee, thereby widening the borders of his property. After the architect must then flee himself in the 1950s, the property retains many of the features he has developed there. The Nazi influence on the very concept of *Heimat* is lasting.

While Goodbody theorizes *Heimat* as the exertive efforts of humans within their material environment, Gillian Pye goes a step further in her discussion of the materiality of home. She describes houses and the objects that fill them as "partners in relational interdependencies with humans. As such, things deter-

---

[8] Axel Goodbody, "*Heimat* and the Place of Humans in the World," 138. Here Goodbody builds on the work of Sven Kramer, who addresses the constructedness of *Heimat*. See Sven Kramer, "Reconsidering 'Heimat,'" 200.
[9] Jenny Erpenbeck, *Visitation*, 24. Originally: "Heimat planen, das ist sein Beruf." Jenny Erpenbeck, *Heimsuchung*, 38.

mine, as much as they are determined by, human activities and behaviors."[10] Thus for both Goodbody and Pye, the characters' security in their house is contingent upon not only political forces, but also natural and material agencies. The landscape, objects, building materials, and the materiality of bodies can alternately assist or frustrate the individual in their endeavors, and none are impervious to the deleterious effects of time.

Heimat is not only a material construct; it proves to be an emotional one as well.[11] At best, *Heimat* in Erpenbeck's novel is a short-lived feeling of happiness or peace in the home before one must leave it. For most of the characters in the novel, however, this happiness is corrupt, as *Heimat* requires repression of the knowledge that one has displaced others to obtain it. For example, the architect engages in the willful repression of guilt not only when he conceals his own Jewish heritage from the authorities in order to join the Reich Culture Chamber, but also when he acquires the neighboring property. As he prepares to leave the house over a decade later, he continues to rationalize his decision to profit from the neighbors' desperation: "Still, he'd paid the Jews a full half of market value for the land. And this was by no means a paltry sum. They'd never have managed to find another buyer in so short a time."[12] Erpenbeck foregrounds the repression of guilt and the intimacy of this injustice by zooming in on one of the most meaning-laden objects in the entire novel: a towel. After a dip in the lake, the architect dries himself with a towel he finds hanging in the boathouse. He does not give the object a moment of thought, but the reader knows that it was manufactured by the murdered family's textile company and had likely been used by the family after they enjoyed a swim in the lake. This most intimate of acts, of casually wiping his skin with a towel made and used by those he has displaced, and whose murder he has contributed to, eloquently shows his indifference to the tragedy his neighbors have endured. This act of drying himself with the towel does not signify an attempt to wipe his guilt away. On the contrary, this material gesture of touching skin to towel shows just how directly, just how concretely and materially, he is responsible for his neighbors' fates – and just how little he thinks about that fact. His con-

---

10 Gillian Pye, "Jenny Erpenbeck and the Life of Things," in *Transitions: Emerging Women Writers in German-Language Literature*, ed. Valerie Heffernan and Gillian Pye (Amsterdam: Rodopi, 2013), 113.
11 See also Sven Kramer, "Reconsidering 'Heimat,'" 201.
12 Jenny Erpenbeck, *Visitation*, 29. Originally: "Immerhin die Hälfte des Verkehrswerts hatte er den Juden gezahlt. Und das war schon nicht wenig gewesen. Auf die Schnelle hätte sich gar kein anderer Käufer gefunden." Jenny Erpenbeck, *Heimsuchung*, 43–44.

science can never be clean, since he has made a life out of the material sacrifices of the persecuted.

In its historical, material, and emotional contingency, *Heimat* is fleeting and troubled, and Erpenbeck's rendering of time foregrounds that fact. In the aggregate, *Visitation* presents a chronology of the house and property over the course of the twentieth century and thereby a microcosm of the human drama and trauma that took place within the national context and on an international scale. But as regimes change over the course of the novel, disrupting the characters' sense of continuity and their relationship to home, the novel foregrounds rupture as an organizing principle of the narrative structure. As Monika Shafi has pointed out, it is important that *Visitation* presents the twentieth century not through the lineage of a family, as family sagas (*Familienromane*) do, "which would suggest continuity anchored by traditions and possessions," but rather as "the accounts of *different* owners whose property rights cease to exist when the political regimes change."[13] The order of the chapters, as well as the novel's experimentation with time within individual chapters, frustrate a linear chronology and go beyond depicting time as simply the fourth dimension of space. The narrator tells events out of order, and within chapters time accelerates and decelerates erratically, jumps, stops altogether, and blends itself with other timelines through memory and flashback. Thus time acts with an agency much closer to that which Pye and Goodbody attribute to materiality, inserting itself on place, rending humans from it, and complicating their relationships to it in the present. Time is no dimension of space nor a product of human perceptual organization, but rather a force that does with humans what it will.

When Erpenbeck zooms far out, situating the century within a long scope of natural time and agency that spans millennia, human actions within one century seem trivial. And yet, Erpenbeck avoids diminishing human suffering. The fates her characters suffer are all the more tragic because as time marches forward, they will be forgotten. She also manages not to relativize the traumas of the twentieth century, even though, as Katharina Gerstenberger has pointed out "[t]he line between victim and perpetrator is often blurred, with one character occupying both positions at different times."[14] Women are more frequently the

---

[13] Monika Shafi, *Housebound*, 33.
[14] Katharina Gerstenberger, "Fictionalizations: Holocaust Memory and the Generational Construct in the Works of Contemporary Women Writers," in *Generational Shifts in Contemporary German Culture*, ed. Laurel Cohen-Pfister and Susanne Vees-Gulani (Rochester: Camden House, 2010), 96. See also Elisabeth Krimmer, "The Representation of Wartime Rape in Julia Franck's *Die Mittagsfrau* and Jenny Erpenbeck's *Heimsuchung*," *Gegenwartsliteratur: A German Studies Yearbook*, 14 (2015): 45–52.

victims of expropriation and loss in the novel, and those who are named (rather than being marked as types like "the architect," "the visitor," etc.) almost always suffer the worst fates.¹⁵ Klara's expropriation and suicide usher in the century of injustice and death to come, and the chapter focused on the Jewish family's murder recites their first names repeatedly throughout the chapter:

> Hermine and Arthur, his parents.
> He himself, Ludwig, the firstborn.
> His sister Elisabeth, married to Ernst.
> Their daughter Doris, his niece.
> Then his wife Anna.
> And now the children: Elliot and baby Elisabeth, named for his sister.¹⁶

The most devastating chapter of the novel depicts the murder of the twelve-year-old Doris, the niece of the Jewish neighbor, after spending her last days hiding in a cabinet in the Warsaw ghetto and dreaming of her Uncle Ludwig's property in Brandenburg. Doris's chapter is placed in the middle of the book – her murder is recounted on almost the exact middle page of the novel – and thus her death is framed as the novel's central loss. This death is also situated between two chapters detailing the encounter between the architect's wife and a Russian soldier, each chapter from one of those perspectives. Doris's death interrupts the narration of one place and one instance, thus representing the deepest rupture of time and place in the novel.¹⁷

While the timeline of human events has a loosely chronological structure, interludes appear between each chapter that foreground the cyclical timelines

---

15 See Katharina Gerstenberger, "Fictionalizations," 96 and 110; Axel Goodbody, "*Heimat* and the Place of Humans in the World," 142; Nancy Nobile, "'Ihr Erbteil': The Legacy of Romanticism in Jenny Erpenbeck's *Heimsuchung*." *Gegenwartsliteratur: A German Studies Yearbook* 14 (2015): 68.
16 Jenny Erpenbeck, *Visitation* 33, 39, and 42. Originally: "Hermine und Arthur, seine Eltern. / Er selbst, Ludwig, der Erstgeborene. / Seine Schwester Elisabeth, verheiratet mit Ernst. / Die Tochter der beiden, seine Nichte, die Doris. / Dann seine Frau Anna. / Und nun die Kinder: Elliot und die kleine Elisabeth, / genannt nach seiner Schwester. Jenny Erpenbeck, *Heimsuchung*, 48, 55, and 59. Halina Ludorowski describes the listing of names in this chapter as a practice of litany prayer and remembrance. Halina Ludorowska, "Deutsche Geschichte in den Augen der Enkelkinder," in *Geschichte und Gedächtnis in der Literatur vom 18. bis 21. Jahrhundert*, ed. Janusz Golec and Irmela von der Lühe (Frankfurt am Main: Peter Lang, 2011), 258.
17 Elisabeth Krimmer argues that by interrupting the architect's wife's experience with Doris's story, Erpenbeck puts the architect's wife's suffering in perspective and thereby avoids creating false equivalency in suffering in her novel. Elisabeth Krimmer, "The Representation of Wartime Rape," 50.

of nature. These interludes feature an almost mythical character known only as "the gardener," who belongs to the land rather than owning any himself. As the narrator explains, the gardener has inhabited and worked the land for as long as anyone can remember and is its only consistent human inhabitant over the course of the twentieth century. As such, he provides a counter-example to time as historical chronology, attuned instead to the seasonal and cyclical timelines of nature as he tends the trees and flowers and waters the lawns.[18] Yet, the gardener does not belong wholly to nature, working rather at the nexuses of nature and aesthetics. He is responsible for curating the land for the home owners' aesthetic sensibilities, felling trees to create lawns and gardens and planting new ones to frame the view of the lake. His seasonal work maintains the illusion of control over chaos, a necessary condition of home.

Like the gardener, who perceives time cyclically, each of the major characters has a different perception of time. For example, as the architect prepares to flee from his house in the early 1950s, he is plagued (visited!) by memories that are both happy and cruel of the life he and his wife shared there. Erpenbeck employs simultaneity as a way to break with linear time when the architect perceives two timelines at once, acting in the present but experiencing the house and property as he did in the past. Moreover, gaps in memory and misrecognition complicate his concept of time. For example, the architect realizes with some dismay that he cannot remember the last time he swam in the lake because he had not recognized it as such when it happened. Some things can only be understood in retrospect, and, even then, understanding can be elusive, "As if time, even when you grip it firmly with our hands, can still flail and thrash about and twist which way it will."[19]

Erpenbeck dispenses with linear time altogether in the chapter focalized through Ludwig, the architect's former neighbor. Blending Ludwig's memories and the narrator's knowledge in a dizzying fashion, this chapter tells Ludwig's story in four different timelines and places that are difficult to disentangle. Epi-

---

[18] Ulrike Vedder has posited three types of time functioning in Erpenbeck's works: that which she calls "Menschenzeit," or historical time'; "Dingzeit,"or the lifespan of objects that outlive us and thus stretch Menschenzeit beyond actual human lifespans; and "Naturzeit," or the cyclical time of nature. For Vedder, the gardener belongs to the "Naturzeit." Ulrike Vedder, "Lebensläufe: Zeit und Genealogie in Jenny Erpenbecks Literatur," in *Wahrheit und Täuschung: Beiträge zum Werk Jenny Erpenbecks*, ed. Friedhelm Marx and Julia Schöll (Göttingen: Wallstein Verlag, 2014), 62–64.

[19] Jenny Erpenbeck, *Visitation*, 28. Originally: "Als könne die Zeit sich, auch wenn man sie ganz fest in der Hand hält, herumwerfen und zappeln und sich einem, wie sie grad will, verdrehen." Jenny Erpenbeck, *Heimsuchung*, 43.

sodes from 1936, when Ludwig and his father planted trees on the property in Brandenburg and planned the construction of the bathing house, combine with memories of his parents visiting him, his wife, and children later at their newly adopted home in South Africa. His parents' efforts to emigrate in 1939 are interspersed among these memories, as they sell the property at half its market value to the architect next door but are nonetheless detained and murdered outside of Łødz in Poland. Ludwig's sister, Elisabeth, and her daughter, Doris, also attempt to flee but are never heard from again. All of these timelines and memories intermingle with the present, as Ludwig watches his baby daughter Elisabeth, named after his murdered sister, and son Elliot playing in safety in their yard in South Africa. The disjunction of past(s) and present is his lived trauma and contributes to his alienation in exile.

Time can also evade perception. In Erpenbeck's most devastating chapter, Ludwig's niece, the twelve-year-old Doris waits silently in the dark with no ability to track time. She and her mother have been deported to the Warsaw ghetto, and she is hiding in a pitch-black cabinet from Nazi officers while her mother is at work. Alone in the dark with no ability to move and only her memories and reflections, she wonders about two things: time and her own existence. The narrator relays her thoughts in free indirect speech: "Who was she? Whose head was her head? To whom did her memories now belong? Did black time keep going on and on, even when a person was no longer doing anything but just sitting there, did time keep going on, dragging even a child who has turned to stone away with it?"[20] With no sense of whether time is continuing or standing still, Doris cannot know if she continues to exist or not. Time persists only as her memories: of her visit to Uncle Ludwig in South Africa, of the days in which she steeled herself up for her eventual deportation to Poland by wearing thin shoes in the winter, and of her visits to her family's lakeside property in Brandenburg. The "black time" is interrupted, however, when Doris is eventually found, deported in a boxcar, and shot into a mass grave. In the moments before her death, Doris experiences another kind of simultaneity, not the blending of places or the duality of the past and present. Rather, Doris experiences simultaneity of time and place through misrecognition. She believes ever so briefly that she is not in Poland after all, but at her family's property in Brandenburg. She

---

[20] Jenny Erpenbeck, Visitation, 59. Originally: "Wer war sie? Wessen Kopf war ihr Kopf? Wem gehörten jetzt ihre Erinnerungen? Lief die schwarze Zeit immer weiter, auch wenn der Mensch nur noch saß, lief die Zeit immer weiter und riß selbst ein versteinertes Kind noch mit sich fort?" Jenny Erpenbeck, Heimsuchung, 80.

can smell the pines – "Has she really come home?"[21] – just before she is murdered.

Doris wonders whether the "black time" is eternal, and it is, but not in the way she means. In *Visitation*, the only eternity is in loss. Although Doris does not know it yet as she hides in the cabinet, she has eternally lost her mother who was arrested that day. At the end of the chapter, Doris is murdered and thus eternally gone. The murder of Doris is so utterly unjust, so utterly and absurdly senseless that it represents a reversal in the achievements of humanity:

> For three years the girl took piano lessons, but now, while her dead body slides down into the pit, the word piano is taken back from human beings, now the backflip on the high bar that the girl could perform better than her schoolmates is taken back, along with all the motions a swimmer makes, the gesture of seizing hold of a crab is taken back, as well as all the basic knots to be learned for sailing, all these things are taken back into uninventedness, and finally, last of all, the name of the girl herself is taken back, the name no one will ever again call her by: Doris.[22]

The murder of Doris is not only an erasure of what she had ever been, a reversal of everything she had ever achieved and contributed to the world, but an eternal corruption of everyday activities, childhoods, and human achievements as time marches on.

Some characters in the novel believe that they have found eternity in other ways, but turn out to be mistaken. The architect's wife believes she has found an eternity of happiness in the *Heimat*, yet her feeling of eternity ends when she encounters a Russian soldier. He discovers her hiding in a secret compartment of the master bedroom closet and holds her down. Believing he will rape her, she fights back by forcing herself on him and then urinating on him.[23] However, it is arguably not the rape that punctures her sense of eternity, but rather, as she

---

21 Jenny Erpenbeck, *Visitation*, 68. Originally: "Ist sie tatsächlich nach Hause gekommen?" Jenny Erpenbeck, *Heimsuchung*, 91.
22 Jenny Erpenbeck, *Visitation*, 68. Originally: "Drei Jahre lang hat das Mädchen Klavierspielen gelernt, aber jetzt, während sein toter Körper in die Grube hinunterrutscht, wird das Wort Klavier von den Menschen zurückgenommen, jetzt wird der Rückwärtsüberschlag am Reck, den das Mädchen besser beherrschte als seine Schulkameradinnen, zurückgenommen und auch alle Bewegungen, die ein Schwimmender macht, das Greifen nach Krebsen wird zurückgenommen, ebenso wie die kleine Knotenkunde beim Segeln, all das wird ins Unerfundene zurückgenommen, und schließlich, ganz zuletzt, auch der Name des Mädchens selbst, bei dem niemals mehr jemand es rufen wird: Doris." Jenny Erpenbeck, *Heimsuchung*, 91–92.
23 In her reading of the scene, Elizabeth Krimmer argues that the blurred line between seduction and violence that characterizes this rape is typical of rape narratives as told from the perpetrator's perspective. Elizabeth Krimmer, "The Representation of Wartime Rape," 48.

indicates, that he calls her "Mama." This word denies her of her desire to be eternally young.[24] In a later chapter, a neighbor believes he has found eternity in a memory he cannot rid himself of, having witnessed a rape in the woodshed as a youth and not stopped it. However, these are not eternities in any real sense. They do not stop time and exist forever. Rather, they are prolonged moments, no more eternal than the glacier, the Wurrach family line, or the gardener, all of which seem endless but nevertheless disappear eventually. The only thing eternal is loss. Death is eternal; the loss of one's home is as well.

As the novel's focalization aligns with various perspectives, Erpenbeck speeds up, reverses, stops, and cycles through time within the individual lives of the characters. Yet in the aggregate, there is still a forward movement of time from the late nineteenth century at the beginning of the novel to the turn of the millenneum at the novel's end. As time progresses it does not leave the reader, or the characters in the story, with a coherent view. Rather, it advances in much the same way as the potato beetles do who ravage the Brandenburg countryside in 1938, leaving the gardener in tears, or as the Russian horses do at the end of the war. Time devours almost everything in its path, leaving only the twigs and stems of memory from which to reconstruct what once was. From chapter to chapter the characters exhibit little awareness of the events that took place on the property before them. The gardener, who has inhabited the property the longest, has a somewhat more complete view, although even he has gaps in his knowledge of the history of the area. When he digs past the bedrock and into the sandy soil below, he does not recognize the significance of the zigzag pattern on the sand, which the narrator explains is a physical trace of the wind once blowing across the lake. The reader, as the recipient of the narrator's explanations, has perhaps the most comprehensive perspective, yet it is riddled with gaps. No one has a continuous perspective, as time reveals itself to be a patchwork of experiences, memories, the histories one constructs; that which one pays attention to, interprets, and makes sense of; and that which one hopes or expects for the future.

When the writers' granddaughter loses her home to the heirs of the architect's wife at the end of the novel, her behavior within the house makes no sense if time is to be conceived of as linear. Day after day, she trespasses to re-

---

[24] Krimmer argues convincingly that the rape is what ruptures the architect's wife's sense of eternity, dividing her life into a "before" and "after" that is typical of many rape survivors' experience. She also reads the rape as a capitulation to the processes of aging. Elizabeth Krimmer, "The Representation of Wartime Rape," 49–50. Nancy Nobile points out the birth imagery in the scene, reading it as an intertextual reference to Kleist's "Die Marquise von O..." Nancy Nobile, "'Ihr Erbteil'," 71.

store the home's dignity after it has fallen into disrepair. She sweeps up the dust covering the once dazzling cork floorboards, returns the wooden table that was removed from the house to protect it from dry rot, cleans the windows, and removes spider webs and marten feces. Since the utilities having been cut off, she cleans the floors and other surfaces with water from the lake. The labor of cleaning up the home is inexplicable as a forward-looking practice, especially once the house is scheduled to be demolished. Rather, her actions constitute a mourning ritual reminiscent of the rituals of marriage and death detailed in the chapter about the Wurrach family. Rituals harken back to another era, to a cyclical understanding of time. This repetitive work engaging with the materiality of the house also resembles the labor and time perception associated with the gardener, and these intra-actions within the material environment transform both the house and its last occupant. As the house is restored to order again, this last inhabitant transforms into a ghost-like figure, embedding herself in the house – she hides in the closet and watches from windows when real estate agents bring prospective buyers to the property – before she can part with it altogether.

The novel at its end appeals to the reader's sense of justice in two ways. The first has to do with our emotional attachment to place. The house has been awarded to people who have neither visited it, interacted with it, intra-acted within it, nor have memories attached to it. As the writers' granddaughter engages in the work of restoring the home, the abstruse legal explanation for awarding the house to the heirs of the Nazi architect's wife runs through her head. The language is alienating and incomprehensible, contrasting with the simple, uncomplicated love with which she cleans the home. How could the house be awarded to people who do not actually care for it? The second appeal is to our sense of historical justice. Ultimately, the descendant of resisters is being displaced by the heirs of Nazis, not to mention the fact that the resisters were Jewish, a detail mentioned only once in an earlier chapter. In the present day, the history of culpability and victimhood appears not to matter. The architect's purchase of the property from Wurrach is deemed a legitimate transaction, while the writers' acquisition of the property through appointment in the GDR is not. What is more, in the era of privatization and neoliberalism, Germany's genocidal past is to be capitalized on, serving as a selling point for prospective buyers who are charmed by the fact that the architect who built the house worked on Speer's Germania project. That the writers' granddaughter loses this house that she cherishes feels particularly unjust, and yet, the way in which time has functioned in the novel all along should indicate that the past does not necessarily affect the present in the way we expect it to. Time has consistently rent those with an emotional connection with the house and *Heimat* from it. Here, with the restitution case, separation from home is again a matter of inevitability.

Time as Accountability in Kathrin Gerlof's *Now That's a Story*

In an interview in 2008 following the publication of *Visitation*, Jenny Erpenbeck was asked what kind of relationship one should have to one's past. The bluntness with which she answered the question undercut its very premise: "You cannot choose your relationship to the past. Because the past is the past is the past."[25] Since the past is something we are all bound to, it makes no sense to think about it in individual terms. While Erpenbeck uttered this statement in an interview about *Visitation*, it speaks even more directly to the second novel to be discussed in this chapter, Kathrin Gerlof's *Now That's a Story*. In this novel, each of the majors characters seeks out an individual relationship to the past, attempting to manipulate it for their own purposes in the present. The characters' collective mistake is not recognizing that "the past is the past is the past" to which they are all beholden.

Now That's a Story takes place over several months in the present day, as citizens of the fictional town of Warenberg face a class action compensation and restitution case filed by the heirs of two Jewish brothers who lost property there during the Nazi era. The heirs of Hermann Weinreb seek restitution of the undeveloped land and villas that their ancestor had established as the Gut Tannenhof, while the heirs of his brother, Salomon Weinreb, are petitioning for financial compensation for the parceled land on which homes now sit. Tensions run high as the residents, most of whom are working class citizens of the former GDR, face losing their houses. While the heirs are seeking financial compensation rather than restitution of the land, many of the residents would be forced to sell their houses in order to pay their share of the settlement. To defend their case in court, each of the major characters in the novel engages in research about their own family history and the Weinrebs, seeking out a version of the past that will secure their right to their property in the present day. However, when the residents produce multiple, even conflicting, histories of the area, it becomes clear that they will fail. Their disparate accounts of the past cannot be rectified.

In *Now That's a Story*, the past intervenes on the present, but not in the multiple ways it does in *Visitation*. Whereas in *Visitation*, time does with people what it will, in *Now That's a Story*, time expresses its autonomy by refusing to be ma-

---

25 The question, in the original: "Was denken Sie, welche Beziehung sollte man zur eigenen Vergangenheit haben?" The answer: "Man kann sich sein Verhältnis zur Vergangenheit nicht aussuchen. Weil die Vergangenheit ist die Vergangenheit, ist die Vergangenheit." Jenny Erpenbeck, interview by Maren Schuster and Martin Paul, *Planet Interview*, Sept 1, 2008, http://www.planet-interview.de/interviews/jenny-erpenbeck/34662/.

nipulated. In order to secure their material well-being in the present, the residents must build a legal defense that makes particular arguments about the past: that their own families had purchased the houses in good faith and that the Weinrebs' sale of the property during the Nazi regime was fair and uncoerced. By the end of the novel, however, when they have arrived at conflicting histories of the area, it becomes apparent that some community members have manipulated the past in order to serve themselves in the present. Above all else, history is a narrative that must be arrived at honestly, and any attempt to manipulate facts creates a liability for the entire community.

By presenting historical responsibility as a collective obligation, *Now That's a Story* offers a different premise than the narratives depicting property disputes discussed in this monograph so far do. In *Taxi to Rathenow*, *Our House*, *Eduard's Homecoming*, and (in its last chapters) *Visitation*, the rightful ownership of a home hinges on two individuals' or families' competing histories. In *Now That's a Story*, the unjust history of the area implicates everyone. The novel's narrative strategy reflects this shared responsibility, as the narrator shifts focalization from character to character each chapter. The reader is restricted to the characters' perspectives, and with no prior knowledge of this town because it is fictional, is dependent upon their renderings, research, and personal memory. With this mode of narration, some characters reveal themselves to be more trustworthy of handling the past than others.

The scenario of a community collectively deciding whether to pay out or fight for their right to remain in their houses evokes important questions about the material impacts of collective responsibility. The central question of the novel is not, as one might expect, whether Germans today, having no personal culpability for Nazism, are still subject to a collective responsibility for that past. The novel takes a clear position that they do. Rather, the novel probes the material stakes of reparations. Is collective responsibility for the past, when practiced by the individual, a matter of rhetoric, attitude, or identity, or should it be more materially demanding? Do people who are not personally responsible for Nazism, but whose lives today are built upon the losses suffered by people persecuted under the Nazi regime, have an obligation to atone for the past in a way that jeopardizes their material security?

To engage with these questions about the nature and extent of atonement, the characters take strong positions within the so-called "Schlussstrichdebatte," the debate about whether Germany has sufficiently answered for the atrocities of the Holocaust or whether it must continue to do so. One character, the elderly Ilse Bock, argues for a blanket responsibility among Germans to pay reparations to Jewish victims. For Ilse, it is precisely *because* history has been obscured in the area that the Warenbergers should pay whatever the Jewish heirs demand.

She is the longest-standing resident of Warenberg, her father having purchased the family's plot of land in 1936 and built the family home in which she still lives. Her father's purchase of the land was technically at a fair price and legally above board. However, Ilse doubts that the proceeds actually went to the Weinreb family because a known Nazi had brokered the deal. Ilse thus has first-hand knowledge of how property transactions took place during the Nazi period, something the other residents lack. Moreover, Ilse understands the way in which time can conceal and reveal truths. She grew up believing that her father had been only a passive follower of National Socialism. However, when in his last years dementia weakened his ability to keep secrets, he told stories of raping a Polish woman during the war and killing Russians with relish. Ilse could no longer be certain of the extent of his crimes. Because of time's ability to conceal truths, Ilse believes that all Germans have a responsibility to contribute to Jewish compensation claims.

Another major character, the lawyer Johanna Wollweber, feels a similar responsibility to the past. However, she offers a counter-position to Ilse in that she does not believe in assigning guilt in such an undifferentiated manner. Johanna is not a resident of Warenberg herself, but rather, is the lawyer that the residents have sought out because of her previous successes defended against restitution suits. This would be Johanna's first case defending against a Jewish reparations claim, however, which gives her pause. For the past two years, she has obsessively engaged in research about her father, suspecting that he may have been involved in nefarious deeds during his tenure as a war correspondent during World War II. In her spare time, she has travelled throughout Europe to towns where her father was stationed, visiting concentration campus, museums, and archives. She will not take on the Warenbergers' case unless she can prove to herself that her father had not been involved in murderous activities. Unlike Ilse, Johanna believes that truths about the past can be discovered if one undertakes sufficient research.

While a few residents intend to pay the heirs out of guilt or in order to purchase their peace, others disavow any personal responsibility altogether. Ute Graf, a "Change Management" consultant from the West who has moved to Warenberg since unification and hopes to purchase a home there, represents an opposing view from that of Ilse and Johanna. As her job title implies, Ute is forward-looking, believes in adapting to the times as they change, and disavows any connection between the present and the past. She is focused solely on the future, and she has profited handily from this mindset, working in an advisory capacity to help East German companies transition to the new capitalist system. She refutes the very idea of collective guilt, arguing instead that the state, not individuals, carries the responsibility for the past.

The Warenbergers' lack of clarity about the area's history, coupled with their varying attitudes about their responsibility to it, leads them to employ a number of tactics to support their legal defense. One strategy that the community favors is to relativize the Weinrebs' suffering in order to see themselves as the true victims of history in the present day. They thus practice what Aleida Assmann calls "offsetting," one of the five strategies she has identified Germans employing today to deny their historical responsibility for Nazism.[26] Ute states, for example, that "In this story there are only victims [...] you just can't see it any other way. The Jews are victims of National Socialism and the people here are victims of Communism. You can't demand that they pay their way out of this in installments."[27] Here, Ute speaks in an undifferentiated manner about the kind and degree of suffering that people experienced under National Socialism and Communism. As she sees it, the current residents are suffering once more in a long line of injustices in the area.

More egregiously, the Warenbergers engage in another strategy related to what Assmann calls "falsification." Assmann explains that falsification occurs when a family memory does not align with official memory, especially as it pertains to a family member, and one chooses to adapt, or falsify, the memory of that person: "The falsification of personal history takes place under the pressure to adapt to new moral standards. Under these conditions, problematic family members are transformed into moral beacons according to the new framework of memory."[28] While it is unclear to what extent the Warenbergers have falsified their own family histories to accord with the narrative they require to secure their rights to their homes, they certainly do manipulate the image of the Weinreb family to delegitimize the heirs' claims. This manipulation of the past comes to light when their various accounts are compiled:

> In one account the Weinrebs farmed the land, in another they didn't at all, in another they raised a few chickens and geese. In one account they had a bank in the city, in another a

---

[26] In her monograph *Shadows of Trauma*, Aleida Assman describes five such strategies. Relativizing suffering, or what she calls "offsetting," is the first on her list. The others include externalizing, erasure, remaining silent, and falsification. Aleida Assmann, *Shadows of Trauma: Memory and the Politics of Postwar Identity*, trans. Sarah Clift (New York: Fordham University Press, 2016), 141–153.

[27] Originally: "In dieser Geschichte gibt es nur Opfer [...] das kann man gar nicht anders sehen. Die Juden sind Opfer des Nationalsozialismus und die Leute hier Opfer des Kommunismus. Denen kann man nicht abverlangen, dass die jetzt eine Abschlagzahlung leisten, um sich freizukaufen." Kathrin Gerlof, *Das ist eine Geschichte* (Berlin: Aufbau, 2014), 88. All translations of Gerlof are my own.

[28] Aleida Assman, *Shadows of Trauma*, 152.

grain store, in another a monopoly on matchstick production.[...] The same people, at least by name, had seats on either all the advisory councils of the world or on none at all.[29]

These different renderings of the Weinreb family lead the Warenbergers to draw conclusions about their relative power in the community and thus their relative ability to evade suffering under the Nazis. Martin Leber, the only trained historian participating in the citizens' initiative, recognizes the multitude of false conclusions the residents have drawn because of their shoddy research. They have made assumptions, confused names, and concealed facts. What is more, this false information makes its way into the collective knowledge of the group so that, as Martin regrets, historical truth will now become impossible to decipher.[30] Hedwig Gottwald, the leader of the citizens' initiative, understands the consequences of having discrepancies in the final report: "if someone reads that, they will take us for liars. We can't put that in anyone's hands without making ourselves uncredible."[31]

The community members' objective in constructing their narratives about the past is not to produce a truthful rendering. Rather, they are trying to maintain their material security, and this labor is not dissimilar from the material practices of one of the characters, Martina Leber, who suffers from a severe obsessive-compulsive disorder that forces her to clean repetitively. Martina feels a deep insecurity about her environment, and her daily efforts at scrubbing, tidying up, and maintaining order are devoted to controlling it. Her husband, Martin, notes that her behaviors have intensified since the reparations case began; the possibility that others might take her house intensifies her need for control. Indeed, Martina's behavior is one manifestation of the insecurity that the community feels at large. Her tireless scrubbing mirrors the obsessive research and narrative-building the other community members are engaged in, scouring and polishing the area's history to remove any dark spots so that they can feel secure about their rights to their houses.

---

29 Originally: "Mal haben die Weinrebs Landwirtschaft betrieben, mal gar nicht, mal nur zum Schein ein paar Hühner und Gänse gehalten. Mal hatten sie in der Stadt eine Bank, mal ein Getreidegeschäft, mal das Zündholzmonopol. [...] Dieselben Personen, zumindest dem Namen nach, saßen entweder in allen Aufsichtsräten der Welt oder in gar keinem." Kathrin Gerlof, *Das ist eine Geschichte*, 368.
30 Kathrin Gerlof, *Das ist eine Geschichte*, 137.
31 "Aber wenn das jemand liest, werden sie uns für Lügner halten. Das kann man niemandem in die Hand drücken, ohne dass wir uns unglaubwürdig machen." Kathrin Gerlof, *Das ist eine Geschichte*, 369.

While most of the residents of Warenberg lack clarity about the past and attempt to make arguments that best suit their interests in the present, the reader occupies a privileged position. In a number of shorter chapters, Salomon and Heinrich Weinreb, the brothers whose heirs seek reparations, speak from beyond the grave, recounting the respective eras of good fortune, insecurity, and tragedy that the family faced in Warenberg from the mid-nineteenth century into the Nazi period. The reader thus knows more than the current residents do and can evaluate the accuracy of their research. Moreover, Gerlof employs a particular narrative technique to lend certain characters more authority than others. Most characters' perspectives are narrated in the third person through free indirect speech, and thus their inner conflicts and justifications are made apparent. However, characters who are the most secure in their understanding of the past, for example Ilse Bock, speak for themselves in the first person. This narrative technique – the expression of opinion and facts without the inner turmoil – lends these characters' positions a more commanding tone. The Weinreb brothers have the most authority in the novel, as they are the only characters to narrate in the first person for chapters at a time.

While the main characters harbor a range of views on Germany's responsibility to its Nazi past, the novel's overall stance is for reparations, casting those characters who attempt to make arguments in bad faith in a negative light. For example, the residents draw on a number of antisemitic assumptions and stereotypes in order to position themselves as victims of the Weinrebs' heirs. One resident writes in the city newspaper that "Weinreb was a capitalist and a sponge, and I don't care if he was a Jew or not," employing anti-capitalist rhetoric from the GDR to justify drawing on an antisemitic stereotype of Jews being capitalist profiteers.[32] Yet the reader knows that this characterization of the Weinreb family is untrue, having already read Salomon and Hermann's accounts of the hard work they invested in creating a space where the family could feel safe, not amassing wealth for wealth's sake. At the same time, the residents disavow any responsibility for harboring antisemitic assumptions, seeing their upbringing as a safeguard: "We grew up in an antifascist state and aren't capable of being antisemitic."[33]

The community members' arguments intensify when a photograph surfaces that pictures the Weinrebs' suitcases. Perhaps the suitcases were filled with cash as they were leaving, and if so, was the family really all that persecuted? If the

---

[32] Originally: "Weinreb war ein Kapitalist und Schmarotzer, und es interessiert mich nicht, ob er Jude war oder nicht." Kathrin Gerlof, *Das ist eine Geschichte*, 113.
[33] Originally: "Wir sind in einem antifaschistischen Staat aufgewachsen und können gar nicht antisemitisch sein." Kathrin Gerlof, *Das ist eine Geschichte*, 112.

family has prospered elsewhere since the Nazi period, do the heirs really need to be compensated today, especially if that compensation puts the working-class citizens of Warenberg at financial risk? The residents allow themselves to engage in such speculation, but when more extreme sentiments arise from it, they are unsettled, faced with the noxious premise of their logic. When a community member states aloud in a meeting that – "None of their ancestors were directly persecuted, none ended up in a concentration camp. Instead, they received money from the sale of their land here and emigrated"[34] – the residents are uncomfortable with that conclusion. The notion that one had not suffered persecution under the Nazi regime unless they were in a concentration camp is a step too far for most of the residents, yet their practice of relativizing suffering has implied this argument all along. At the same time, when the town historian, Marischka, makes the point "But if the Weinrebs hadn't sold everything they owned at the last minute, they would have ended up in the gas chambers. You can't forget that," the residents ignore him.[35] They require a narrative in which the Weinrebs left the area successful, not persecuted.

Gerlof exposes the assumptions and omissions the residents allow themselves, but she also foregrounds the fact that these characters are in a difficult situation, financially, socially, and emotionally. The residents of Warenberg are themselves only achieving a modest (if also comfortable) lifestyle, which is now threatened by the possibility of having to pay a debilitating debt left them by a previous generation. The residents are being asked to atone for the past in a way that most Germans have not, to make material sacrifices rather than merely agree with the idea of atonement. Even the legal battle the residents face requires a material sacrifice. As Hedwig Gottwald explains, "This legal battle will draw out over many years. Those are years of insecurity for us all. We can't take a mortgage on our houses as long as the restitution claim encumbers them."[36] While Ilse Bock is prepared to relinquish her home and leave Warenberg, most of the residents see this as an extreme and undue sacrifice.

---

34 Originally: "Von ihren Vorfahren ist niemand direkt verfolgt worden, keiner ist ins Konzentrationslager gekommen. Stattdessen haben sie alle ihr Geld vom Verkauf der Grundstücke bekommen und sind ausgereist." Kathrin Gerlof, *Das ist eine Geschichte*, 136.
35 Originally: "Aber hätten die Weinrebs nicht in letzter Minute alles verkauft, was ihnen gehörte, wären sie ins Gas gegangen. Das dürft ihr nicht vergessen." Kathrin Gerlof, *Das ist eine Geschichte*, 101.
36 Originally: "dieser Rechsstreit werde sich über viele Jahre hinziehen. Das sind Jahre der Unsicherheit für uns alle. Wir können keine Hypothek auf unsere Häuser aufnehmen, solange auf denen die Rückgabeforderung lastet." Kathrin Gerlof, *Das ist eine Geschichte*, 112.

Gerlof also lets us draw no easy conclusions about Germany's complicated history. The question of individual obligation becomes tricky, not only because of the economic burden it would create for the current residents, but also because the history of that area has yielded many victims. Like Erpenbeck, Gerlof deftly points to various types of victimization that occurred in the twentieth century, garnering sympathy for a number of characters without relativizing the degree or kind of suffering. Hedwig Gottwald is one of the few characters with a clear grasp of her family history and thus proceeds with the defense of her home with confidence. Hedwig's parents had been Communist resisters to the Nazis. Her father was murdered in Buchenwald, and her mother raised three children while continuing to support a resistance group. When the Warenberg case gains notoriety, and accusations of historical amnesia are cast against the community in the media, Hedwig feels that an additional injustice has occurred. One history of persecution is legitimized whereas the persecution her parents experienced as resisters of the Nazi system is being forgotten. The result is an undifferentiated blame, which she finds unjust: "It's wrong to mix everything together [...]. That is the basic problem with this whole history. Everything is thrown into one pot, and we're supposed to just take the disgusting mush that comes out of it."[37] She believes that her parents' act of resisting the Nazis and the suffering they experienced as a result have earned her the right to her home and peace in the present day.

However, another character whose parents were victims of political persecution under the Nazi regime, Martin Leber, presents a counter-example to Hedwig's perspective. Although Martin's family was also awarded housing in the GDR for his parents' resistance to the Nazi regime and subsequent imprisonment, he does not consider their suffering to be pertinent to the current restitution case. Indeed, he mentions his parents only once, at the beginning of the novel, when he recalls parties they once hosted for other former political prisoners. He wonders how they would see the restitution case today, drawing no certain conclusions about what side they would take. Martin is a historian, has read a number of books about the history of Jews in Prussia, and relays his knowledge to the reader in the chapters focalized through his perspective. Unlike Hedwig, Martin balances his own family history against more established research and is unwilling to presume that his parents' sacrifice in the past earns him material security in the present.

---

37 Originally: "Es ist falsch, alles miteinander zu vermengen [...]. Das ist das Grundübel dieser ganzen Geschichte hier. Alles wird in einen Topf geworfen, und den ekligen Brei, der daraus entsteht, sollen wir auslöffeln." Kathrin Gerlof, *Das ist eine Geschichte*, 210.

The characters who lend us the longest view on the area's history are the Weinreb brothers. However, as a non-Jewish writer, Gerlof exhibits a great deal of self-doubt in authoring Jewish characters. In several instances in the novel, Salomon refers to the "shiksa" writer who has made him speak from beyond the grave: "[...] I [...] narrate, a dead person who still doesn't know if he's only good to the shiksa as an alibi. A harmless dead Jew."[38] In writing in this way, Gerlof investigates her own intentions:

> The shiksa here who is writing this whole story down is probably not doing anything differently [from the residents]. [She] writes her responsibility away, and then everything is fine. Crawls into my skin, as though she had a right to do that. As though I and my people were ever asked if they wanted to be the object of books, school assignment, exhibits.[39]

Such moments of self-reflexivity address the difficulties and potential liabilities of representing the past in narrative form. Whose perspectives should be included in the history of an area? What does it mean to inhabit someone else's skin, to voice someone else's perspective? What are the responsibilities in doing so? These question emerge as the central concerns of this novel as the characters piece together a narrative about the past, its injustices, and the material benefits and possible ramifications of those injustices for the current residents.

Another character, Ulrich Sturm, directly articulates the author's conundrum in deciding what kind of – and whose – story to tell. Ulrich is not a community member himself, but is temporarily renting a house there while he conducts research for a new documentary film. While in Warenberg, he learns that he stands to inherit a property in another town in the former East Germany, his childhood summer home that his parents abandoned when moving to the West. Hesitant to claim a house that might have a compensation claim pending, Ulrich researches its history and finds that his great uncle Konrad Sturm had bought it from a Jewish friend, Ernst David, in the 1930s. Ulrich puts his project on hold and considers making a film about the history of the house instead. In the process, he questions his own motivations for making such a film: "I'm seeking the Jew. I'm seeking the Jew to prove something to him. I'm seeking the Jew to prove to

---

[38] Originally: "[...] ich [...] erzähle, ein Toter, der immer noch nicht weiß, ob er der Schickse nur als Alibi gut ist. Ein harmloser toter Jude." Kathrin Gerlof, *Das ist eine Geschichte*, 125.

[39] Originally: "Die Schickse hier, die diese ganze Geschichte aufschreibt, macht es wahrscheinlich auch nicht anders. Schreibt sich was weg, und dann ist es gut. Schlüpft in meine Haut, als hätte sie ein Recht dazu. Als wären ich und meinesgleichen jemals gefragt worden, ob sie Gegenstand von Büchern, Studienarbeiten, Ausstellungen werden wollten." Kathrin Gerlof, *Das ist eine Geschichte*, 156.

him that neither I nor my ancestors have done anything unjust."[40] As Ulrich's research about Ernst David progresses, he struggles to find the beginning, end, and focus of the film. Should it be about the friendship between Konrad and Ernst? About the fact that Ernst was nearly shot and killed in Berlin during the sailors' rebellion in November 1919, but was spared because his brother took a bullet for him? Should this be a film about the parallel lives of Ernst David and Otto Marloh, the man who shot at the rebelling sailors?[41] Once Ulrich decides not to claim the house, he wonders if that should be the film's focus: "I wanted to make a film about why I stopped seeking the Jew although a whole house depends on it. Even if it's a small one. Now I am starting to tell a completely different story."[42] In the end, Ulrich finds a living heir of Ernst David, meets with him, and speaks directly with him about the house rather than composing his own narrative.

The meeting between Ulrich and the heir of Ernst David, also named Ernst, has a particular resonance. During their meeting, Ernst relinquishes any claim that his family might have to the property because he recognizes Ulrich's emotional connection with it. Ernst never knew his family had owned the property, nor has he any personal memories of it, and he is satisfied with Ulrich's research that indicates that the transaction was most likely fair. In this scene and others, Graf shows a nimble ability to represent a plurality of perspectives. Unlike the exchange between Eduard and Edita in *Eduard's Homecoming* discussed in chapter 5, in which Edita, the only Jewish character in the novel, serves to absolve Eduard and thus Germans more generally of guilt, Ernst in *Now That's a Story* is one of many Jewish characters with a range of perspectives. The Weinreb brothers, for instance, argue about their differing experiences of living in Germany. Salomon speaks with some nostalgia about times of relative security and happiness, having always identified more than his brother did with the German majority culture. Hermann, by contrast, was always burdened by a sense of unease and rarely felt safe leaving the Gut Tannenhof, his refuge. The brothers also have differing opinions about their heirs' motivations for engaging with the cur-

---

40 Originally: "Ich suche den Juden. Ich suche den Juden, um ihm etwas zu beweisen. Ich such den Juden, um ihm zu beweisen, dass weder ich noch meine Vorfahren irgendetwas Unrechtes getan haben." Kathrin Gerlof, *Das ist eine Geschichte*, 100.
41 For more on Otto Marloh as a historical figure, see "Marloh, Otto," *Das Bundesarchiv*, accessed January 2, 2020, https://www.bundesarchiv.de/aktenreichskanzlei/1919-1933/0000/adr/adrmr/kap1_1/para2_56.html.
42 Originally: "Ich wollte doch einen Film darüber machen, warum ich aufgehört habe, den Juden zu suchen, obwohl ein ganzes Haus dranhängt. Wenn es auch klein ist. Jetzt fange ich an, eine ganz andere Geschichte zu erzählen." Kathrin Gerlof, *Das ist eine Geschichte*, 238.

rent residents. They argue about whether their descendants should have any interest in that land at all, the site of so much pain for the family, or whether the dispute is about something else entirely: the German majority culture telling Jews that they no longer have a right to mourn their past.

Whereas Ulrich is someone who thoughtfully crafts narratives about the past, another character who creates stories for public consumption, Dieter Drühmer, must learn this responsibility over the course of the novel. Dieter is the editor of the town newspaper, the *Warenberger Bote* (*Warenberg Mercury*), and is initially delighted by the uproar that the compensation and restitution claim has caused. Letters to the editor come flowing in, and Dieter, enjoying the still relatively new freedoms of speech and press, prints all perspectives. However, the anonymity with which residents can express their views in the paper emboldens them to voice extreme opinions. After the heightened rhetoric leads to antisemitic vandalism of the heirs' lawyer's office building, Dieter realizes that as a member of the media, he has a responsibility to steer the conversation. He decides to limit discussion of the restitution case to a small segment, thereby putting its importance into perspective among other news stories to hinder further hysteria.

For the residents of Warenberg, having control over the dominant narrative about the past means having control over their material security in the present. The narratives the characters cannot control present the greatest threats to them. The city historian, Marischke, has long chronicled the history of antisemitism in the area. However, the residents refuse to draw on his expertise because it will not support their claims. While the reader is aware of Marischke's well-researched perspective, we are only indirectly privy to it. He does not speak much in the novel, because the other residents keep him at arm's length. The most obviously threatening narrative to the residents is that of the heirs, precisely because it is straightforward and comprehensive. As Hedwig states in a panic at the end of the novel, "They came here with a complete story, and their lawyers tell it over and over again. And we're behaving like a bunch of scared chickens instead of unifying."[43] Hedwig understands the heirs' advantage in having a collectively agreed upon story, something the residents do not have.

If the citizens of Warenberg cannot arrive at a narrative of the past that will reliably serve them in the present, another function of time, delay, is their best strategy: "We cannot stop. Believe me. We cannot stop. If we come to a conclu-

---

[43] Originally: "Die sind hergekommen mit einer fertigen Geschichte, und deren Anwälte erzählen die wieder und wieder. Und wir benehmen uns wie ein aufgescheuchter Hühnerhaufen, anstatt uns auch zu einigen." Kathrin Gerlof, *Das ist eine Geschichte*, 370.

sion, we will have to make a decision. Like Ilse Bock, who is paying the heirs, selling her house, and moving. If we stop, we will have to determine if we are in the right or the wrong."[44] Like Martina Leber, who repetitively scrubs, the residents must continue to research and rewrite their history, over and over again, without closure. Coming to a conclusion will mean acknowledging that they have not, in fact, scrubbed the dirt away. The novel ends on this sentiment of delay. Not only will the citizens continue to research their past, but Hedwig has also convinced Johanna to delay giving her the bad news that she will not represent them. She seems to have intuited what the reader already knows. Johanna has found evidence that her father was likely involved in the administration of a concentration camp. The legacy of Nazism is pervasive, and thus the citizens will be defeated eventually. Now, at least, they can hold onto their homes by delaying the process of that reckoning.

The Threatening Inevitability of (In)justice

Both *Visitation* and *Now That's a Story* center on the injustices of the nineteenth and twentieth centuries, framing them as the destabilization of home in the face of large-scale historical developments. In Erpenbeck's novel, the characters' individual fates – murder, expropriation, disinheritance, expulsion, flight, and rape – result from the racist and misogynistic ideologies that dominated the last two centuries. With each social or political regime change, a new character finds and loses home on the property that constitutes the novel's setting. *Now That's a Story*, on the other hand, deals with the fallout of Germany's history as the country enters the new millennium, depicting reverberations of historical injustice that continue in unexpected ways in the present.

In both novels, time exercises a particular kind of agency, advancing in a way that ranges from indifference to hostility to humans' security. It acts similarly to the potato beetles and Russian horses in *Visitation*, destroying almost everything in its path as it advances and leaving only twigs and stems – or as Martin Leber puts it in *Now That's a Story*, "shards and fragments" – from which to construct history.[45] In *Visitation*, generation after generation have little awareness of

---

[44] Originally: "Wir können nicht aufhören. Glauben Sie mir. Wir können nicht aufhören. [...] Wenn wir zu einem Ende kommen, müssen wir eine Entscheidung treffen. Wie Ilse Bock, die den Erben das Geld zahlt, ihr Haus verkauft und fortzieht. Wenn wir aufhören, müssen wir für uns festlegen, ob wir im Recht oder im Unrecht sind. Jeder Einzelne muss das tun." Kathrin Gerlof, *Das ist eine Geschichte*, 394.
[45] Originally: "Scherben und Bruchstücke[]." Kathrin Gerlof, *Das ist eine Geschichte*, 371.

what has occurred in the house before them, which allows a sequence of injustices to take place on the same site. Loss thus becomes a matter of inevitability, the quintessential experience of home.[46] By the end of the novel, historical awareness appears only in the form of apathy, as the history of Nazism and persecution becomes commercialized, a selling point in the new economy. In this respect, Gerlof endows time with more dignity than Erpenbeck does. Even though time also destroys almost all memory in *Now That's a Story*, the novel asserts that an objectively true history exists, will make itself known, and will obligate us to its truths. Whereas in *Visitation*, injustice is inevitable, in *Now That's a Story* historical justice becomes the inevitability. Those residents who try to manipulate the past for their own purposes will not be seen favorably. Graf thus exhibits more faith in history as a basis for justice than Erpenbeck does.

Still, both novels probe the limits of justice. While the restitution and compensation laws were intended to respond to a history of expropriation, displacement, and persecution, both novels illustrate the inadequacy of those laws to respond to a complex history of victimhood in Germany. In turn, they produced new injustices. Toward the end of *Visitation*, heirs to Nazis win a restitution case over heirs to resisters because of technicalities in the law. Having been on the right side of history is not enough to entitle one to security and justice in the present. Gerlof makes a similar case with her character Hedwig Gottwald, whose father was shot in Buchenwald as punishment for resisting the Nazis. This background puts her on the right side of history, but that is not enough to secure her exemption from the compensation claim or accusations of historical amnesia.

The novels then agree on one thing: the past does not protect one from the present. Time is an unwieldy foe; it promises only the inevitability of loss. In *Visitation*, time does with people what it will, demonstrating multiple modes and agencies. In *Now That's a Story*, time is a narrative that demands, with material consequences, to be pieced together. While both novels end by looking out into the future, the differences in the respective novels' endings are telling. *Now That's a Story* ends with delay, as the residents of Warenberg draw out their court case in order to retain their homes and disavow their historical responsibility as long as possible. Whereas *Now That's a Story* ends with a focus on the collective future of a community, *Visitation* looks past humans altogether. In the novel's epilogue the house has been razed and the landscape looks briefly as it did before the house was built on it. The epilogue thus mirrors the preface in

---

46 See also Monika Shafi, *Housebound*, 27.

its utter absence of human beings. The future of the area is the future of its material environment, and any human fates met in that environment are only of secondary importance. Whereas Gerlof's novel ends with humans in a vulnerable position, Erpenbeck's novel ends with the erasure of humans altogether. In both novels, time marches forward, out of human control.

Chapter 7
Home in the East as Corporate Overlord: Juli Zeh's *Unterleuten* (2016)

On July 1, 1990, the day on which the currency union took effect, Chancellor Helmut Kohl delivered a television address that would later be referred to, mockingly, as the *Blühende Landschaften* (Blooming Landscapes) speech. In this speech, he foretold a difficult transition away from the Communist system, but promised a bright common future for all Germans:

> There will be much hard work before we achieve unity and freedom, prosperity, and social equality for all Germans. Many of our compatriots in the GDR will have to adapt to new and unfamiliar living conditions – and also to a transition period that will certainly not be easy. But no one will be expected to endure undue hardship. To Germans in the GDR, I can say what Prime Minister de Mazière has already emphasized: No one will be worse off than before – and many will be better off.[1]

Within a year, Kohl's words would prove to have been naïve at best and a lie at worst. The undue hardships that many East Germans experienced as a result of unification included unemployment, de-credentialing, the loss of vital social programs, and the forfeiture of homes. Kohl and de Mazière's promise – that no one would be worse off than before – had been broken.

For those who were skeptical that unification would deliver on such promises, the next words in Kohl's speech did little to assuage fears that it was anything other than a capitalist takeover of the East:

> Only the monetary, economic, and social union offers the chance, yes, even the guarantee, of improving living conditions rapidly and thoroughly. Through our joint efforts, we will

---

[1] Helmut Kohl, "Fernsehansprache des Bundeskanzlers Kohl zum Inkrafttreten der Währungsunion am 1. Juli 1990," *Deutsche Geschichte in Dokumenten und Bildern*, accessed January 3, 2020, http://ghdi.ghi-dc.org/sub_document.cfm?document_id=3101&language=german. Originally: "Es wird harte Arbeit erfordern, bis wir Einheit und Freiheit, Wohlstand und sozialen Ausgleich für alle Deutschen verwirklicht haben. Viele unserer Landsleute in der DDR werden sich auf neue und ungewohnte Lebensbedingungen einstellen müssen – und auch auf eine gewiß nicht einfache Zeit des Übergangs. Aber niemandem werden dabei unbillige Härten zugemutet. Den Deutschen in der DDR kann ich sagen, was auch Ministerpräsident de Maizière betont hat: Es wird niemandem schlechter gehen als zuvor – dafür vielen besser."

soon succeed in transforming Mecklenburg-Vorpommern and Saxony-Anhalt, Brandenburg, Saxony, and Thuringia into blooming landscapes where it is worthwhile to live and work.[2]

The issuance of the West German Deutsche Mark in the GDR confirmed what many had foreseen: that the economic and social union that Kohl spoke of was no true merger. Kohl's rhetoric in this speech even evokes colonialism. The notion that only a Western socio-economic approach could bring about a "blooming landscape" in the East echoes the way in which Europeans had imagined the American and African continents, as well as parts of Asia, for centuries: not as harboring peoples, cultures, and economic systems of their own, but primarily as landmasses with natural resources awaiting development. In this speech, Kohl similarly characterizes the GDR as a place of untapped potential and disregards the fact that many of the people who lived in the GDR already considered it to be a worthwhile place to live and work.

Skeptics immediately made their voices heard. For example, the prominent East German author Volker Braun published a poem in the national newspaper *Die Zeit* one month after Kohl's speech that mourns the loss of East Germans' cultural identity. His poem, "Property" ("Das Eigentum"), begins with an ironic reference to Georg's Büchner's *The Hessian Courier* from 1834. The first two lines,

> Da bin ich noch. Mein Land geht in den Westen.
> KRIEG DEN HÜTTEN FRIEDE DEN PALÄSTEN.
>
> I'm still here. My country's going West.
> WAR ON THE COTTAGES, THE PALACES TAKE THE REST![3]

---

[2] Helmut Kohl, "Fernsehansprache." Originally: "Nur die Währungs-, Wirtschafts- und Sozialunion bietet die Chance, ja die Gewähr dafür, daß sich die Lebensbedingungen rasch und durchgreifend bessern. Durch eine gemeinsame Anstrengung wird es uns gelingen, Mecklenburg-Vorpommern und Sachsen-Anhalt, Brandenburg, Sachsen und Thüringen schon bald wieder in blühende Landschaften zu verwandeln, in denen es sich zu leben und zu arbeiten lohnt." Helmut Kohl, "Kohl's Celebration of the Currency Union, July 1, 1990," trans. Allison Brown and Belinda Cooper, in *Uniting Germany: Documents and Debates, 1944–1993*, ed. Konrad Jarausch and Volker Gransow (Providence and Oxford: Berghahn Books, 1994), 172–174.

[3] Volker Braun, "Das Eigentum," *Die Zeit*, Aug. 9, 1990, https://www.zeit.de/1990/33/das-eigentum. All translations from Braun are my own, adapted from the translations of Michael Hofmann, David Constantine, and Karen Leeder. See: Volker Braun, "Property," trans. Michael Hofmann, *Poetry* 173, no. 1 (1998): 53; Volker Braun, "Property," trans. David Constantine and Karen Leeder, *Rubble Flora: Selected Poems* (New York: Seagull Books, 2014), 46. The original line from Büchner reads: "Friede den Hütten! Krieg den Palästen!" ("Peace to the cottages! War on the palaces!"). Georg Büchner, "Der Hessische Landbote," in *"Friede den Hütten! Krieg den Palästen!" Der Hessische Landbote. Briefe*, ed. Hanjo Kesting (Hamburg: Verlag Lutz Schulenburg, 2002), 23.

invert Büchner's famous call to revolution against the monarchy over a century and a half before and foreground the pro-capitalist ends of the "peaceful revolution" of 1989. In the final two lines of the poem,

> Mein Eigentum, jetzt habt ihrs auf der Kralle.
> Wann sag ich wieder *mein* und meine alle
>
> My property, now you have it in your claws.
> When will I say *mine* again and mean of all

Braun ironically frames Easterners' cultural and social losses as a loss of property, the capitalist terminology being the only language left that holds meaning in the new system.

Some twenty-six years later, Juli Zeh's novel *Unterleuten* (2016) expands on these themes, depicting issues of property, investment, and corporatization as they continue to reshape cultural identity and community in the former East Germany. Far from the "blooming landscapes" that Kohl envisioned, Zeh's novel takes place within a dense forest landscape that hosts and obscures violence spurred on by the competition of capitalism. *Unterleuten* is set in 2010, as the local agribusiness and major employer of the rural town Unterleuten (hence the novel's title) faces insolvency in the midst of the global financial crisis brought on by sub-prime mortgage lending in the United States. The town might be saved, however, when a clean energy firm, *Vento direct*, proposes establishing a wind farm there that will pump money into its struggling economy. One lucky resident in particular will strike it rich, as the most direct and immediate profit will go to the person who leases land to the corporation. There is, of course, a catch. No one resident owns the acreage required to build a wind farm, and the company is not willing to do business with multiple leasers. The few people who own the land under consideration, an area on the edge of the town known as the *Schiefe Kappe* (the crooked cap), must negotiate among themselves to consolidate two tracts of land under one owner. Whoever can secure the purchase of their neighbor's property will win the lucrative contract. Competition soon consumes the town like a dark force, as the residents of Unterleuten divide into camps for and against the wind farm and turn on one another.

Zeh is known for playing with genre expectations, and *Unterleuten* is no exception. This slow burning thriller derives its suspense from the eerie force that finance capitalism seems to wield over the people of Unterleuten. Given the novel's inward focus on a community, it might be best described as a *Dorfroman* (village novel), *Heimatroman* (*Heimat* novel), or even *Anti-Heimatroman*.[4] It reads at times like a Western and at others like a mafia drama, yet the overarching aesthetic bent resembles that of the American Southern gothic story, in which horrific events play out against tranquil pastoral settings. In Zeh's novel, however, the horror does not emerge from within, but rather, results from a capitalism that invades from far away. In that respect, *Unterleuten* is like an alien invasion story inflected with *Heimat* aesthetics.

Beyond referencing the name of the town in which the novel is set, the title *Unterleuten* also reflects the communal and interpersonal nature of its main conflict. This compound word, when broken into its components, "unter Leuten," translates to "among people" and, indeed, the community is the novel's collective protagonist. As a *Dorfroman*, Unterleuten maintains a tight inward focus on the town, and the third-person narration emphasizes the residents' connectedness, shifting focalization among the community members from chapter to chapter and lending the reader access to their thoughts through free indirect speech.[5] At the same time, the title points to the residents' shared responsibility for their collective fate. Although the promise of investment seems like a force invading from far away, the people of Unterleuten are ultimately responsible for how they treat one another. Capitalism, and how one practices it, is determined by humans – among people. Finally, the title hints at the secrecy with which the residents of Unterleuten operate. In German, if something stays "unter uns" (like the English idiom "between us"), it is a secret, and to be sure, the residents of Unterleuten prefer secrecy over openness. The characters repeatedly hold private meetings in the forest that borders the town, a site with a long history of hosting and obscuring the violence that they inflict on one another.

Unterleuten shares similarities with the other narratives discussed in this monograph, for example depicting Westerners acquiring houses in the Eastern countryside and drawing on *Heimat* imagery for its affective force, but it frames the encroachment of capitalism in the East differently. A few Westerners have acquired houses in Unterleuten since unification, but their relative wealth has not

---

[4] For more on Zeh's novel as a *Dorfroman*, see Natalie Moser, "Dorfroman oder Urban Legend? Zur Funktion der Stadt-Dorf-Differenz in Juli Zehs *Unterleuten*," in *Über Land: Aktuelle literatur- und kulturwissenschaftliche Perspektiven auf Dorf und Ländlichkeit*, ed. Magdalena Marszałek, Werner Nell, and Marc Weiland (Bielefeld: Transcript, 2018), 127–129.

[5] The novel breaks from this narrative scheme only once, changing to first-person narration in the epilogue to reveal that the narrator had pieced together the story of Unterleuten after reading a headline about a rural suicide, deciding to investigate in order to write a more in-depth exposé on it, and then visiting the town multiple times to speak with its residents to research the piece. The exposé has ostensibly become the novel we just read.

purchased them social influence or status. Quite the opposite, as the older guard runs the town politics and marginalizes new voices. The real impact of capitalism on social structures in the East lies not with individuals or their transactions, but, as it turns out, with the faceless and faraway power of global corporate investment. In *Unterleuten*, the town's residents – Eastern and Western – become pawns in a hegemonic investment scheme in which faraway banks and investment firms are the only winners.

While *Unterleuten* foregrounds the large-scale impacts of corporate investment rather than the interpersonal and interfamilial injustices of housing transactions, it warrants an examination in the final chapter of this monograph for a number of reasons. For one, it follows up on themes discussed in chapter 3 in conjunction with *The Brocken* (Glowna 1992) and *No More Mr. Nice Guy* (Buck 1993), films from the early 1990s that center on houses in order to address the former East Germany becoming a capitalist battleground. *Unterleuten* depicts this capitalist battleground some twenty years later, after the widespread phenomenon of housing disputes has given way to a new wave of corporate investment. It now pervades all aspects of home, personal relationships, and *Heimat*, and as such, fulfills the neoliberal mission for the market to control all aspects of life.[6] The residents mull over and debate the energy firm's proposal while engaging in their domestic routines, and the interiority of home becomes the site of economic negotiations and decisions. In a few instances, the residents' houses even become the sites of overt attacks on each other in their competition for the investment contract. However, as we will see below, an analysis of the actual houses that Westerners have acquired in the area yields that they, if not their inhabitants, might be the last agents of resistance to the encroachment of capitalism in the area. Houses in Unterleuten wield a non-human agency against their Western inhabitants, similar to that of the houses discussed in chapters 4 and 5 of this monograph, and may have played a role in containing the power of Westerners so far.

The Alien Invasion of Capitalism, or Not Recognizing the Sociomateriality

The novel's intrigue begins when the mayor of Unterleuten, Arne Seidel, calls a town meeting without disclosing an agenda. A plurality of residents attends out

---

6 See the introduction and chapter 3 for my discussions of neoliberalism, which draw on work by Raewyn Connell and David Harvey, among others.

of curiosity, and after allowing a buzz to build in the room, Seidel proudly announces that a wind energy company, *Vento direct*, plans to build a wind farm outside of their town. Predictably enough, the townspeople's reactions are split: some are cautiously enthusiastic and others outright hostile to the idea. It quickly becomes clear, however, that they have been summoned not to vote or give input, but solely to be informed. The important decisions have already been made, and the community's only agency in the process is in securing a large enough plot of land for the site of the wind farm. There is no doubt that the residents of Unterleuten will complete this task since the economic incentive to the town and person who secures an appropriate parcel of land is too great to resist. The company's power is hegemonic. Even its representative in the area, Herr Pilz, has no decision-making power. He acts in a servile capacity rather than as part of the company's administration.

The most direct competition in the novel will take place among the three characters who own land on the *Schiefe Kappe*, the area in question for the wind farm: Gombrowski, a man whose family has managed land in Unterleuten for generations; Linda Franzen, a newcomer from the West who has moved to Unterleuten to stable her beloved horse, Bergemotte; and Konrad Meiler, a speculator living in Ingolstadt who snapped up land cheaply in Unterleuten some years before and has been raising lease rates in the area ever since. While those three play a game of niceties and deception in order to secure a deal for each other's land, a deep and ugly rift emerges among the townspeople, dividing them into camps for and against the wind farm. Those who are in favor of it, led by Gombrowski, see its financial potential. Those against it, led by his longtime rival, Kron, protest out of concerns about animal protection, mental health, and the aesthetics of the landscape. As the camps face off against one another, a number of mysterious events take place. Two children disappear and reappear inexplicably in two separate instances. Authorities detain the local cat lady (an extraordinary event, to be sure, since the people of Unterleuten strictly avoid the attention of bureaucratic agencies or outside law enforcement). A near-fatal car accident sends a resident to the hospital in what was most likely an attempted murder. There are multiple assaults, and in the novel's climax, a resident commits a gruesome suicide that doubles as an act of revenge on the town at large.

Zeh's characters are particularly adept at manipulating their physical environment for discursive purposes, and as such, Zeh treats the themes of home, competition, inheritance, loss of security, time, and collective responsibility – themes discussed in the previous chapters of this monograph – with a careful eye toward the materiality of home and landscape. The town of Unterleuten exists in and for itself as an entanglement of people, the physical environment, and objects, resisting the influence of outside politics or media. As one of the newer residents from Berlin, Gerhard Fließ, observes early in the novel, "Having escaped the notice of politics, media, and science, there existed here a half anarchic, almost completely independent way of life, a kind of pre-state barter society, unintentionally subversive, far from the grasp of the state, forgotten, disregarded, and thus in a strange way free."[7]

Rather than turning to the law to handle conflicts, the residents of Unterleuten routinely manipulate their physical environment for discursive purposes. That is, they send passive aggressive messages to one another by arranging objects in inconvenient and sometimes dangerous ways within the landscape. For instance, when Gerhard Fließ insists that his neighbor, Bodo Schaller, obtain permission from the area's nature protection agency before renovating his barn, Schaller responds by burning tires on their shared property line, sending the smell of burnt rubber into the home of Gerhard, his wife Jule, and their infant daughter for weeks on end. In this way, Schaller punishes his neighbors for their presumption and wages psychological warfare, sending a clear message without having to speak with them. In another instance, when the mayor Arne Seidel is angered by the noise his neighbor makes by mowing incessantly, he blocks the path to his neighbor's septic tank with his car so that it cannot be emptied. The sewage backs up into the neighbor's house, and so Seidel has enacted his revenge. A note left on the car informing the neighbor that mowing is allowed only once a week guarantees that the content of the message is clear. The manipulation of the physical environment communicates the weight of that message.

The tragedy of *Unterleuten*, then, lies in its irony. Whereas the people of Unterleuten are accustomed to controlling their social dynamics by manipulating the physical environment, they do not recognize the material leverage they have in their dealings with *Vento direct*. Both the institutional structure of *Vento direct* and the wealth that it promises seem alien in comparison to the economic drivers that the townspeople are accustomed to. Not only does the town's major employer, the agribusiness Ökologica GmbH, have a physical location in Unterleuten and employ local people, but it also provides the framework – an apparatus, in Karen Barad's terms – for workers' interactions with and intra-actions within the material landscape. *Vento direct*, by contrast, is headquartered

---

[7] Originally: "Unbemerkt von Politik, Presse und Wissenschaft existierte hier eine halb-anarchische, fast komplett auf sich gestellte Lebensform, eine Art vorstaatlicher Tauschgesellschaft, unfreiwilling subversiv, fernab vom Zugriff des Staates, vergessen, missachtet und deshalb auf seltsame Weise frei." Juli Zeh, *Unterleuten* (Munich: Luchterhand, 2016), 29. All translations from Zeh are my own.

in an undisclosed, and presumably faraway, location and is therefore imperceptible and abstract in comparison.[8] The resource the company will make use of – the wind – and the product it will manufacture – energy – are intangible in nature and thus are only abstract to the citizens of Unterleuten. Moreover, the profits that *Vento direct* promises the town will be generated through corporate taxes and investment, not from the actual labor of people or the yields of the earth. The amounts generated, some 200,000 Euro per year for the town and 150,000 for the individual leaser, are unfathomable to the townspeople and, in all practical terms, virtual. This amount of capital flowing into Unterleuten will fundamentally change its society, giving money a new value and the Westerners who have moved there a leg up.

Since the company does not yet have a material infrastructure in Unterleuten, something the residents could manipulate for discursive purposes, the power that it wields in the town seems hegemonic and unassailable to them from the very beginning. Indeed, in his initial presentation to the people of Unterleuten, Pilz appears aware that the company derives much of its power through this perceived intangibility and expertly manipulates the residents to believe that the construction of a wind farm in their town is inevitable. He meets both their enthusiasm and hostility with the simple response that, "The essential decisions aren't being made in Unterleuten."[9] That is, the wind farm will be constructed regardless of what the townspeople think or do, and he supports this claim with graphics in his presentation that are designed to confuse and thereby disempower them. Even the discord among the community members works in the favor of the company since it will eventually exhaust the residents and give way to submission. As Seidel recounts it in his thoughts:

> It was necessary to let the refusal rise to a critical point, then to let the anger smolder, and finally to put arguments forth that make it seem like there is no alternative to the project. In this way, the impression arises that it is a complex matter with a certain inescapability. That confuses people. Pilz didn't need approval. He needed resignation.[10]

---

[8] See the introduction and chapter 2 for discussions of Barad's terms "apparatus" and "intra-action."
[9] Originally: "'Das Wesentliche wird nicht in Unterleuten entschieden.'" Juli Zeh, *Unterleuten*, 160.
[10] Originally: "Es galt, die Ablehnung bis zum kritischen Punkt zu steigern, dann die Wut verrauchen zu lassen und anschließend Argumente nachzulegen, die das ganze Projekt alternativlos erscheinen ließ. Auf diese Weise entstand der Eindruck, es handele sich um eine komplexe Materie mit einer gewissen Ausweglosigkeit. Das verwirrte die Leute. Pilz braucht keine Zustimmung, er braucht nur Resignation." Juli Zeh, *Unterleuten*, 153–154.

If the construction of the wind farm is inevitable, the only question remaining is which resident will provide the tract of land and secure a lucrative contract. The notion that the investment is inevitable – that capitalism itself is inevitable – sets the ground for competition.

Pilz has engineered a sense of inevitability and helplessness among the townspeople by foregrounding the virtual and intangible aspects of the transaction, that is, the financial investment, and by concealing the fact that the company is depending upon the people of Unterleuten to provide the material conditions for the wind farm. The residents' fatal flaw is that even though they are adept at manipulating the physical environment for discursive purposes, they do not perceive *Vento direct* as a materially dependent system that can be manipulated. Indeed, this type of misrecognition is so common in our contemporary world that a field of study within the discipline of Management Studies has been developed to explain it. Scholarship on the topic of "sociomateriality" conceives of the mutual construction of the physical and the social aspects of systems typically considered to be primarily social, intersubjective, or discursive, such as organizational management, finance capitalism, and telecommunications.[11]

Pratima Bansal and Janelle Knox-Hayes illustrate sociomateriality as a concept with the example of googling:

> At face value, the Internet user appears to possess the power to search for information, yet that search effort depends on the physical infrastructure that Google built, including its servers, directories, and databases. Embodied in those material elements are the ideas, priorities, and preferences of the individuals and groups involved in developing the material objects. Google searching, then, becomes a mangle of the sociological and the material, giving rise to sociomateriality.

Not only does the practice of googling, which is largely considered to be an intersubjective and virtual experience, rely on material infrastructure, but more importantly, this material infrastructure has been shaped by our human needs, priorities, and values. Neither the material nor the intersubjective aspects of googling is more important or a priori, but rather, both shape one another. In their introductory work on materiality in organization studies, Paul. R. Carlile,

---

[11] In their work on the ecological impacts of corporate organizational practices, Pratima Bansal and Janelle Knox-Hayes have written that "research on sociomateriality acknowledges the importance of the physical world in management and organizations, arguing that organizational life is the result of the coproduction or mutual constitution of the social and physical worlds." Pratima Bansal and Janelle Knox-Hayes, "The Time and Space of Materiality in Organizations and the Natural Environment," *Organization & Environment* 26, no. 1 (2013): 62.

et al., emphasize just how central materiality is to all human social interactions: "What makes human sociality distinctive [...] is that practices are not merely constellations of intersubjectivity, they are also constellations of 'interobjectivity.'"[12]

The residents of Unterleuten fail to recognize the material and "interobjective" potential for controlling their interactions with *Vento direct*. For example, if the residents were to decide not to host a wind farm in Unterleuten, they might employ the material-discursive tactic of manipulating the land in a way that is inconvenient, even dangerous, for *Vento direct* to use. This is, after all, a tactic they routinely use on one another. Alternatively, if the residents could agree that they did want to host a wind farm, they might negotiate with the company on its placement, the number of wind turbines, the yields they would receive from it, or any number of other conditions. However, capitalism's appeal is to the individual, not the collective, and as we will see in a moment, the town of Unterleuten has a long history of parceling and consolidating the very same land for the benefit of a few individuals and at the cost of others. The corporation will ultimately profit from the residents' history of competing over control of the land.

Violent Capitalism(s)

While *Vento direct*'s promise of investment compels unexplained mysteries and violence in the present day, it soon becomes apparent that the townspeople have a history of enacting violence on one another whenever a major shift in political regime affects the ways in which people inhabit and control land. Perhaps Zeh's greatest achievement with this novel is that she reveals different material-discursive practices that operate according to the prevailing political and economic paradigm. She effectively draws lines of continuity between commercial investment in the present day and a much longer history of hegemonic land ownership in the area, connecting the dots between the large land holdings of the Prussian nobility, the collectivization of farmlands during Soviet occupation and in the early years of the GDR, the establishment of the agricultural co-op and its privatization after unification, the acquisition of houses in the area by Westerners, and the global effects of finance capitalism in the twenty-first century.

---

[12] Paul. R. Carlile, et al., "How Matter Matters: Objects, Artifacts, and Materiality in Organization Studies: Introducing the Third Volume of 'Perspectives on Organization Studies'" in *How Matter Matters: Objects, Artifacts, and Materiality in Organization Studies*, ed. Paul R. Carlile, et al. (Oxford: Oxford University Press, 2013) 7.

Zeh achieves this continuity by structuring it along the lines of rivalry between two longtime residents of Unterleuten, Gombrowski and Kron, who represent a dialectic of power and resistance that dates back for decades. In the post-unification era, this dialectic aligns with the ideological competition between capitalism and communism. Gombrowski, effectively a personification of industrial capitalism, runs the Ökologica GmbH and sees himself as a father figure and provider in the community. In a chapter devoted to Gombrowski's point of view, we learn how he came into the position of controlling the company, and thus, most of Unterleuten's land. As a child, he watched as his father led the Soviet-era land reform in the area in order to protect the family's landholdings.[13] Through a combination of politicking, coercion, and physical violence, the elder Gombrowski then attained a leadership position in what became the LPG Gute Hoffnung (agricultural co-op Good Hope), a position that his son would later occupy. After German unification, the younger Gombrowski implemented similar tactics of politicking, coercion, and physical violence in his own efforts to retain control when the *Landwirtschaftsanpassungsgesetz* (Agricultural Adjustment Act) mandated the privatization of large-scale agricultural co-ops in the former East Germany.[14]

Kron, on the other hand, hails from a family of landless peasant farmers, was a devoted Communist up to the end of the GDR, and counters Gombrowski at every opportunity. He was a visible part of the resistance to collectivization efforts in the GDR and was among the mob that burned down the Gombrowski family's grain silo in the "socialist spring" of 1960 – an incident that hints at a long history of material-discursive acts taking place in the area. After German unification, Kron has continued to oppose Gombrowski's efforts, challenging the initiative to privatize the agricultural co-op and championing instead a return of the land to the people who had owned it before collectivization. Feeling that the people are being expropriated all over again, he refers to the privatization efforts of the 1990s as "Raubtierkapitalismus" (predatory capitalism).[15] Today, Kron opposes the wind farm out of suspicion that Gombrowski will find a way to profit from it and further strengthen his social influence in the town: "He had seen

---

13 See chapter 1 for a discussion of Soviet-era (SMAD) land reforms and what resulted from them after unification.
14 Agricultural Restructuring Act (Gesetz über die strukturelle Anpassung der Landwirtschaft an die soziale und ökologische Marktwirtschaft in der Deutschen Demokratischen Republik [Landwirtschaftsanpassungsgesetz]), 29 June 1990.
15 Juli Zeh, *Unterleuten*, 115.

enough to understand the world as a place where changes primarily existed so that the dreadfulness could dress in ever brighter clothing."[16] Referring to Gombrowski's *Junkergesicht* (nobleman's face),[17] Kron points to the fact that the Gombrowski family has had continuous control over the land since their time as landed nobility in Prussia.

The violence the town inflicts upon itself in the present day recalls the rash of violence that took place some twenty years before in Unterleuten, when Gombowski led efforts to privatize the agricultural co-op and convert it to the Ökologica GmbH. Unlike in Erpenbeck's novel *Visitation*, discussed in chapter 6, in which violence takes place repeatedly on the same tract of land in large part due to a lack of continuous memory from generation to generation, in *Unterleuten* memory proves to be no safeguard against violence. To the contrary, Gombrowski's first-hand memory of his father's brutal tactics guided his approach to maintaining control over the land in the 1990s and does so again in 2010. Like his father before him, Gombrowski is attuned to the political climate, taking on whatever leadership role and employing whatever tactics will ensure his dominance in the new era.

One of the most climactic scenes in the novel depicts Gombrowski's violence twenty years before, when he arranged a meeting in the woods to discuss the privatization of the co-op with Kron. In this scene, Kron arrives at the meeting place to find another resident there, Bodo Schaller, who beats him mercilessly. Even worse, the incident leaves another resident, Erik Kessler, dead. Mistrustful of Gombrowski, Kron brought Erik with him for back-up. However, a tree branch falls on Erik in an apparent freak accident when a thunderstorm sets in. Through violent means, possibly the manipulation of the physical environment (Gombrowski determined the location of the attack, and it is unclear whether he had manipulated the tree branch in advance as a way to injure Kron), and the use of the woods to hide his deeds, Gombrowski has managed to gain control over the privatization process, and thus the land. Some twenty years later, Kron still walks with a limp, a physical reminder of that fateful meeting.

In the present day, finance capitalism and supranational decision-making are the impetus to repeat this history of violent competition over control of the land. We learn, for example, in a chapter devoted to Konrad Meiler's perspective why Westerners are suddenly attracted to this particular area outside of Berlin some twenty years after unification:

---

16 Originally: "Er hatte genug gesehen, um die Welt als einen Ort zu begreifen, an dem Veränderung vor allem darin bestand, die Ungeheuerlichkeit in immer neue bunte Gewänder zu kleiden." Juli Zeh, *Unterleuten*, 115.
17 Juli Zeh, *Unterleuten*, 492.

Since the American mortgage crisis put a strain on the national budgets and the realization spread that running a deficit could also become a problem for national economies, the Treasury did what any private citizen would do. It didn't polish the table silver, per se, but rather the large-area junk lands that had ended up in the Federal Republic at unification in the form of former people's property.[18]

The financial crash of 2008 brought on by the predatory lending practices of Lehmann Brothers and other similar institutions has forced Germany to sell off assets at a low price. Westerners such as Meiler are then able to snap up those properties in the East and drive up rent and sales prices on the land. As Meiler recalls: "At the auction that Wanka and Meiler visited, the successor organization of the Treuhand brought 250 hectares under the hammer. Because the starting price was downright ridiculous, Konrad Meiler bid, and once he had begun, he couldn't stop."[19] Meiler has no personal attachment to the area, instead seeing the purchase of land there as a more secure investment than stocks. With the area around Berlin promising to boom, he will sell at a premium when, for example, the state decides to build a new highway or a grocery store chain plans to open a location in Unterleuten. To his delight, the fact that Westerners are purchasing more land in the area only makes his properties more valuable, so that he can inflate rents and optimize sales prices.

Similarly, Linda Franzen's purchase demonstrates how middle-class citizens from the West were able, with some help, to benefit from the global economic crash. When Linda finds the house of her dreams in Unterleuten, an abandoned farmhouse with a pasture and silo, she is able to secure a low-interest bank loan to finance purchasing it. Property values have been driven up by speculation to the point that Easterners are unable to maintain control of their land. At the same time, banks have cut interest rates in order to fight the recession, which plays to the advantage of Westerners with enough capital for a down payment. Such economic decisions coming out of Berlin and Brussels are now wresting

---

18 Originally: "Seit die amerikanische Immobilienkrise die Staatshaushalte unter Druck setzte und sich die Erkenntnis ausbreitete, dass Überschuldung auch für Volkswirtschaften zum Problem werden konnte, machte das Finanzministerium, was jeder Privatmensch auch tun würde: Es verscheuerte zwar nicht das Tafelsilber, wohl aber den großflächigen Ramsch, der bei der Wiedervreinigung in Form von ehemaligem Volkseigentum in das Eigentum der Bundesrepublik gelangt war." Juli Zeh, *Unterleuten*, 52.
19 Originally: "Bei der Auktion, die Wanka und Meiler besuchten, brachte die Nachfolgeorganisation der Treuhand 250 Hektar unter den Hammer. Weil der Ausgangspreis geradezu lächerlich war, bot Konrad Meiler mit, und als er einmal damit angefangen hatte, konnte er nicht mehr aufhören." Juli Zeh, *Unterleuten*, 52–53. See chapter 1 for an explanation of the *Treuhand*.

control of the land from Gombrowski, placing it instead in the hands of Westerners like Konrad Meiler and Linda Franzen.

While the presence of Westerners in the area over the past two decades has seemed innocuous, not having altered the social dynamics of the town in any meaningful way, it now actually assists the corporation in gaining influence in the area. The same three characters who are most closely attuned to capitalist thinking are the best situated to compete for the contract with *Vento direct*. Gombrowski, Linda Franzen, and Konrad Meiler all own land on the *Schiefe Kappe* and are ready to compete for one another's land while the rest of the town wages war on itself by manipulating the materiality of home and the landscape. None of these three main competitors for the contract represent the kind of resistance to hegemonic capitalism that someone like Kron does and, in the end, the Westerners win out – at least seemingly. After leading Gombrowski to believe that she will sell to him, Linda Franzen cuts a deal with Konrad Meiler behind Gombrowski's back. Konrad can leave Unterleuten happy with the deal he made with Linda, and she can secure the contract with *Vento direct*.

However, Linda is ultimately foiled by the physical war being waged by the town at large. As soon as Linda has secured Meiler's land in a secret meeting with him in Berlin, her boyfriend, Frederik, races back to Unterleuten, hoping to manage the town's expectations and prevent retaliation against Linda. On his way, however, he is nearly killed in an automobile collision while driving around a sharp curve entering Unterleuten. By his account, someone likely recognized Linda's car and was attempting to murder or severely injure her. After this extreme act of violence against them, in which objects were once again manipulated within the physical environment for discursive purposes, Linda and Frederik leave the area without contracting their land to *Vento direct*. This is no matter to the company, however, who will get its land regardless of who has been injured, traumatized, or even killed because of the competition. It turns out that Kron also holds a suitable piece of land that could be developed, but given his history of resistance to hegemonic capitalism, he had been largely overlooked as an eligible party to lease to the energy firm. In the end, he gives the land to his daughter so that the contract will secure the financial wellbeing of his beloved granddaughter Krönchen.

Gombrowski, having been cut out of the deal with Linda that would have made his contract with *Vento direct* possible, will no longer be in a position to control the land and "provide," as he sees it, for the town. With the Ökologica GmbH failing, the Gombrowski family's reign of control in the area has come to an end. In the novel's gruesome climax, he asserts his final material-discursive act, committing suicide in a performative act of simultaneously exercising and abdicating his power. Carefully descending into the depths of the municipal drinking well on which the community depends, he cuts open his wrists and bleeds out into the water. The drinking well is one of Gombrowski proudest accomplishments since it has secured the town's independence from the administrative district. His suicide there is thus designed to draw attention to his role as a provider in the town. However, Gombrowski's acts of providing have long been coupled with coercion and violence, and his final act reflects both aspects of his power. Not just his blood, but also the decomposing matter of his corpse will eventually enter the water. The people of Unterleuten will drink of his body and become ill.[20] As such, the materiality of his body becomes discursive, too, a message of revenge through provision.

Kron dies soon thereafter from natural causes, and with Kron's death comes the end of the opposition to hegemonic control over the land. There is woefully little prospect of resistance to hegemony among the younger generation. Kron's daughter Kathi will succeed Arne Seidel as mayor of Unterleuten, but she has remained neutral in her father's feud with Gombrowski. Moreover, she stands to profit from the contract with *Vento direct* and thus has little reason to oppose its influence or power in the area. Placated by money flowing into the town, the new generation also does not understand – and is not motivated to learn – how to manipulate the materiality in which they live for discursive purposes. They are not interested in the feuds of their fathers and are perhaps not aware that they can manipulate the sociomateriality of finance capitalism for the purposes of gaining control in the new system. *Vento direct* and finance capitalism will continue to exist with an abstract, alien power in the town.

But perhaps there is another site of resistance as yet unaccounted for in this discussion of the sociomaterial dynamic. At times, the houses that Westerners have bought seem to exercise their own agency. For example, when Gerhard Fließ recalls his initial visit to the house as a prospective buyer, a door handle practices a particular attraction on him:

> Gerhard had stared at the door handle, a beautiful piece made out of brass, curved with a spiral embellishment on the end. The handle must have been over a hundred years old, and this realization paralyzed him like a shock. When the handle was affixed to the door, the people who had paid for it hadn't yet known of two impending world wars. They had been happy to move into a newly built house with every comfort. They probably hadn't given the door handle any particular attention. No one had considered that the handle would easily outlive its owners. [...] Suddenly Gerhard wanted the exact same thing to hap-

---

20 Toxicity is a motif that occurrs with consistency throughout the novel. Bodo Schaller poisons the air that his neighbors, Gerhard and Jule, breathe by burning rubber tires on the property line they share. Linda foreshadows the possibility of the town being poisoned when she and Frederik come across the well and note the flimsy security system.

pen with him. He wanted also to be a phase in the life of the door handle, which would still be in its place after his death. He knew then that he had to buy the house.[21]

Houses have the power to draw Westerners to the area, bewitching them and promising to satisfy their needs. For Gerhard, who is tired of the fast-paced, goal-oriented, neoliberal society in Berlin, the house is something permanent, something that has already survived war and dictatorship and will long survive him. Rather than the door handle belonging to Gerhard, he wants to belong to the life of the door handle. He submits to the house.

A house with even more agency is the Villa Kunterbunt, which Linda and her boyfriend Frederik have purchased. The ghostly nature of the house is apparent, and even attractive, to Linda when she first sees it profiled on a real estate website: "Wood-frame sunroom, stucco over the windows, and a strangely shaped roof. Overgrown garden, old trees. A house like out of a fairytale, bewitched and almost a little threatening."[22] Linda is drawn to this combination of charm and danger. Later, when she and Frederik visit the house as prospective buyers, she gazes through a window to discover a fully furnished room, "as though [the abandoned furniture] has waited for years on the return of their owners"[23] – an eerie picture, to be sure. The piece-de-resistance in the room is a rocking horse, an abandoned plaything that prompts questions about the fate of the previous owners. Linda, however, interprets it as a sign that she, a lover of horses, is fated to live there with Bergemotte. The residents of Unterleuten acknowledge the house's agency, believing it to be cursed since its last few owners met terrible fates. As the narrator reports, "One after the other had landed on Kathrin's table in the pathology department. Brain tumor, stroke, suicide.

---

21 Originally: "Gerhard hatte die Türklinke angestarrt, ein schönes Stück aus Messing, geschwungen und mit einer schneckenförmigen Verzierung am Ende. Die Klinke musste seit über hundert Jahre alt sein, und diese Erkenntnis lähmte ihn wie ein Schock. Als die Klinke an der Tür befestigt wurde, hatten die Leute, die das bezahlten, noch nichts von zwei bevorstehenden Weltkriegen gewusst. Sie hatten sich gefreut, ein frisch gebautes Haus mit allem Komfort zu beziehen. Der Türklinke hatten sie vermutlich keine besondere Beachtung geschenkt. Niemand hatte darüber nachgedacht, dass die Klinke ihre Besitzer spielend überleben würde. [...] Plötzlich wollte Gerhard, dass es ihm genauso erginge. Auch er wollte eine Phase im Leben der Klinke sein, die sich nach seinem Tod immer noch an ihrem Platz befinden würde. Er wusste jetzt, dass er dieses Haus erwerben musste." Juli Zeh, *Unterleuten*, 15.
22 Originally: "Hölzerner Wintergarten, Stuck über den Fenstern, dazu ein seltsam geformtes Dach. Verwilderter Garten, alte Bäume. Ein Haus wie aus dem Märchen, verwunschen und fast ein bisschen bedrohlich." Juli Zeh, *Unterleuten*, 35.
23 Originally: "als wartete sie seit Jahren auf die Rückkehr ihrer Besitzer." Juli Zeh, *Unterleuten*, 36.

Only a car accident was missing to complete the quartet of most popular causes of death."²⁴ Indeed, Frederik's car accident toward the end of the novel fulfills the narrator's prophecy.

While the townspeople believe that the house is cursed, and Linda anthropomorphizes it by imagining its ability to wait for and miss its owners, this house – and the one Gerhard purchased – may have an agency more in line with the houses discussed in chapters 4 and 5 of this monograph. Like the eighteenth-century estate in "Summerhouse, Later" that enchants Stein but threatens to collapse and trap the narrator, Gerhard and Jule's house draws Gerhard in but traps Jule. Also like the narrator in "Summerhouse, Later," Jule eventually retreats to Berlin. The Villa Kunterbunt is even more similar to the house in *Rain*, as it seems to be actively trying to murder its inhabitants, enacting an agency that threatens the lives of the Westerners who have acquired it. In trapping Westerners or chasing them away, these houses are perhaps the last form of resistance to capitalism's encroachment in the area. The people of Unterleuten are no longer able to resist the hegemonic powers that control the land; perhaps the houses will have another role to play.

The Fallacy of Misrecognition

If Kohl envisioned investment bringing "blooming landscapes" into the East German countryside, Zeh's novel counters that vision with an image of utter destruction of the *Heimat*. In *Unterleuten*, investment spurs on competition and violence that lead to trauma, injury, death, decline of community, and ultimately, submission to the capitalist superstructure. The finance capitalism that invades the small rural town from without is one of the most abstract antagonists seen in this monograph. Whereas earlier texts and films centering on property disputes frame competition in terms of family histories, claims to *Heimat*, and memory cultures, in *Unterleuten*, competition serves an invisible power that steers decisions remotely.

However, the notion that finance capitalism is an otherworldly force, that it is anything other than a human, material construct, is a terrible mistake. Sociomateriality as a concept reminds us that neither *Vento direct* nor the finance capitalism it practices is virtual, spectral, or otherworldly. The company has physical

---

24 Originally: "Den Vorbesitzern hatte die heruntergekommene Villa kein Glück gebracht. Einer nach dem anderen war auf Kathrins Tisch in der Pathologie gelandet. Hirntumor, Schlaganfall, Selbstmord. Fehlt nur noch ein Autounfall, um das Quartet der beliebtesten Todesursachen zu komplettieren." Juli Zeh, *Unterleuten*, 169.

headquarters somewhere, and the bank that is likely funding the project – banks like Deutsche Bank and Goldman Sachs routinely fund such projects globally – also has headquarters and branch locations with material vulnerabilities and impacts.[25] More locally, *Vento direct*'s ability to create profits in Unterleuten depends upon its access to the material landscape, which the residents of Unterleuten control. In failing to recognize the company's dependence upon them to lease the tract of land in question, the residents also fail to recognize their leverage, and thus their options. From the beginning, Pilz has engineered this misrecognition among the residents by framing the investment as an inevitability and masking the fact that he is asking them to secure the vital material conditions for the wind farm.

When seen only in abstract terms, capitalism seems as inevitable and uncontrollable as the weather or as impossible to defend against as an alien invasion. This is where the wind farm itself has some didactic value. *Vento direct* generates energy and profits from one of the least material, visible, or predictable aspects of the natural environment, the wind. If *Vento direct* can harness the material impact of something so abstract, then the same possibility exists for the people of Unterleuten to identify the power they hold by controlling the materiality of their environment. The novel's tragedy is not that the people of Unterleuten sell to the company; it is that they feel compelled to because they do not recognize the sociomaterial dynamic and thus do not employ their material-discursive power. Instead, they wield this power against one another, rending the community apart in order to do the company's bidding. This same power could instead have been used collectively to benefit them as a whole. The corporation relies on and profits from this lack of perspective on the residents' part.

As the older generation dies off, and with it the dialectic of hegemony and resistance that Gombroski and Kron embody, one is left to wonder whether it is all for the best. After all, the previous generation was a violent one. Yet the lack of resistance to hegemony left in Unterleuten as the town makes the transition from industrial to finance capitalism is far more unsettling. The novel's epilogue jumps forward in time by some eight weeks. Windmills already stand on the horizon, even though the residents' wounds are still fresh from the death, injuries, and traumas they inflicted on one another. *Vento direct* has wasted no time in

---

25 Pratima Bansal and Janelle Knox-Hayes, "The Time and Space of Materiality," 68. See, for example, "Our Energy and Climate Strategy, *Deutsche Bank*, accessed January 6, 2020, https://www.db.com/cr/en/concrete-energy-and-climate-strategy.htm and "Alternative Energy Investing," *Goldman Sachs*, accessed January 6, 2020, https://www.goldmansachs.com/what-we-do/investing-and-lending/middle-market-financing-and-investing/alternative-energy/.

profiting from the community's tragedies, the wind turbines looming as a sinister indication of the company's dispassion. Arne Seidel implies this when he asks the now diegetic first-person narrator, the reporter Lucy Finkbeiner, ironically: "They actually look innocent, don't you think?"[26] For outsiders, the sight of wind turbines slowly and silently rotating in the wind might be a thing of meditative beauty or evidence of progress on ecological measures – or at worst an irritating mark on the landscape. For the people of Unterleuten, however, the wind turbines are a monument to the violence the town inflicted upon itself in its competition for the investment contract and its submission to the company's will.

---

26 Originally: "Sehen eigentlich ganz unschuldig aus, finden Sie nicht?" Juli Zeh, *Unterleuten*, 634.

Coda
Home in the East as an Ongoing Issue: Sonja Blattner's *drüben* Series and the Importance of Considering Medium

The walls of Sonja Blattner's studio in Berlin are lined with her paintings of houses. Dozens of them, with bright, contrasting colors and irregular, expressive lines. Her sculptures, tall, thin houses tottering upon absurdly long stilts like giraffes, line shelves. Blattner's studio is an intriguing universe of houses that variably invite or repel, intimidate or ease. They exist as though on their own planets, where the sky can be green or white or yellow and the ground purple or blue. Standing in her studio is like standing in the center of a colorful, wonderful alternate universe of houses.

While her paintings appear to depict fantastical worlds, they are actually based on real houses in Europe and the United States. Perhaps her most impressive series comprises houses in the former GDR, a series she calls *drüben* ("over there," formerly the colloquial West German term for East Germany). Blattner has produced over 3,400 paintings in the *drüben* series over the last twenty years, mostly 6 by 8.5 inches in gouache and acrylic, and the project is ongoing. If you didn't know from the series title that these were houses in the former East Germany, you wouldn't suspect it. She has endowed them with new life, giving them bright, vibrant colors in place of the famously ubiquitous brown-gray of the GDR. What is perhaps most impressive about this series, however, is that despite consisting of thousands of paintings, no two are alike in composition or color scheme. Her unflinching use of color and distinctive style lend the series its continuity.

Viewing the hundreds of paintings she selected for me to consider, some stand out as the kind of house that might appear in the films and novels discussed in this monograph. I picked one, and as though to confirm my impulse, its title reads *One of the Beloved Ones* (2004, see fig. Coda.1). One of the paintings with a more realistic color scheme, it depicts a friendly looking yellow house with a red addition and a playful blue-green roof. As a viewer you see the house from the side, and at first glance the painting evokes familiar *Heimat* imagery. The house is situated in a green landscape, and something gray, perhaps even a mountain range, stands high in the background. It's a tranquil and gentle, yet bright and cheery place, somewhere you might want to live. And then the details – or rather, lack of them – become apparent. This house has no door.

https://doi.org/10.1515/9783110673975-010

Fig. 1: *One of the Beloved Ones*, Sonja Blattner, 2004, Gouache, 14.8 x 21 cm

There are only three tiny, strangely placed windows. If this is a house in the former East, then the gray in the background is not mountains. What could it be?

Looking even more closely, the overall impression gives way to estrangement. The house leans in funny ways, making it all the more soft and endearing as an idea of home, but all the more strange as anyone's actual house. Moreover, it does not sit solidly on the ground. The red and yellow of the walls spill into the green of the grass. The house has no hard lines; its contours dissolve into its environment. The blue-green paint of the roof smudges into the blue paint of the sky. Some green paint from the ground appears to be rising up into the house, not growing like a plant, just color. One wall differentiates itself from another wall and the house from the sky by the variation in color and the direction of brushstrokes. Bits of white placed here and there help distinguish between the blue of the roof, the blue of the sky, and the green of the tree, but a smudge of white on the lower left side of the painting is inscrutable. It does not appear to represent anything. Is it there for the sake of composition? To evoke a feeling? To irritate the viewer? And then come other questions. What is the brown smudge in the bottom left corner? And what is behind the fence?

Perhaps most striking of all, there are no people, no traces of a human life led in this house. No car outside or laundry hanging in the yard, no flowers planted in window boxes or other typical elements of life in the *Heimat* that one sees in visual representations. This house exists purely for itself in its environment. Perhaps that is the reason there is no door. A door would put the house in the service of humans. The windows are also not functional. Small and oddly situated, they do not lend us a view into an interior, but rather, resemble the opacity of eyes and mouth. These windows are not the product of human design, but rather, vital organs of the house.

Blattner's houses exist in environments that are largely devoid of human objects. In some of her paintings, fences and street signs might remain. Once in a while a car is visible. (They're western cars, she explained to me, since Westerners often come looking for such houses to buy.) As such, the houses' individual characters come to the fore. Some are inviting, like in "One of the Beloved Ones." Others seem to want to avoid human contact. In some of the paintings, the perspective lends the viewer the sense of rushing past and only catching a glimpse of the house. In others, the viewer stands at an uncertain position to the house, simultaneously near to it and far away, as though with a zoomed-in perspective.

Blattner's houses do something special, arousing a strange combination of defamiliarization and mesmerizing attraction. The houses are abstracted, existing as form, color, and brushstroke direction. Free of inhabitants and the traces of human life, they do not evoke the typical emotional attachment or material meaning of home, exhibiting instead an array of other emotions that seem to emanate from the houses themselves. Some of the houses even seem to speak for themselves. "Huuh!" is the onomatopoetic title of one of her works, as if to express exhaustion. "Einsam" ("lonesome") is another. The texture and materiality of these houses also do not evoke an association with the materiality and textures of home. Rather, their texture and materiality originate from the medium of representation (most of them gouache or acrylic), the thick brushstrokes, and the layering of colors. Blattner's houses defamiliarize, asserting their independence from humans and defying the *Heimat* ideals of coziness, belonging, and stasis held so dear in the German cultural imagination. But then, somehow, they also draw the viewer in and fascinate us with the dignity and character they have gained by being untethered from the usual, familiar associations with home.

Although these houses appear to be unencumbered by human activity, Blattner's source material is anything but that. The *drüben* series depicts houses in the former GDR that are up for auction. Some are abandoned and have fallen into disrepair. Some presumably have owners who want or need to rid themselves of the house and its financial burdens. None of them are inhabited, which explains the emptiness with which Blattner works as a theme. (It is only in this state that they can speak for themselves, according to Blattner.) However, to know of this source material also provokes questions about the fates of the humans who once owned and inhabited them. Why have these houses been abandoned or why are they being given up? Did their owners leave after unification (or perhaps before)? Were they forced to sell more recently out of financial distress? And who will be their future owners? Who buys these houses in the East?

Blattner's houses, each painted in the first decades of the twenty-first century and at a time when they were currently on the market, make a fitting coda to this study of cultural productions that depict the new property relations in the former East Germany. In Blattner's paintings, as in the narratives discussed in previous chapters, houses have an enduring materiality and form that place them at the interface of a newly capitalist present and a difficult national past. Like the houses imagined by Judith Hermann, Karen Duve, and Juli Zeh, Blattner's houses have agency and personality. Like the house at the center of Jenny Erpenbeck's *Visitation*, her houses exist in harmonious relationship to the landscape, as though organically part of the environment. And like every house to appear in the news media, television, films, and fictional texts discussed in this monograph, their ownership is up in the air. What is then perhaps so fascinating about Blattner's paintings is the simultaneous play on and resistance to the thorough commercialization of home. Unlike in the literary depictions of home in Erpenbeck and Zeh, capitalism is not so pervasive that it determines all aspects of her houses. Blattner takes houses that are considered in the real world primarily as real estate, as the potential property of consumers, and then gives them life in unconventional ways, not as the containers of human lives, but as themselves in their own expressive materiality and form.

This de-commercialization of home provides some relief within the landscape of cultural productions that depict houses in the former East Germany. The news reports, made-for-television films, cinematic releases, and prose fiction texts discussed in this monograph all depict houses to foreground the destabilization of home as an effect of the market-infused world. Each demonstrates that the new property relations have been one of the most devastating outcomes of German unification for Easterners. Far from depicting the "blooming landscapes" that Kohl envisioned, these texts and visual productions preserve the memory of deep insecurities that Easterners felt in the aftermath of unification about their position within the social and material worlds. They pose important questions. Who has a right to inhabit a place and conceive of it as home? What grounds one more closely to home: one's habitation of it in the present or the memory (or family memory) of a home once inhabited? What happens when two parties have competing emotional ties to a home? Do those who depend financially upon retaining a home have a greater right to it than those who have the financial power to purchase the house and *Heimat* of their desires? What role does engagement with the materiality of house and landscape play? For many East Germans, the question of home has boiled down to a question of alienation in the new society: How can one feel at home in the new Germany if one faces losing one's home quite literally?

In the cultural productions discussed in the first three chapters of this monograph – those news media reports, television films, and cinematic releases of the early 1990s – the question of home ownership rights is framed as face-to-face competition between individuals or families. In these narratives, the threat to one's home is visible and concrete. However, proceeding in a somewhat chronological order, we see that the literary texts discussed in chapters 4 through 7 produced more abstract themes than had appeared in the earlier visual productions. Rather than facing a rival party, characters in these texts face the threats of national and family history, time, and neoliberalism. These foes are less tangible, harder to identify, and less assailable than a competing individual or family would be. Judith Hermann's short story "Summerhouse, Later," which appeared in 1998, was the first critically acclaimed literary text to depict a Westerner's acquisition of a home in the former East, as well as the displacement of another family that results from this acquisition. The narrative tension builds when the house at the center of the story threatens to trap and fall in on the narrator. Given that the house is a dilapidated, eighteenth-century estate, what perhaps really threaten to trap and suffocate her are the symbolic weight of history and the traditional role of women in the domestic sphere. In the novels that followed, such as *Eduard's Homecoming* and *Rain*, houses pose dire threats to those from the West who have acquired them, including financial ruin, danger to one's health, and an apparent desire on the house's part to expel or consume its inhabitants. In these texts, the materiality of the houses themselves gains in agency, at times harboring an invisible, intangible will that the protagonists must fight against. In this respect as well, Sonja Blattner's paintings show us the next step in this defamiliarization and abstraction. Her houses appear to enact a will and agency even without human inhabitants to act against.

In the texts of the early 2000s, the main threats the characters face are no longer individuals, groups of people, or the agentic materiality of nature, but rather, are much more abstract forces. The unrelenting forward march of time in Jenny Erpenbeck's *Visitation* guarantees loss for her characters, and in Kathrin Gerlof's *Now That's a Story*, it is the continued presence of the past that jeopardizes a community's feelings of security. In Juli Zeh's *Unterleuten*, the superstructure of capitalism itself takes hold, overpowers the individuals in a community, and reshapes their interactions with one another and the material environment. The irony of *Unterleuten* is that the main characters do not recognize their own agency in creating the competition that overtakes them, nor do they recognize their potential to fight back against the power that finance capitalism seems to wield. Time and capitalism are human constructs, fairytales that we have created and endow with agency and power. Our systems are the most threatening.

As the foes in these literary works have become less and less individual, so have the protagonists. Whereas in the earlier productions, the narrative hinges on individual or family history, in later works, such as *Visitation*, *Now That's a Story*, and *Unterleuten*, the conflict is shared more collectively. In *Visitation*, each chapter is focalized through a different character who represents a "type" or typical outlook for their generation. These characters' perspectives add up to a picture of the twentieth century. *Now That's a Story* and *Unterleuten* are narrated in a similar manner, through the free-indirect speech of a variety of characters. Rather than spanning a century, however, they depict a limited time period in the present day.

The increasingly abstracted foe and increasingly collective protagonist in these narratives might reflect the distance that time has put between us and the initial shocks of unification. As East and West have become less concretely divided (and thus less representable as feuding families), the abstract forces of privatization and neoliberalism have weighed more heavily and the burdens of memory and history have made themselves known to a new generation. On the other hand, the increased abstraction of both protagonist and antagonist might also be an effect of the respective medium of these narratives. The earliest productions, made-for-television films, were designed to quickly and directly address the anxieties of the nation as the processes of unification and privatization were taking place. As we move from those initial television films to cinematic releases to prose fiction, we see the foes becoming more abstract and the fights more complicated, less concrete, and harder to grapple with. In Sonja Blattner's paintings, an ongoing project since 2001, these conflicts become so abstract that they nearly dissolve altogether. The very same kinds of homes depicted in narrative form in television, films, and prose fiction become abstracted in her work and untethered from human strife. Her *drüben* series almost completely obscures the market-based underpinnings of her source material and thereby transforms those houses into something that we can engage with in a new way.

This variety of productions across different media attests to just how ubiquitous the changing property relations in the former East Germany were as a social problem. A conversation that takes place at the end of *The Same Old Song* between Katharina's granddaughter, Sophie, and Alf's grandson, Stefan, may shed light on the ways in which these different types of narratives, told through different media, reach different audiences and thus have complementary effects. In an early scene, Sophie and Stefan discuss whether Easterners are equipped to engage critically with a Western media system that is built to serve the free market. They agree that ideology and media are necessarily linked. However, Sophie and Stefan differ in their opinions about how best to communicate messages that will have a social impact. Stefan sees the potential of mass media to inform large groups of people, whereas Sophie is disillusioned by the mass media, arguing that it caters to the status quo and thus cannot raise a society's consciousness. Sophie believes in a grass-roots approach to social change, maintaining that real contact with a few people at a time is more effective than superficial contact with a mass audience.

The conversation between Stefan and Sophie on the value of media speaks directly to the value of differing types of media depicting the issue of property ownership in the former East Germany. While many of the cultural productions discussed in this monograph have similar messages – that *Heimat* must be situated within a national history, that Westerners have at best a problematic claim to properties in the East, that family inheritance is no longer viable given the ruptures caused by twentieth- and early twenty-first-century politics, and that Westerners' acquisition of property in the East often results in the unjust displacement of Easterners from their homes – they employ varying strategies to communicate these messages. Made-for-television films like *Taxi to Rathenow*, *Our House*, and *The Brocken* enjoyed a national audience by virtue of being broadcasted on public television, but also by drawing on a conventional understanding of *Heimat* with its attendant traditional gender roles and by being somewhat forgiving, even neglectful, of German history. The arthouse film, *The Same Old Song*, on the other hand, attends in a more unforgiving manner to Germany's past and attempts a critical engagement with the processes of unification through an examination of gender, property, and history. At the same time, its audience is presumably much smaller and more targeted, the kind of engagement that Sophie sees as valuable. It is also worth noting that while prose fiction texts presumably reach a smaller audience than television and popular film, Jenny Erpenbeck, Judith Hermann, Peter Schneider, and Juli Zeh are among the best-selling contemporary German authors. To be sure, their engagements with the new property relations have reached a sizeable audience. The question of which medium or approach is more effective is perhaps moot in itself, but a consideration of medium provokes thought. In the last three decades, a variety of cultural productions from different political and ideological standpoints, in different forms and media, have taken a stance on the property disputes in the East, thereby underscoring the enduring importance of home and *Heimat* in the new nation.

To date, the issue of property ownership in the East remains unresolved. A number of restitution cases are still pending, and both state-level and national offices for the Regulation of Open Property Questions continue to exist. Just as telling, Sonja Blattner's *drüben* project carries on, and she sees little reason for it to conclude anytime soon. While she has painted over 3,400 houses so far, this is only a sampling of the houses that have stood, or now stand, empty in the former East Germany. Her project is not exhaustive, but rather, catalogs houses in a representative manner that attests, simultaneously in its selectivity and scale, to the continuing uncertainty about property relations of home in the former East Germany.

Works Cited

Primary Texts

Améry, Jean. "Wieviel Heimat braucht der Mensch?" *Werke*, 2nd ed., edited by Irene Heidelberger-Leonard, 68–117. Stuttgart: Klett-Cotta, 2002.
Arslan, Thomas, dir. *Ferien*. 2007; Berlin: Filmgalerie 451. DVD.
Blattner, Sonja. *One of the Beloved Ones*. 2004. Gouache, 14.8 x 21 cm. Berlin.
Braun, Volker. "Das Eigentum." *Die Zeit* 33, no. 9 (August 1990). Accessed 23 January 2020. https://www.zeit.de/1990/33/das-eigentum.
Braun, Volker. "Property." In *Rubble Flora: Selected Poems*. Translated by David Constantine and Karen Leeder, 46. New York: Seagull Books, 2014.
Braun, Volker. "Property." Translated by Michael Hofmann. *Poetry* 173, no. 1 (1998): 53.
Büchner, Georg. "Der hessische Landbote." In *"Friede den Hütten! Krieg den Palästen!" Der Hessische Landbote. Briefe*, edited by Hanjo Kesting, 23–35. Hamburg: Verlag Lutz Schulenburg, 2002.
Buck, Detlev, dir. *Wir können auch anders*. 1993; Munich, Germany: universum film, DVD.
Duve, Karen. *Rain*. Translated by Anthea Bell. New York: Bloomsbury, 2002.
Duve, Karen. *Regenroman*. Berlin: Eichborn Verlag, 1999.
Engel, Thomas, dir. *Taxi nach Rathenow*. 1991; Mainz, Germany: ZDF Sendungsmitschnitt, 2017. DVD.
Erpenbeck, Jenny. *Heimsuchung*. Frankfurt am Main: Eichborn Verlag, 2008.
Erpenbeck, Jenny. *Visitation*. Translated by Susan Bernofsky. New York: New Directions, 2010.
Gerlof, Kathrin. *Das ist eine Geschichte*. Berlin: Aufbau, 2014.
Glowna, Vadim, dir. *Der Brocken*. 1992; Hamburg, Germany: NDR Sendungsmitschnitt, 2016, DVD.
Grass, Günter. *Ein weites Feld*. Göttigen: Steidl, 1995.
Griesmayr, Hartmut, dir. *Unser Haus*. 1991; Mainz, Germany: ZDF Sendungsmitschnitt, 2012. DVD.
Hermann, Judith. *Aller Liebe Anfang*. Frankfurt am Main: S. Fischer Verlag, 2014.
Hermann, Judith. "Sommerhaus, später." In *Sommerhaus, später*. 9. Aufl., 139–156. Frankfurt am Main: S. Fischer Verlag, 2003.
Hermann, Judith. "Summer House, Later." In *Summer House, Later*. Translated by Margot Bettauer Dembo, 185–205. New York: HarperCollins, 2001.
Hermann, Judith. *Where Love Begins*. Translated by Margot Bettauer Dembo. London: The Clerkenwell Press, 2016.
Heym, Stefan. *Filz: Gedanken über das neuste Deutschland*. Munich: C. Bertelsmann, 1992.
Hochhuth, Rolf. *Wessis in Weimar: Szenen aus einem besetzten Land*. Berlin: Volk & Welt, 1993.
Kara, Yadé. *Selam Berlin*. Zurich: Diogenes, 2004.
Kirsch, Sarah. *Allerlei-Rauh*. Stuttgart: Deutsche Verlags-Anstalt, 1988.
Petzold, Christian, dir. *Jerichow*. 2008; New York: Cinema Guild. DVD.
Schneider, Peter. *Eduards Heimkehr*. 2. Aufl. Reinbek bei Hamburg: Rowohlt Taschenbuch Verlag, 2005.
Schneider, Peter. *Eduard's Homecoming*. Translated by John Brownjohn. New York: Farrar, Straus and Giroux, 2000.

https://doi.org/10.1515/9783110673975-011

Schneider, Peter. *Paarungen*. Berlin: Rowohlt, 1992.
Schulze, Ingo. *Simple Storys: Ein Roman aus der ostdeutschen Provinz*. Berlin: Berlin Verlag, 1998.
Stöckl, Ula, dir. *Das alte Lied*. 1992; Berlin, Germany: Basis Film, DVD.
Wolf, Christa. *Sommerstück*. Frankfurt am Main: Luchterhand, 1989.
Zeh, Juli. *Unterleuten*. Munich: Luchterhand, 2016.

Secondary Literature and Theoretical Works

Alaimo, Stacy. "Trans-Corporal Feminisms and the Ethical Space of Nature." In *Material Feminisms*, edited by Stacy Alaimo and Susan Hekman, 237–264. Bloomington and Indianapolis: Indianapolis University Press.

"Alte Rechte Neues Unrecht," *Der Spiegel Online* 27 (June 29, 1992). https://www.spiegel.de/spiegel/print/d-13689057.html.

"Alternative Energy Investing," *Goldman Sachs*. Accessed January 6, 2020. https://www.goldmansachs.com/what-we-do/investing-and-lending/middle-market-financing-and-investing/alternative-energy/

Applegate, Celia. *A Nation of Provincials: The German Idea of Heimat*. Berkeley: University of California Press, 1990.

"Arme Jungs!" Special section of *Focus* 32 (2002): https://www.focus.de/magazin/archiv/jahrgang_2002/ausgabe_32/.

Assmann, Aleida. *Shadows of Trauma: Memory and the Politics of Postwar Identity*. Translated by Sarah Clift. New York: Fordham University Press, 2016.

Aydemir, Fatma, and Hengameh Yaghoobifahah, editors. *Eure Heimat ist unser Albtraum*. Berlin: Ullstein fünf, 2019.

Baer, Hester, Maria Stehle, and Carrie Smith. "Digital Feminisms and the Impasse: Time, Disappearance, and Delay in Neoliberalism." *Studies in Twentieth and Twenty-First Century Literature* titled *Neoliberalism and the Undoing of Time* 40, no. 2 (2016): Article 3. Accessed Jan 22, 2020, https://doi.org/10.4148/2334-4415.1881.

Baer, Ulrich. "The Hubris of Humility: Günter Grass, Peter Schneider, and German Guilt after 1989." *Germanic Review* 80, no. 1 (2005): 50–73.

Bansal, Pratima, and Janelle Knox-Hayes. "The Time and Space of Materiality in Organizations and the Natural Environment." *Organization & Environment* 26, no. 1 (2013): 61–82.

Barad, Karen. *Meeting the Universe Halfway: Quantum Physics and the Entanglement of Matter and Meaning*. Durham: Duke University Press, 2007.

Barad, Karen. "Posthumanist Performativity: Toward an Understanding of How Matter Comes to Matter." *Signs: Journal of Women in Culture and Society* 28, no. 3 (2003): 801–831.

Baudrillard, Jean. *For a Critique of the Political Economy of the Sign*. St. Louis: Telos Press, 1981.

Bauer, Esther K. "Narratives of Femininity in Judith Hermann's *Summerhouse, Later*." *Women in German Yearbook* 25 (2009): 50–75.

Bauerkämper, Arnd. "Collectivization and Memory: Views of the Past and the Transformation of Rural Society in the GDR from 1952 to the Early 1960s." *German Studies Review* 25, no. 3 (May 2002): 213–255. http://www.jstor.org/stable/1432990

Berlant, Lauren. *Cruel Optimism*. Durham: Duke University Press, 2001.
Biendarra, Anke. "Gen(d)eration Next: Prose by Julia Franck and Judith Hermann." *Studies in Twentieth and Twenty-First Century Literature* 28, no. 1 (2004): 211–239. Accessed Jan 22, 2020, https://doi.org/10.4148/2334-4415.1574.
Biendarra, Anke. "Globalization, Travel, and Identity: Judith Hermann and Gregor Hens." *Gegenwartsliteratur: A German Studies Yearbook* 5 (2006): 233–251.
Blacksell, Mark, Karl Martin Born, and Michael Bohlander. "Search for a Unified Justice." *Geographical Magazine* 67, no. 2 (Feb 1995). Accessed Jan 30, 2020. Academic OneFile, https://go-gale-com.er.lib.k-state.edu/ps/i.do?p=AONE&u=ksu&id=GALE|A18541072&v=2.1&it=r&sid=AONE&asid=c6e79fdd.
Blacksell, Mark, Karl Martin Born, and Michael Bohlander. "Settlement of Property Claims in Former East Germany." *Geographical Review.* 86, no. 2 (Apr. 1996): 198–215. Accessed Jan 22, 2020, DOI: 10.2307/215956 https://www.jstor.org/stable/215956
Blickle, Peter. *Heimat: A Critical Theory of the German Idea of Homeland*. Rochester: Camden House, 2002.
Boa, Elizabeth. "Lust or Disgust? The Blurring of Boundaries in Karen Duve's *Regenroman*." In *Pushing Boundaries: Approaches to Contemporary German Women Writers from Karen Duve to Jenny Erpenbeck*, edited by Heike Bartel and Elizabeth Boa, 57–72. Amsterdam: Rodopi, 2006.
Boa, Elizabeth, and Rachel Palfreyman. *Heimat – A German Dream: Regional Loyalties and National Identity in German Culture 1890–1990*. Oxford: Oxford University Press, 2000.
"Bodenpolitik Brandenburg," *Brandenburg Aktuell*. Aired Feb 11, 1993 on ORB.
Boehringer, Michael. "Introduction." *Seminar: A Journal of Germanic Studies* 44, no.1 (2008): 1–5.
Bogdal, Klaus-Michael. "Hard-Cold-Fast: Imagining Masculinity in the German Academy, Literature, and the Media." In *Conceptions of Postwar German Masculinity*, edited by Roy Jerome, 13–42. Albany: State University of New York Press, 2001.
Borgstedt, Thomas. "Wunschwelten: Judith Hermannn und die Neuromantik der Gegenwart." *Gegenwartsliteratur: A German Studies Yearbook* 5 (2006): 207–232.
Breger, Claudia. "Hegemony, Marginalization, and Feminine Masculinity: Antje Rávic Strubel's *Unter Schnee*." *Seminar: A Journal of Germanic Studies* 44, no. 1 (2008): 154–173.
Brouër, Dirk, et al. *Offene Vermögensfragen: Ein Ratgeber: Der Streit um Häuser, Datschen und Grundstücke; zur veränderten Rechtslage in den neuen Ländern*. Reinbek bei Hamburg: Rowohlt, 1995.
Brown, Wendy. *Undoing the Demos: Neoliberalism's Stealth Revolution*. New York: Zone Books, 2015.
Bundesamt für zentrale Dienste und offene Vermögensfragen. Accessed September 17, 2019. https://www.badv.bund.de
Bundesministerium für Raumordnung, Bauwesen und Städtebau. *Wohnungsprivatisierung in den neuen Bundesländern. Informationen für Kaufinteressenten und Mieter*. Bonn, 1993.
"Bundesrat: Vorrang von Investitionen im Bau/Fristen für Alteigentümer," *Heute*. Aired July 10, 1992 on ZDF.
Bütfering, Elisabeth. "Frauenheimat Männerwelt. Die Heimatlosigkeit ist weiblich." In *Heimat: Analysen, Themen, Perspektiven. Bd. 1*, edited by Will Cremer and Ansgar Klein, 416–426. Bielefeld: Westfalen-Verlag, 1990.

Carlile, Paul. R., et al. "How Matter Matters: Objects, Artifacts, and Materiality in Organization Studies: Introducing the Third Volume of 'Perspectives on Organization Studies.'" In *How Matter Matters: Objects, Artifacts, and Materiality in Organization Studies*, edited by Paul R. Carlile, et al., 1–15. Oxford: Oxford University Press, 2013.

Chronister, Necia. "Domestic Disputes: Envisioning the Gender of Home in the Era of Reprivatization in Eastern Germany." In *Heimat Goes Mobile – Hybrid Forms of Home in Literature and Film*, edited by Gabriele Eichmanns and Yvonne Franke. 146–169. Newcastle: Cambridge Scholars Publishing, 2013.

Chronister, Necia. "Judith Hermann's 'Sommerhaus, später': Gender Ambiguity and Smooth versus Striated Spaces." In *German Women Authors and the Spatial Turn: New Perspectives*, edited by Carola Daffner and Beth Ann Muellner, 149–165. Berlin and Boston: De Gruyter, 2015.

Chronister, Necia. "Narrating the Fault Lines: German Literature since the Fall of the Wall." *World Literature Today*, Nov. 14 issue, https://www.worldliteraturetoday.org/2014/november/narrating-fault-lines-german-literature-fall-wall-necia-chronister.

Chronister, Necia. "The Poetics of the Surface as a Critical Aesthetic in Judith Hermann's *Alice* (2009) and *Aller Liebe Anfang* (2014)." *Gegenwartsliteratur: A German Studies Yearbook* 14 (2015): 265–289.

Colvin, Sarah, and Peter Davies, editors. *Masculinities in German Culture*, special issue of *Edinburgh German Yearbook* 2 (2008).

Connell, R. W. *Masculinities*. Berkeley and Los Angeles: University of California Press, 1995.

Connell, Raewyn. "Understanding Neoliberalism." In *Neoliberalism and Everyday Life*, edited by Susan Braedley and Meg Luxton, 22–36. Montréal and Ithaca: McGill-Queen's University Press, 2010.

Cormican, Muriel, and Gary Schmidt. "Introduction: Masculinity in Contemporary German Culture." *Colloquia Germanica* 46, no. 1 (2013): 1–3.

Costabile-Heming, Carol Anne. "Peter Schneider's *Eduards Heimkehr* and the Image of the 'New Berlin.'" *German Studies Review* 25, no. 3 (2002): 497–510.

Costabile-Heming, Carol Anne. "Tracing History through Berlin's Topography: Historical Memories and Post-1989 Berlin Narratives." *German Life and Letters* 58, no. 3 (2005): 344–356.

Crary, Jonathan. *24/7: Late Capitalism and the Ends of Sleep*. London and New York: Verso, 2013.

Deleuze, Gilles, and Félix Guattari. *A Thousand Plateaus: Capitalism and Schizophrenia*. Translated by Brian Massoumi. Minneapolis: University of Minnesota Press, 1987.

"Diskussion über Landvergabepraxis mit Herrn Zimmerman," *Vor Ort in Satzkorn/Brandenburg*. Aired Oct 6, 1993 on ORB.

Dornberger, Gerhard. *Offene Vermögensfragen nach dem 2. Vermögensrechtsänderungsgesetz*. Berlin: Verlag Die Wirtschaft GmbH, 1992.

Doyle, Jonathan J. "A Bitter Inheritance: East German Real Property and the Supreme Constitutional Court's 'Land Reform' decision of April 23, 1991." *Michigan Journal of International Law* 13, no. 4. (1992): 832–864.

"Eigenheim ist nun 'Privateigentum.'" *Leipziger Volkszeitung* (Leipzig, Germany), December 3, 1990.

Eigler, Friederike. "Critical Approaches to Heimat and the 'Spatial Turn.'" *New German Critique* 39, no. 1 (2012): 27–48. Accessed Jan 22, 2020, https://doi.org/10.1215/0094033X-1434497.

"Entschädigungsgesetz verabschiedet," *Tagesschau*. Aired May 20, 1994 on ARD.

Fehrenbach, Heide. *Cinema in Democratizing Germany: Reconstructing National Identity after Hitler*. Chapel Hill and London: The University of North Carolina Press, 1995.

Frank, Rainer. "Privatization in Eastern Germany: A Comprehensive Study." *Vanderbilt Journal of Transnational Law* 27 (1994): 809–868.

Ganeva, Mila. "Female Flâneurs: Judith Hermann's *Sommerhaus, später* and *Nichts als Gespenster*." *Gegenwartsliteratur: A German Studies Yearbook* 3 (2004): 250–277.

Gehrmann, Wolfgang, and Nikolaus Piper. "Der Häuserkampf." *Die Zeit* (March 20 1992). https://www.zeit.de/1992/13/der-haeuserkampf/komplettansicht.

Gerstenberger, Katharina. "Fictionalizations: Holocaust Memory and the Generational Construct in the Works of Contemporary Women Writers." In *Generational Shifts in Contemporary German Culture*, edited by Laurel Cohen-Pfister and Susanne Vees-Gulani, 95–114. Rochester: Camden House, 2010.

Goodbody, Axel. "*Heimat* and the Place of Humans in the World: Jenny Erpenbeck's *Heimsuchung* in Ecocritical Perspective." *New German Critique* 43, no. 2 (2016): 127–51. Accessed Jan 22, 20202, https://doi.org/10.1215/0094033X-3511907.

Goodbody, Axel. "Nature's Revenge: The Ecological Adaptation of Traditional Narratives in Fifty Years of German-Speaking Writing." *Tamkang Review* 37, no. 1 (2006): 1–27.

Gordinsky, Natasha. "Das Draußen im Eigenen entdecken: Judith Hermanns *Sommerhaus, später*." *Gegenwartsliteratur: A German Studies Yearbook* 11 (2012): 301–323.

Graves, Peter J. "Karen Duve, Kathrin Schmidt, Judith Hermann: 'Ein Literarisches Fräuleinwunder'?" *German Life and Letters* 55, no. 2 (2002): 196–207.

Gremler, Claudia. "Country Escapes and Designs for Living: Christa Wolf, Sarah Kirsch and Judith Hermann." In *Women's Writing in Western Europe: Gender, Generation and Legacy*, edited by Adalgisa Giorgio and Julia Water, 118–131. Newcastle upon Tyne: Cambridge Scholars Publishing, 2007.

Gremler, Claudia. "Diesseits und jenseits der Oder: Judith Hermanns literarische Auseinandersetzung mit Theodor Fontane in *Sommerhaus, später*." *Neophilologus* 97 (2013): 523–540.

Gremler, Claudia. "Intertextualität und Vergangenheitsarbeit in Judith Herman *Sommerhaus, später*." *Text & Kontext: Zeitschrift für Germanistische Literaturforschung in Skandinavien* 37 (2015): 7–35.

Gruber, Reinhard P. "Heimat ist, wo das Herz weh tut. 35 Fragmente eines konkreten Beitrags zu einer antiutopischen Heimatentheorie." In *Die Ohnmacht der Gefühle. Heimat zwischen Wunsch und Wirklichkeit*, edited by Jochen Kelter, 89–115. Weingarten: Drumlin, 1986.

"Grundbedürfnis: Was ist Heimat?" *Stern Online* (December 15, 2004). https://www.stern.de/politik/deutschland/grundbeduerfnis-was-ist-heimat-3554102.html.

Hancock, Nicholas, and Hans-Dieter Schulz-Gebeltzig. "Recovering Expropriated Property in Eastern Germany." *New Law Journal*. 1 March 1991.

Harvey, David. *A Brief History of Neoliberalism*. Oxford and New York: Oxford University Press, 2005

Harvey, David. *The Enigma of Capital and the Crisis of Capitalism*. Oxford: Oxford University Press, 2011.
Heilig, Karen. "From the Luxembourg Agreement to Today: Representing a People." *Berkeley Journal of International Law* 20 (2002): 176–196.
"Heim ins Eigene? Enteignete wollen einklagen." *Leipziger Volkszeitung* (Leipzig, Germany). August 30, 1990. 2.
Henderson, Heike. "Re-Thinking and Re-Writing Heimat: Turkish Women Writers in Germany." *Women in German Yearbook* 13 (1997): 225–243.
Heslop, Jessica, and Joel Roberto. "Property Rights in the Unified Germany: A Constitutional, Comparative, and International Legal Analysis." *Boston University International Law Journal* 11 (1993): 243–298.
Hill, Alexandra M. "The Violent Turn: West German Women as Victims of Neoliberalism." *The German Quarterly* 91, no. 2 (2018): 138–152.
Huhn, Klaus. *Raubzug Ost. Wie die Treuhand die DDR plünderte*. Berlin: Das Neue Berlin, 2009.
Jacobsen, Ann. "Edith Wharton's Houses Full of Rooms." *Women's Studies* 44 (2015): 516–536.
"Jährliche Zuschaueranteile seit 1990" (PDF) *Kommission zur Ermittlung der Konzentration im Medienbereich*. kek-online.de
Jeffress, Dorothy Ames. "Resolving Rival Claims on East German Property upon German Unification." *The Yale Law Journal* 101, no. 2 (Nov. 1991): 527–549. Accessed Jan 22, 2020, DOI: 10.2307/796809 / Stable URL: http://www.jstor.org/stable/796809
Jerome, Roy, editor. *Conceptions of Postwar German Masculinity*. Albany: State University of New York Press, 2001.
Kinzer, Stephen. "Anguish of East Germans Grows with Property Claims by Former Owners." *The New York Times*, June 5, 1992. https://www.nytimes.com/1992/06/05/world/anguish-of-east-germans-grows-with-property-claims-by-former-owners.html
Kohl, Helmut. "Fernsehansprache des Bundeskanzlers Kohl zum Inkrafttreten der Währungs-Wirtschafts- und Sozialunion am 1. Juli 1990." *Bulletin des Presse- und Informationsamtes der Bundesregierung* 86 (July 3, 1990): 741–42.
Kohl, Helmut. "Kohl's Celebration of the Currency Union, July 1, 1990." Translated by Allison Brown and Belinda Cooper in *Uniting Germany: Documents and Debates, 1944–1993*, edited by Konrad Jarausch and Volker Gransow, 172–174. Providence and Oxford: Berghahn Books, 1994.
Kohl, Sebastian. *Homeownership, Renting and Society: Historical and Comparative Perspectives*. London and New York: Routledge, 2017.
Köhler, Andrea. "'Is That All There Is?' Judith Hermann oder Die Geschichte eines Erfolgs." In *Aufgerissen: Zur Literatur der 90er*, edited by Thomas Kraft, 82–89. Munich and Zurich: Piper, 2000.
Köhler, Astrid. "Plagiat oder Intertextualität? Zur literarischen Beziehung zwischen Klaus Schlesinger und Peter Schneider." In *Justiziabilität und Rechtmäßigkeit: Verrechtlichungsprozesse von Literatur und Film in der Moderne*, edited by Claude D. Conter, 97–108. Amsterdam: Rodopi, 2010.
Köhler, Otto. *Die große Enteignung. Wie die Treuhand eine Volkswirtschaft liquidierte*. Munich: Knaur, 1994.

Kramer, Sven. "Reconsidering 'Heimat': Jenny Erpenbeck's Novel *Heimsuchung* (2008)." In *Readings in Twenty-First-Century European Literatures*, edited by Michael Gratzke, Margaret-Anne Hutton, and Claire Whitehead. 197–210. Oxford: Peter Lang, 2014.

Krimmer, Elisabeth. "The Representation of Wartime Rape in Julia Franck's *Die Mittagsfrau* and Jenny Erpenbeck's *Heimsuchung*." *Gegenwartsliteratur: A German Studies Yearbook*, 14 (2015): 35–60.

Kristeva, Julia. *The Powers of Horror: An Essay on Abjection*. Translated by Leon S. Roudiez. New York: Columbia University Press, 1982.

Laabs, Dirk. *Der deutsche Goldrausch. Die wahre Geschichte der Treuhand*. Munich: Pantheon, 2012.

"Die Lage ist trostlos," *Der Spiegel* 41 (Oct 8, 1990). https://www.spiegel.de/spiegel/print/d-13501112.html.

Langman, Lauren. "Globalization, Alienation, and Identity." In *The Evolution of Alienation: Trauma, Promise, and the Millennium*, edited by Lauren Langman and Devorah Kalekin-Fishman, 179–200. Lanham: Rowman & Littlefield Publishers, 2006.

Langman, Lauren, and Devorah Kalekin-Fishman. "Introduction." *The Evolution of Alienation: Trauma, Promise, and the Millennium*, edited by Lauren Langman and Devorah Kalekin-Fishman, 1–20. Lanham: Rowman & Littlefield Publishers, 2006.

Leeder, Karen. "'Another Piece of the Past': 'Stories' of a New German Identity." *Oxford German Studies* 33 (2004): 125–147.

Linklater, Beth. "'Philomela's Revenge': Challenges to Rape in Recent Writing in German." *German Life and Letters* 54, no. 3 (2001): 253–271.

Ludden, Teresa. "Nature, Bodies, and Breakdowns in Anne Duden's *Das Landhaus* and Karen Duve's *Regenroman*." In *Pushing at Boundaries: Approaches to Contemporary German Women Writers from Karen Duve to Jenny Erpenbeck*, edited by Heike Bartel and Elizabeth Boa, 41–55. Amsterdam: Rodopi, 2006.

Ludorowski, Halina. "Deutsche Geschichte in den Augen der Enkelkinder." In *Geschichte und Gedächtnis in der Literatur vom 18. bis 21. Jahrhundert*, edited by Janusz Golec and Irmela von der Lühe, 253–262. Frankfurt am Main: Peter Lang, 2011.

Lützeler, Paul Michael. "'Postmetropolis': Peter Schneiders Berlin-Trilogie." *Gegenwartsliteratur: A German Studies Yearbook* 4 (2005): 91–110.

Mallett, Shelley. "Understanding Home: A Critical Review of the Literature," *The Sociological Review* 52, no. 1 (2004). Accessed Jan 22, 2020, doi: 10.1111/j.1467-954X.2004.00442.x.

"Marloh, Otto." *Das Bundesarchiv*. Accessed Sept 23, 2019. https://www.bundesarchiv.de/aktenreichskanzlei/1919-1933/0000/adr/adrmr/kap1_1/para2_56.html.

Marx, Karl. *Ökonomisch-philosophische Manuskripte aus dem Jahre 1844*. Berlin: Hofenberg, 2019.

Mein, Georg. *Erzählungen der Gegenwart: von Judith Hermann zu Bernhard Schlink*. Munich: Oldenbourg, 2005.

Meise, Helga. "Mythos Berlin: Orte und Nicht-Orte bei Julia Franck, Inka Parei und Judith Hermann." In *Fräuleinwunder Literarisch. Literatur von Frauen zu Beginn des 21. Jahrhunderts*, edited by Christiane Caemmerer, Walter Delabar, and Helga Meise, 125–150. Frankfurt am Main: Lang, 2005.

Merkl, Peter H. "An Impossible Dream? Privatizing Collective Property in Eastern Germany." In *German Unification: Process and Outcomes*, edited by M. Donald Hancock and Helga A. Welsch, 199–221. Boulder: Westview Press, 1994.

Moser, Natalie. "Dorfroman oder Urban Legend? Zur Funktion der Stadt-Dorf-Differenz in Juli Zehs *Unterleuten*." In *Über Land: Aktuelle literatur- und kulturwissenschaftliche Perspektiven auf Dorf und Ländlichkeit*, edited by Magdalena Marszałek, Werner Nell, and Marc Weiland, 127–140. Bielefeld: Transcript, 2018.

Müller-Adams, Elisa. "'De Nymphis, Sylphis, Pygmaeis et Salamandris': Zur Verwendung eines Motivkreises in Texten von Michael Fritz, Julia Schoch und Karen Duve." In *Pushing at Boundaries: Approaches to Contemporary German Women Writers from Karen Duve to Jenny Erpenbeck*, edited by Heike Bartel and Elizabeth Boa, 73–88. Amsterdam: Rodopi, 2006.

Murphy, John. "Philosophical Reflection, Self-Management, and the Disappearance of the Market." In *Toward a Post-Market Society*, edited by J. W. Murphy and Karen A. Callaghan, 159–178. Hauppauge: Nova Science Publishers, 2011.

Nobile, Nancy. "'Ihr Erbteil': The Legacy of Romanticism in Jenny Erpenbeck's *Heimsuchung*." *Gegenwartsliteratur: A German Studies Yearbook* 14 (2015): 61–83.

Nobile, Nancy. "A Ring of Keys: Thresholds to the Past in Judith Hermann's *Sommerhaus, später*." *Gegenwartsliteratur: A German Studies Yearbook* 9 (2010): 288–315.

"Our Energy and Climate Strategy." *Deutsche Bank*. Accessed January 6, 2020. https://www.db.com/cr/en/concrete-energy-and-climate-strategy.htm.

Palfreyman, Rachel. "Reflections of the 'Heimat' Genre: Intertextual Reference in Reitz's *Heimat*." *German Life and Letters* 50, no. 4 (1997): 529–543.

Pye, Gillian. "Jenny Erpenbeck and the Life of Things." In *Transitions: Emerging Women Writers in German-Language Literature*, edited by Valerie Heffernan and Gillian Pye, 111–130. Amsterdam: Rodopi, 2013.

Richards, Anna. "'Ob Mädchen oder Hunde': Women and Animals in Karen Duve's *Regenroman*." *German Life and Letters* 71, no. 4 (2018): 495–510.

Rink, Christian. "Nichts als Gespenster: Zur Identitätsproblematik in den Erzählungen Judith Hermanns." In *Autobiographisches Schreiben in der deutschsprachigen Gegenwartsliteratur, Band 1: Grenzen der Identität und der Fiktionalität*, edited by Ulrich Breuer and Beatrice Sandberg, 112–125. Munich: Iudicium, 2006.

Rinner, Susanne. *The German Student Movement and the Literary Imagination: Transnational Memories of Protest and Dissent*. New York and Oxford: Berghahn: 2015.

Rinner, Susanne. "Intergenerational Conflicts and Intercultural Relations: Peter Schneider's *Eduards Heimkehr*." *Gegenwartsliteratur: A German Studies Yearbook* 7 (2008): 204–222.

Riordan, Colin. "German-Jewish Relations in the Works of Peter Schneider." In *Jews in German Literature since 1945: German-Jewish Literature?*, edited by Pól O'Dochartaigh, 625–636. Amsterdam: Rodopi, 2000.

Rölleke, Lothar. "Rückgabe vor Entschädigung: Im größten Restitutionsprozess geht es um 1400 Grundstücke in Teltow und Kleinmachnow." *Die Welt* 94, April 23 2003.

Salerno, Roger A. "Alienated Communities: Between Aloneness and Connectedness." In *The Evolution of Alienation: Trauma, Promise, and the Millennium*, edited by Lauren Langman and Devorah Kalekin-Fishman, 253–268. Lanham and Boulder: Rowman & Littlefield Publishers, 2006,

Schmale, Wolfgang. *Geschichte der Männlichkeit in Europa (1450–2000)*. Vienna, Cologne, and Weimar: Böhlau Verlag, 2003.

Schuster, Maren, and Martin Paul. "Man kann sich sein Verhältnis zur Vergangenheit nicht aussuchen," interview with Jenny Erpenbeck. *Planet Wissen*. September 1, 2008. http://www.planet-interview.de/interviews/jenny-erpenbeck/34662/.

Schwalm, Dagmar. "Unser Haus," *g* 27 (no date). Archived material, Stiftung deutsche Kinemathek.

Shafi, Monika. *Housebound: Selfhood and Domestic Space in Contemporary German Fiction*. Rochester: Camden House, 2012.

Shafi, Monika. "Spaces of Violence: On the Role of Home, Nature and Gender in Narratives by Karen Duve and Felicitas Hoppe." In *Violence, Culture and Identity: Essays on German and Austrian Literature, Politics and Society*, edited by Helen Chambers, 373–388. Oxford: Peter Lang, 2006.

Stack, Heather M. "The 'Colonization' of East Germany?: A Comparative Analysis of German Privatization." *Duke Law Journal* 46, no. 5 (March 1997): 1211–1253. Accessed Jan 22, 2020, DOI: 10.2307/1372919. Stable URL: http://www.jstor.org/stable/1372919.

"Statistische Übersichten 31.12.2015." *Bundesamt für zentrale Dienste und offene Vermögensfragen*. Accessed February 14, 2020. file:///C:/Users/nchroni/Downloads/akt_Statistik.pdf.

Stephan, Inge. "Undine an der Newa und am Suzhou River. Wasserfrauen-Phantasien im interkulturellen und intermedialen Vergleich." *Zeitschrift für Germanistik* 12, no. 3 (2002): 547–563.

"Taxi nach Rathenow," Press Material. *ZDF Presseproduktion Berlin*. Archived material, Stiftung deutsche Kinemathek.

Theweleit, Klaus. *Male Fantasies*. Translated by Stephen Conway, Erica Carter, and Chris Turner. Minneapolis: University of Minnesota Press, 1987.

Thomerson, Michael J. "German Reunification: The Privatization of Socialist Property on East Germany's Path to Democracy." *Georgia Journal of International and Comparative Law* 21, no. 1 (1991): 123–143. Accessed Jan 22, 2020, http://digitalcommons.law.uga.edu/gjicl/vol21/iss1/5.

Tomlinson, John. *Globalization and Culture*. Chicago: University of Chicago Press, 1999.

"Unser Haus," Press Material. *ZDF Presseproduktion Berlin*. Archived material, Stiftung deutsche Kinemathek.

Vedder, Ulrike. "Lebensläufe: Zeit und Genealogie in Jenny Erpenbecks Literatur." In *Wahrheit und Täuschung: Beiträge zum Werk Jenny Erpenbecks*, edited by Friedhelm Marx and Julia Schöll, 55–66. Göttingen: Wallstein Verlag, 2014.

Vegso, Roland, and Marco Abel. "Biopolitical Education: The Edukators and the Politics of the Immanent Outside." *Studies in Twentieth and Twenty-First Century Literature* titled *Neoliberalism and the Undoing of Time* 40, no. 2 (2016): Article 7. Accessed Jan 22, 2020, https://doi.org/10.4148/2334-4415.1885.

Viana Guarda, Filomena. "Gedächtnis, Raum und Identität in Peter Schneiders Postwenderoman." *Estudios Filológicos Alemanes* 22 (2011): 403–413.

Vollmer, Hartmut. "Die sprachlose Nähe und das ferne Glück. Sehnsuchtsbilder und erzählerische Leerstellen in der Prosa von Judith Hermann und Peter Stamm." *Literatur für Leser* 29, no. 1 (2006): 59–79.

Von Moltke, Johannes. *No Place Like Home: Locations of Heimat in German Cinema*. Berkeley: University of California Press, 2005.
Wehdeking, Volker. *Generationenwechsel: Intermedialität in der deutschen Gegenwartsliteratur*. Berlin: Erich Schmidt Verlag, 2007.
Weigel, Sigrid. *Topographien der Geschlechter*. Reinbek bei Hamburg: Rowohlt Taschenbuch, 1990.
Zeller, Josef, and Tatiana Wait. "Safeguarding Property Claims in the Former GDR." *International Financial Law Review* 11, no. 3 (Mar 1992): 29–32.
"*Das zerbrechliche Geschlecht*," special section of *Der Spiegel* 36 (2001): https://www.spiegel.de/spiegel/print/index-2001-36.html.
"Zwangsenteignete wollen Progresslawine." *Leipziger Volkszeitung* (Leipzig, Germany), August 4–5, 1990. 1.

Laws, Legal Decisions, and Treaties

Agreement between the State of Israel and the Federal Republic of Germany. Signed at Luxembourg, on 10 September 1952 [Luxembourg Agreement]. *United Nations Treaty Series, Treaties and International Agreements Filed and Recorded from 20 March 1953 to 31 March 1953*. United Nations Treaty Series (in English and French), 205–311. https://treaties.un.org/doc/Publication/UNTS/Volume%20162/v162.pdf#page=215.
Agricultural Restructuring Act (Gesetz über die strukturelle Anpassung der Landwirtschaft an die soziale und ökologische Marktwirtschaft in der Deutschen Demokratischen Republik [Landwirtschaftsanpassungsgesetz]), 29 June 1990. *Gesetze im Internet*, Bundesministerium der Justiz und für Verbraucherschutz. https://www.gesetze-im-internet.de/lanpg/DDNR006420990.html.
Article 3(1), Basic Law of the Federal Republic of Germany (Grundgesetz der Bundesrepublik Deutschland). *Gesetze im Internet*, Bundesministerium der Justiz und für Verbraucherschutz, https://www.gesetze-im-internet.de/gg/BJNR000010949.html.
Article 14, Basic Law of th Federal Republic of Germany (Grundgesetz der Bundesrepublik Deutschland). Gesetze im Internet, Bundesministerium der Justiz und für Verbraucherschutz, https://www.gesetze-im-internet.de/gg/BJNR000010949.html.
Article 23, Basic Law of the Federal Republic of Germany (Grundgesetz der Bundesrepublik Deutschland). *Gesetze im Internet*, Bundesministerium der Justiz und für Verbraucherschutz, https://www.gesetze-im-internet.de/gg/BJNR000010949.html.
Article 41, Treaty of 31 August 1990 between the Federal Republic of Germany and the German Democratic Republic on the Establishment of German Unity [Unification Treaty] (Vertrag vom 31. August zwischen der Bundesrepublik Deutschland und der Deutschen Demokratischen Republik über die Herstellung der Einheit Deutschlands [Einigungsvertrag]). *Gesetze im Internet*, Bundesministerium der Justiz und für Verbraucherschutz, https://www.gesetze-im-internet.de/einigvtr/BJNR208890990.htm.
Article 143, Basic Law of the Federal Republic of Germany (Grundgesetz der Bundesrepublik Deutschland). *Gesetze im Internet*, Bundesministerium der Justiz und für Verbraucherschutz, https://www.gesetze-im-internet.de/gg/BJNR000010949.html.

Basic Law of the Federal Republic of Germany (Grundgesetz der Bundesrepublik Deutschland). *Gesetze im Internet*, Bundesministerium der Justiz und für Verbraucherschutz, https://www.gesetze-im-internet.de/gg/BJNR000010949.html.
Decision of the Federal Constitutional Court of 23 April 1991 (Entscheidung des Bundesverfassungsgerichts BVerfGE, 23 April 1991), 1BvR 1170/90, 1174/90, 1175/90. *Bundesverfassungsgericht*, https://www.bundesverfassungsgericht.de/EN/Das-Gericht/Geschichte-des-Bundesverfassungsgerichts/geschichte-des-bundesverfassungsgerichts.html.
Decision of the Federal Constitutional Court of 26 October 2004 (Entscheidung des Bundesverfassungsgerichts BVerfG, 26 Oktober 2004), 2 BvR 1038/01. *Bundesverfassungsgericht*, https://www.bundesverfassungsgericht.de/SharedDocs/Entscheidungen/DE/2004/10/rs20041026_2bvr095500.html.
Joint Declaration of the Governments of the Federal Republic of Germany and the German Democratic Republic on the Settlement of Open Property Questions (Gemeinsame Erklärung der Regierungen der Bundesrepublik Deutschland und der Deutschen Demokratischen Republik zur Regelung offener Vermögensfragen). *Gesetze im Internet*, Bundesministerium der Justiz und für Verbraucherschutz, https://www.gesetze-im-internet.de/reggerkl_einigvtr/RegGErkl_EinigVtr.pdf.
Land Registry Act (Grundbuchordnung). *Gesetze im Internet*, Bundesministerium der Justiz und für Verbraucherschutz, https://www.gesetze-im-internet.de/gbo/BJNR001390897.html.
Law for Public Compensatory Payment for Expropriations Based on the Law or Sovereignty of Occupation, which Cannot Be Made Reversible (Gesetz über staatliche Ausgleichsleistungen für Enteignungen auf besatzungsrechtlicher oder besatzungshoheitlicher Grundlage, die nicht mehr rückgängig gemacht werden können). *Gesetze im Internet*, Bundesministerium der Justiz und für Verbraucherschutz, https://www.gesetze-im-internet.de/ausglleistg/BJNR262800994.html.
Law for the Privatization and Reorganization of People's Property of 1 July 1990 [Trust Law] (Gesetz zur Privatisierung und Reorganisation des volkseigenen Vermögens vom 1. Juli 1990 (Treuhandgesetz]). *Gesetze im Internet*, Bundesministerium der Justiz und für Verbraucherschutz, https://www.gesetze-im-internet.de/treuhg/DDNR003000990.html.
Law for the Sale of People's Structures of 7 March 1990 (Gesetz über den Verkauf volkseigener Gebäude vom 7. März 1990). *Deutsche Digitale Bibliothek*. https://www.deutsche-digitale-bibliothek.de/item/76OOKOQZM3ZC7LS5OIVECXQ6SK5WRZJM.
Law on the Regulation of Open Property Questions of 23 September 1990 (Gesetz zur Regelung offener Vermögensfragen vom 23 September 1990). *Gesetze im Internet*, Bundesministerium der Justiz und für Verbraucherschutz, https://www.gesetze-im-internet.de/vermg/BJNR211590990.html.
Law to Remove Impediments to Privatization of Enterprises and for the Promotion of Investments, 22 March 1991 (Gesetz zur Beseitigung von Hemmnissen bei der Privatisierung von Unternehmen und zur Förderung von Investitionen vom 22. März 1991). *Bundesgesetztblatt Online*, https://www.bgbl.de/xaver/bgbl/start.xav?start=%2F%2F*%5B%40attr_id%3D%27bgbl191s0766.pdf%27%5D#__bgbl__%2F%2F*%5B%40attr_id%3D%27bgbl191s0766.pdf%27%5D__1600091745248.
Order No. 124 of the Soviet Military Administration in Germany, (Befehl Nr. 124 der sowjetischen Militäradministration für Deutschland), 30 October 1945. *Wikimedia*

Commons, https://upload.wikimedia.org/wikipedia/commons/1/13/Befehl_Nr._124_der_Sowietischen_Milit%C3%A4r-Administration.pdf.

Paragraph 1 and 1(2), Law on Special Investments in the German Democratic Republic of August 31, 1990. (Gesetz über besondere Investitionen in der Deutschen Demokratischen Republik vom 31. August 1990). *Verfassungen.de*, http://www.verfassungen.de/ddr/investitionsgesetz90.htm.

Paragraph 295(2), Civil Code of the GDR, (Zivilgesetzbuch der Deutschen Demokratischen Republik vom 19. Juni 1975). *Verfassungen.de*, http://www.verfassungen.de/ddr/zivilgesetzbuch75.htm.

Treaty Establishing a Monetary, Economic and Social Union (Vertrag über die Schaffung einer Währungs-, Wirtschafts- und Sozialunion zwischen der Deutschen Demokratischen Republik und der Bundesrepublik Deutschland), May 18, 1990. *Gesetze im Internet*, Bundesministerium der Justiz und für Verbraucherschutz, https://www.gesetze-im-internet.de/wwsuvtr/WWSUVtr.pdf.

Treaty of 31 August 1990 between the Federal Republic of Germany and the German Democratic Republic on the Establishment of German Unity [Unification Treaty], (Vertrag zwischen der Bundesrepublik Deutschland und der Deutschen Demokratischen Republik über die Herstellung der Einheit Deutschlands [Einigungsvertrag]). *Gesetze im Internet*, Bundesministerium der Justiz und für Verbraucherschutz, https://www.gesetze-im-internet.de/einigvtr/BJNR208890990.html.

Treaty on the Final Settlement with Respect to Germany (Two-Plus-Four Treaty on Germany), 12 September 1990. *Germany History in Images and Documents*, http://ghdi.ghi-dc.org/sub_document.cfm?document_id=176.

Index

Abbey in the Oakwood 65
agency, non-human 5, 13f., 59, 65, 89, 100, 139–142, 148f., 152, 156, 159f., 167, 178, 185, 195–197, 204
agential cut 13, 59f., 62, 71
Alaimo, Stacy 13f., 141f., 147f.
alienation
– in capitalism 75, 79–81, 84, 86f., 94–96
– in exile 163
– in the unified Germany 204
– women's in the patriarchy 100, 108, 111–114, 120f.
– women's in the patriarchy in literary history 108
Aller Liebe Anfang See *Where Love Begins*
Améry, Jean 61
Amt zur Regelung offener Vermögensfragen See Office for the Regulation of Open Property Questions
Applegate, Celia 9, 11
Arslan, Thomas 18
Article 3(1) of the Basic Law 27
Article 14 of the Basic Law 2f., 24, 50
Article 23 of the Basic Law 21
Aryanization See expropriation under National Socialism
Assmann, Aleida 15, 170

Bansal, Pratima 189
Barad, Karen 13f., 59f., 62, 71, 187
Berlant, Lauren 86, 89
Berlin
– as deterritorialized space 102f.
– as opposed to Brandenburg 101f., 106
Blattner, Sonja 6, 200, 202–205, 207
Blickle, Peter 9, 11f., 58
Blooming Landscapes speech / *Blühende Landschaften* (Rede) 181, 197, 203
Boa, Elizabeth 11
body armor, Theweleit 142, 147
Bogdal, Klaus-Michael 16, 128–130, 141
Bohr, Niels 13

Böser, Knut 123
Brandenburg, as opposed to Berlin 104–107
Braun, Volker 1, 182f.
Breger, Claudia 16, 124
Brief History of Neoliberalism, A 14
Brown, Wendy 14, 95f.
Buck, Detlev 5, 18, 46, 86, 185

collective guilt 126, 133–135, 169, 174, 177
collectivization 24, 190f.
colonialism, rhetoric evoking 3–5, 62, 182
colonization of women 16, 109
Communism 15, 24f., 35, 54f., 72f., 170, 174, 181, 191
Conference on Jewish Material Claims against Germany 25, 135
Connell, Raewyn or R. W. 14, 95f.
construction of consent 14f.
Crary, Jonathan 95
creative destruction 80
cruel optimism 86, 89, 94

Das alte Lied See *The Same Old Song*
Das ist eine Geschichte See *Now That's a Story*
DEFA 38
Deleuze, Gilles 103, 121
Der Brocken See *The Brocken*
deterritorialization 103, 107, 110–112, 121f.
– and reterritorialization 103, 121f.
dilapidation 58, 65, 89, 91f., 130, 137, 204
– as non-human agency 14, 142
displacement 49, 73, 106, 108, 111–113, 122, 159, 179, 204, 206
domestic violence 18, 120
Dresden, bombing of 65–67
drüben series 200, 202, 205, 207
Duve, Karen 6, 15f., 100, 123, 137, 141–143, 149, 151, 203

https://doi.org/10.1515/9783110673975-012

Index — **221**

Eduards Heimkehr / Eduard's Homecoming 6, 16–18, 100, 123–126, 130, 137, 150f., 153, 168, 176, 204
embodiment 147f., 150
Engel, Thomas 4, 21
erasure, Assmann 15
Erpenbeck, Jenny 6, 15, 153, 155–160, 162f., 165, 167, 174, 178–180, 203f., 206
expropriation 24f., 161, 178f.
– after unification 3, 20, 191
– in the GDR 3, 24f., 30, 190f.
– under National Socialism 2, 24f., 30, 68, 134
– under SMAD 24, 27f., 30, 158, 190f.
externalizing, Assmann 15

falsification, Assmann 15, 170
Federal Agency for the Settlement of Open Property Questions 36
Federal Office for Central Services and Unresolved Property Issues (BADV) 36
finance capitalism 76, 183, 185, 189f., 192, 195, 197f., 205
Friedrich, Caspar David 65

GDR *See* German Democratic Republic
gender as performance 143, 151
generation 68 132f.
– and memory 69, 127, 154, 178, 192, 195, 205
– role in interfamily conflicts 41, 57f., 62f.
Gerlof, Kathrin 1, 6, 15, 153f., 167, 172–175, 179f., 204
German Democratic Republic 2f., 11, 25, 35, 42, 57, 219
Germania project 157, 166
globalization 11f., 76, 78, 80f., 84, 90, 102f., 121f., 183, 185, 193
Glowna, Vadim 5, 46, 73
Grass, Günther 18
Griesmayr, Hartmut 1, 38, 50
Guattari, Félix 103, 121

Harvey, David 14, 75, 80, 95f.
Heim, Stefan 18

Heimat 1, 6, 8–13, 41, 44–46, 48, 50f., 55, 57–60, 62–64, 66, 68, 70–72, 106, 125, 140–142, 149, 155–160, 164, 166, 184f., 197, 200, 202, 206
– and the agential cut, Barad 60f., 71
– as a foil to modernity 11
– as a utopian ideal 12
– films 10, 52
– in National Socialism and the Holocaust 9f., 61
– in the Weimar Republic 9
– materiality of 12
– matrilineal 68
– miniseries, Edgar Reitz 52
– patrilineal 53
– symbolic separation with the mother 58
– Turkish-German 10, 61
Heimsuchung See Visitation
Hermann, Judith 5, 15, 18, 98, 100, 123, 151, 153, 203f., 206
heteronormativity 7, 15f., 62, 93, 99–101, 105f., 109, 111–113, 120f., 128
hoarding 117, 122
Hochhuth, Rolf 18
home
– and national history 8, 15, 50f., 64, 70, 107, 127, 153f., 190, 203, 206
– as a trope of loss 12, 58, 113, 156
– as real estate 2, 6, 15, 24, 56, 78, 83, 91, 166, 196, 203
– as threatening 5, 8, 16, 99f., 108, 157
home ownership in the GDR 32, 41–43
homelessness 18, 20, 40, 68, 71, 105
Housebound: Selfhood and Domestic Space in Contemporary German Fiction 7

inheritance 17, 63, 67–71, 87f., 91f., 95, 125, 127, 133, 206
– matrilineal 15, 51, 63, 68
– patrilineal 53, 62, 127f., 156
– social 127, 150
intra-action 13f., 59, 78, 142, 162, 166, 187
– and Heimat 17, 61f., 71f., 141, 149, 158

JCC *See* Conference on Jewish Material Claims against Germany

222 — Index

Joint Declaration of the Governments of the Federal Republic of Germany and the German Democratic Republic on the Settlement of Open Property Questions 26f., 30

Kara, Yadé 18
Knox-Hayes, Janelle 189
Kohl, Helmut 181f., 197, 203
Kombinate 23
Körperpanzer *See* body armor, Theweleit
Kristeva, Julia 106

land reform under SMAD 2, 24, 191
Law for Public Compensatory Payment for Expropriations Based on the Law or Sovereignty of Occupation, Which Cannot Be Made Reversible 28
Law for the Sale of People's Structures 22
Law on Special Investments in the German Democratic Republic 33
Law on the Regulation of Open Property Questions *See* Property Law
Law to Remove Impediments to Privatization of Enterprises and for the Promotion of Investments 34
lawyers, in the East after unification 35
LGBTQ 18, 109f., 143
Luxembourg Agreement / *Luxemburger Abkommen* 25

made-for-television films
 – as artifacts 4, 39
 – pedagogical function 4, 21, 38, 42, 48
Male Fantasies 17, 142
Mallett, Shelley 7
Marx, Karl 80
masculinity 16, 93, 123, 125, 127–130, 137, 141, 143–146, 148, 150f.
 – crisis 6, 16, 124–126, 131, 133, 136f., 142, 147f., 150f.
 – hegemonic 16, 128f., 136f., 141, 146, 150f.
Meeting the Universe Halfway 13, 59
Mercedes 39f., 79, 123, 137, 140, 146

National Socialism / Nazi 5, 8, 10, 15, 25, 29, 55, 66, 157, 169
 – and the Holocaust 2, 9, 24, 29, 50, 64, 68, 125, 133f., 154, 157–159, 161, 163f., 167–169
neoliberalism 5, 14, 73, 75, 77f., 80, 84, 94–97, 102, 112, 122, 143, 166, 184f.
No More Mr. Nice Guy 5, 18, 46, 73–75, 86, 94–96, 99
Now That's a Story 1, 6, 15, 153–155, 167f., 176, 178f., 204f.

Office for the Regulation of Open Property Questions 36, 207
offsetting, Assmann 15, 170
One of the Beloved Ones 200
Our House 1f., 5, 15, 18, 38, 50–53, 55, 62–64, 67, 69–73, 86, 141, 153, 168, 206

Palfreyman, Rachel 11, 58
Petzold, Christian 18
polyamory 101f., 105f., 109f.
privatization 3, 11, 73, 83
Privatization and Reorganization of Publicly Owned Assets Act *See* Trust Law
Property Law 30, 33, 42, 54, 82
Prussia, large land holdings 190, 192

Rain 6, 15–17, 100, 123–126, 137, 141f., 147, 150f., 197, 204
Reagan, Ronald 14
Regenroman See Rain
remaining silent, Assmann 15
restitution before compensation / Rückgabe vor Entschädigung 25–27, 35, 50

Salerno, Roger A. 95
Schlussstrichdebatte 168
Schmale, Wolfgang 16, 128–130, 141
Schneider, Peter 6, 16, 18, 100, 123, 126, 131, 133f., 151, 206
Schulze, Ingo 18
Second Party Congress 24
SED *See* Socialist Unity Party of Germany
sexual assault 144, 146, 157, 164f.
Shafi, Monika 7

SMAD *See* Soviet Military Administration in Germany
sociomateriality   189, 195, 197 f.
"Sommerhaus, später" *See* "Summerhouse, Later"
Soviet Military Administration in Germany   24 f., 27–29, 54, 218
Speer, Albert   15, 157, 166
squatting   18, 130
stalking   111, 114, 118–120, 122
Stöckl, Ula   5, 15, 50 f., 63, 67 f.
suburb, as nondescript place   112
"Summerhouse, Later"   5, 98–101, 103, 109, 111 f., 114 f., 119–123, 153, 197, 204

Taxi nach Rathenow / Taxi to Rathenow   4 f., 21, 38 f., 41, 44, 46, 48, 50, 53, 62, 73, 86, 123, 141, 153, 168, 206
Thatcher, Margaret   14
The Brocken   5, 46, 73–75, 81, 86 f., 90, 95–97, 123, 206
The Same Old Song   5, 15, 18, 50 f., 63 f., 67–73, 86, 141, 153, 205 f.
The *Treaty of 31 August 1990 between the Federal Republic of Germany and the German Democratic Republic on the Establishment of German Unity*   *See* Unification Treaty
Theweleit, Klaus   17, 142, 145

Tomlinson, John   103
trans-corporal space   13, 141 f., 147, 149
Treaty Establishing a Monetary, Economic and Social Union   23
Treuhand   3, 17, 29, 34–36, 193
Two-Plus-Four Treaty   27

Unification Treaty   21, 25, 33
Unser Haus   *See* Our House
Unterleuten   6, 183–185, 197, 204 f.

Visitation   6, 15, 153–155, 157 f., 160, 164, 167 f., 178 f., 192, 203–205
volkseigene Betriebe   23
von Moltke, Johannes   9 f.
vulnerability, within the home   115, 119, 121, 151

water, and the feminine   17, 138, 142–144, 148 f.
Weigel, Sigrid   16, 108
West Germany, social market economy   23
Where Love Begins   5, 18, 100 f., 111 f., 114, 119–123, 130
Wir können auch anders   *See* No More Mr. Nice Guy
World War II   2, 23 f., 66, 157

Zeh, Juli   6, 183 f., 190 f., 197, 203 f., 206

www.ingramcontent.com/pod-product-compliance
Lightning Source LLC
Chambersburg PA
CBHW071739150426
43191CB00010B/1633